DATE DUE

Phenomenological Sociology

Theory, Culture & Society

Theory, Culture & Society caters for the resurgence of interest in culture within contemporary social science and the humanities. Building on the heritage of classical social theory, the book series examines ways in which this tradition has been reshaped by a new generation of theorists. It also publishes theoretically informed analyses of everyday life, popular culture, and new intellectual movements.

EDITOR: Mike Featherstone, *Nottingham Trent University*

SERIES EDITORIAL BOARD
Roy Boyne, *University of Durham*
Mike Hepworth, *University of Aberdeen*
Scott Lash, *Goldsmiths College, University of London*
Roland Robertson, *University of Aberdeen*
Bryan S. Turner, *University of Singapore*

THE TCS CENTRE
The *Theory, Culture & Society* book series, the journals *Theory, Culture & Society* and *Body & Society*, and related conference, seminar and postgraduate programmes operate from the TCS Centre at Nottingham Trent University. For further details of the TCS Centre's activities please contact:

Centre Administrator
The TCS Centre, Room 175
Faculty of Humanities
Nottingham Trent University
Clifton Lane, Nottingham, NG11 8NS, UK
e-mail: tcs@ntu.ac.uk
web: http://www.tcs.ntu.ac.uk

Recent volumes include:

Globalization and Belonging
Mike Savage, Gaynor Bagnall, Brian Longhurst

The Sport Star
Barry Smart

Diaspora and Hybridity
Kalra, Kaur and Hutnyk

The Postcolonial Challenge
Couze Venn

Phenomenological Sociology

Insight and Experience in Modern Society

Harvie Ferguson

SAGE Publications
London ● Thousand Oaks ● New Delhi

SAGE Publications Ltd
1 Oliver's Yard
55 City Road
London EC1Y 1SP

SAGE Publications Inc.
2455 Teller Road
Thousand Oaks, California 91320

SAGE Publications India Pvt Ltd
B-42 Panchsheel Enclave
Post Box 4109
New Delhi 110 017

British Library Cataloguing in Publication data

A catalogue record for this book is
available from the British Library

ISBN: 978-0-7619-5986-1 (pbk)
ISBN: 978-0-7619-5987-8
Library of Congress control number available

Typeset by C&M Digital (P) Ltd., Chennai, India

For Sandra

Gentil pensero che parla di vui,
sen vene a dimorar meco sovente.

Dante, *Vita Nuova* (xxxviii)

Contents

Acknowledgements

British universities are in danger of abandoning scholarship for research (commissioned and paid for by private and public bodies with their own, non-academic, agendas), knowledge for expertise (narrowly conceived and eminently saleable), and learning for teaching (reduced to a process of assessment that serves simultaneously to certify the quality of both students and teachers). A book which claims that serious philosophical reflection is the best way of gaining knowledge of the most important aspects of contemporary experience and, in doing so, engages in the real difficulty of learning is, then, written against the grain of current academic policy. That it was written at all is due in large measure to the genuine intellectual support of its publisher, Chris Rojek, at Sage. His admirable, old-fashioned patience would have been severely tested, however, had it not been for the timely award of a fellowship from the Japan Foundation. The author was the grateful, and somewhat bemused, recipient of that august body's generosity during the academic session 2003–4, which he spent at the Institute for Research in the Humanities, Kyoto University. The latter part of the book was conceived and written in the inspiring surroundings of Japan's ancient, aristocratic capital and owes something to *The Tale of Genji* as well as the Kyoto School of Phenomenology.

The author's major intellectual debts are recorded in the References, and he alone is responsible for the distortions, errors of interpretation, and misunderstandings that constitute the text. His infinite personal debt is acknowledged in the Dedication.

Introduction: Phenomenology and Sociology

Philosophy is essentially homesickness – the universal impulse to be at home.

Novalis, *Logological Fragments*

As soon as ever a philosophy begins to believe in itself, it always creates a world in its own image.

Nietzsche, *Beyond Good and Evil*

To reach the starting point not only for the human sciences but also for philosophy we must go behind its scientific elaboration and grasp life in its natural state.

Dilthey, *The Formation of the Historical World in the Human Sciences*

Should sociologists concern themselves with philosophy? Ought philosophers pay any attention to sociology? The most fruitful response to these and related questions is surprising. Put simply, it is that sociologists must concern themselves with (some) philosophy if they are to produce incisive *sociology*; and philosophers have to attend to (some) sociology if they are to realize the promise of *philosophy*. Philosophy was and remains a rich source of description and reflection that is central to a proper sociological understanding of modern society; and sociology yields insights essential to the historic project of philosophical enquiry. Each requires, in their own interests, the complementary perspectives afforded by the other. This can hardly be regarded as a radical proposal; yet, both disciplines having grown increasingly isolated and inward-looking, it is doubtless contentious and requires some justification at the outset.

The pursuit of academic and disciplinary autonomy has encouraged a kind of technical specialization that has made each of these subjects impenetrable to all but the most determined general reader, and made academics in what were at one time adjacent and interrelated fields of study mutually suspicious and dismissive of each other's work. The hermeticism of contemporary research, which is demanding, fascinating, and rewarding for the specialist, not only has the effect of arbitrarily and artificially separating sociological and philosophical issues but also distances both from their real subject matter. However it is presently conceived (and there are several contested models on offer), sociology cannot adequately grasp society through its unique methods and concepts; and however philosophy is understood (and here too bewildering variation breaks out), its self-conception frustratingly leads it away from just that reality it sets out to seize. Neither society nor reality falls easily within those schemata of understanding provided by the disciplines that now claim a special obligation and competence to define them. More importantly, neither society nor reality waits upon the outcome of expert reflection to decide the future – our future. The issues that founded sociological and philosophical discourse are matters of vital practical importance for everyone – including sociologists and philosophers. And in order to return disciplined reflection to the vital issues of contemporary life and to restore its relevance and credibility to a wider public, it is essential that academics first of all clarify and make more general their insights by sharing them more openly with each other.

Put otherwise and more precisely: *historical* sociology needs to develop a relationship with *phenomenology*, not only, as it will subsequently be argued in detail, because this offers the most immediately fruitful point of contact between the two disciplines, but also because each is in danger of being ignored by established positions within their own disciplines. Thus, particularly in Britain, phenomenology is paid scant attention by academic philosophers who tend airily to dismiss it as 'continental philosophy'; and, equally, historical sociology is ignored by many sociologists insufficiently interested in pursuing research into matters they regard as falling outside their own, contemporary society. In what follows it will be argued that, unlikely as at first it may seem, a powerful affinity already exists between these two discourses. Historical sociologists have, in fact, been compelled to develop their own phenomenological insights, and phenomenologists have been forced to acknowledge the significance for their own thought of specific social-historical forms.

The Disciplinary and the Interdisciplinary

Of course, it is tempting to exaggerate and, no doubt, the above statement caricatures a situation that is neither without a rational basis in an unavoidable intellectual division of labour nor the balancing influence of many well-known scholars who have developed interdisciplinary or inclusive programmes of research. Such qualifications notwithstanding, the following discussion finds its point of departure in the view that well-established and powerful tendencies towards overspecialization, technical language and methods, and disciplinary autonomy have for some time obstructed genuine intellectual development of just those subjects which claim to deal most directly with issues of 'real life'. And while pleas to broaden the scope of enquiry and cross disciplinary boundaries are frequently acknowledged as worthy aims, they are rarely acted upon. The exigencies of academic life make other assumptions all too appealing. Would not sociology and philosophy (as well as other disciplines) do better to cultivate their own fields of study, using their own hard-won techniques and methods? Is not any dialogue likely to be fertile only of misunderstanding and confusion?

For many students of sociology, certainly, philosophy seems to be remote from their interests. In fact, they frequently anathematize philosophy as an intellectual obstacle to the full development of clarity about the most fundamental and pressing questions that confront us. The urgent need to grasp more adequately the real character of the society in which we live makes us impatient and even intolerant of anything that, pretending profundity, lacks real seriousness. Was it not philosophy even more than religion, after all, that was responsible for the view of the world that sociology had most strenuously to struggle against to establish its own validity? Abstract, formalistic, and self-indulgent, philosophy, even where it does not block or divert the course of practical reflection on the human reality in which we are implicated, often enough presents itself as an intellectual game which, like all such absorbing and inessential activities, finds its primary significance as nothing more than a *pastime*.

Of course a symmetrical indictment informs the prejudices of the philosophy student. For the serious-minded philosopher it is sociology that now distracts the enquiring mind from any more strenuous engagement with the essential task of self-understanding. Works of sociology are choked with meaningless neologisms, trivial conceptual distinctions, incomprehensible diagrams, and empty theoretical speculation. Sociology is the new scholasticism – strident rather than principled, opinionated rather than critical, formalistic rather than systematic; it is the diseased language of academic modernism.

It is not just that such views overstate their case, make the division of intellectual labour too neat and tidy, tend to overlook borderline disputes, and ignore the *variety* of positions espoused by both philosophers and sociologists; more significantly, they misdescribe both philosophy and sociology, and misconstrue their aims. This more basic misunderstanding, furthermore, is common to those who see a *positive* relationship between the disciplines. The issue is not solely, or even primarily, one of academic politics or dogmatic conflict; it is, rather, a matter of recovering the sense in which principled reflection is rooted in and refers to an undivided world of *experience*. It is important, therefore, critically to consider the positive as well as the negative view; this at least avoids the immediate threat of sliding into a playground game of name-calling.

The situation is made more difficult by the failure to establish a suitable historical context for any such discussion. Philosophy clings to the aura of a venerable tradition; sociology welcomes the mantle of novelty. Both views are deceptive. The *academic* study of philosophy is, like other disciplines, of quite recent origin, while sociology, by a host of other names, was one of the central intellectual preoccupations of premodern western societies (Anderson and Valente 2002; Gouldner 1968).

In a general way, and for the most part reluctantly, many sociologists (as well as other academic specialists) have been willing to accord philosophy the special role of providing a 'methodological foundation' for their particular studies. Philosophy legislates on the laws of clear conceptualization, compelling argumentation, and adequate explanation. In this view philosophy is an art of thinking; a purely formal and procedural discipline to be observed with equal rigour whatever the subject matter under discussion and the special techniques developed for its investigation. It is just the clarification of the formal principles of rational thought, irrespective of what the thought is about, that guarantees the coherence of the sciences and furnishes the modern view of the world with its unity. Sociology, in its preoccupation with society as its particular subject matter and in seeking to analyse and explain this content, develops its own concepts and procedures. But in doing so it is guided by general rules of thought. Sociology, that is to say, must be consistent with methodological principles, the articulation of which is the proper field of philosophy, which is the only legitimate 'meta'-science.

In the western tradition, however, it is only rarely that conceptual clarity, rigour, and the explication of rules for adequate thought have been taken to be the real subject matter of philosophical discourse. John Locke, for example, describes his own philosophical efforts with apparent modesty: 'Ambition enough to be employed as an Under-Labourer in clearing Ground a little, and removing some of the Rubbish, that lies in the way to Knowledge' (1975, 10).

It quickly transpires, of course, that the task of 'under-labourer', far from being restricted to the modest role Locke pretends, arrogates to itself the essential and not just the preliminary form of all systematic thinking and, more significantly, claims to establish the normative framework of practical life as well as reflection upon it.

More frequently, in fact, philosophers have claimed a pre-eminent position among the sciences as the most general and inclusive of all disciplined reflection. It is not so much a particular method that distinguishes philosophy as its ambitious inclusiveness; uniquely, it sets out intellectually to grasp reality in its fullness. It is, therefore, not to be compared with the perspective and approach of any more specific discipline such as sociology, economics, or mathematics, as it is to be viewed in the light of other, non-philosophical modes of grasping and exploring reality. For such a view, philosophy might more reasonably be considered in relation to religion or art, which similarly seek and respond to reality in a genuinely comprehensive way, than to the more limited ambitions of any academic discipline (including, of course, the academic study of philosophy!). And it is just this view that is challenged by the rise of sociology, which claims for itself the privilege of being the only genuinely comprehensive account of the *modern* world (Lepenies 1988).

Any such view emasculates philosophy and leaves it with a purely judicial role. Yet philosophy 'does not conclude the long series of natural and human sciences' but treats 'problems which it, and only it, raises ... it is not a summary of accomplishments attained elsewhere; and it is absolutely not a totalizing universal science ... philosophizing means the capacity and need to question even where everything is supposed to be matter-of-course' (Funke 1987, 6).

4

Every major philosophical innovation, thus, as every religious reformation and artistic movement, justifies itself first of all by invoking its own version of a primal world as the source of its critically inquiring spirit. Every radical departure justifies itself in the claim to be nothing other than a determination once again to grasp the spirit of its *original* foundation; to return philosophy to the genuine path of dialogue; to revitalize empty forms of worship; to liberate the image latent in things. Yet every effort to delineate the origin of our world and grasp precisely the experience of its *worldness* sooner or later becomes distracted and ends in formalism and the pursuit of technical sophistication.

Descartes, to take an outstanding example, sought in a fundamental way to establish or, rather, to re-establish a relation between philosophy and the most immediate forms of life. He prefaces his discussion of philosophical method with a personal narrative and initially claims 'not to teach the method which everyone must follow in order to direct his reason correctly, but only to reveal how I have tried to direct my own' (1985, 113). He claims to be 'presenting this work only as a history' distinguished by its 'frankness'. Descartes begins his philosophy by recounting his lurch into doubt. He tells us that 'as soon as I had completed the course of study at the end of which one is normally admitted to the ranks of the learned, I completely changed my opinion. For I found myself beset by so many doubts and errors that I came to think I had gained nothing from my attempts to become educated but increasing recognition of my ignorance' (1985, 113).

In addition to assimilating the best formal education Descartes had read everything that came his way, and found in 'abstruse and unusual' sources much that seemed the equal to authoritative texts. He came across unresolved disagreement in every field of learning and, worse, found that knowledge remained remote from the vital human issues of morality, salvation, and hope. Knowledge disconnected from life was useless and, more significantly, hardly deserved to be called knowledge at all. Consequently, his *desire* to grasp the world intensified rather than diminished by doubt, he resolved on an unorthodox programme of study:

> as soon as I was old enough to emerge from the control of my teachers, I entirely abandoned the study of letters. Resolving to seek no knowledge other than that which could be found in myself or less in the great book of the world, I spent the rest of my youth travelling, visiting courts and armies, mixing with people of diverse temperaments and ranks, gathering various experiences, testing myself in the situations which fortune offered me, and at all times reflecting upon whatever came my way so as to derive some profit from it. For it seemed to me that much more truth could be found in the reasonings which a man makes concerning matters that concern him than in those which some scholar makes in his study about speculative matters. (1985, 115)

Descartes's autobiographical account of the origin of his philosophy is more subtly ambivalent than Locke's apparently modest self-effacement. For Descartes, the personal experience of doubt is no extraneous motive, but enters into the constitution of knowledge itself. What is often read as an interesting but superfluous 'Preface' to the argument of the *Discourse on Method* remains its essential and vital starting point. Modern philosophy begins, thus, with the overthrow of authority and an appeal to *experience* as the only secure ground of knowledge. For Descartes, philosophical knowledge is nothing other than a secure grasp of experience itself. Yet Descartes's philosophy was rapidly transformed into the autonomous starting point for a technical rationalism or an equally technical empiricism that treated the 'mind' rather than experience as its subject matter and, furthermore, sought to establish normative standards for its 'correct' operation.

The ambition to characterize and account for a system of 'pure' reason, thus, retrospectively rooted in Descartes's *thought*, animates much of modern philosophy. And for many that ambition was realized, at least in a schematic and preliminary way, by Immanuel Kant in his famous *Critique of Pure Reason*. Here, it was felt, was delineated the architectonic structure of *reason* in such a way that reality finally becomes comprehensible in it; the world, *and* our intellectual means of grasping it, become reunited in self-conscious transparency. But this was never Kant's purpose (Ameriks 2000). The *Critique of Pure Reason* has first of all to be understood in the context of yet larger and more pressing problems. Kant's philosophy is concerned to clarify the *limits* of pure reason; to establish the valid domains of faith, practical reason, and aesthetic judgement, each of which raises philosophical issues of its own and none of which is reducible to, or should be regarded as an extension of the structural principles of, the 'mind' (Beiser 1987). Philosophy as a 'scholastic concept' judges itself only in respect of internal clarity, consistency, and systematic unity; it seeks to fulfil itself as a system of interconnected concepts. What Kant refers to as the 'cosmopolitan concept' of philosophy grounds itself and is represented in the archetype of the philosopher. From this point of view the philosopher is designated an 'artist' rather than a logician or scientist, and beyond any logical system immanent in formalized models of thinking the *ends* of action remain the fundamental subject matter of philosophy (Zammito 1992; 2002; Ameriks 2000).

An equally firm and radical commitment to what had become regarded as the extraterritorial aims of philosophy is also magnificently expressed by Hegel at the outset of his *Phenomenology of Spirit*:

> Spirit has not only lost its essential life; it is also conscious of this loss, and of the finitude of its own content. Turning away from the empty husks, and confessing that it lies in wickedness, it reviles itself for so doing, and now demands from philosophy, not so much *knowledge* of what *is*, as the recovery through its agency of that lost sense of solid and substantial being. Philosophy is to meet this need, not by opening up the fast-locked nature of substance, and raising this to self-consciousness, not by bringing consciousness out of its chaos back to an order based on thought, nor to the simplicity of the Notion, but rather by running together what thought has put asunder, by suppressing the differentiations of the Notion and restoring the *feeling* of essential being: in short, by providing edification rather than insight. (1977, 4–5)

Yet here also, and as a consequence of his own subsequent writing as well as the work of enthusiastic followers, rather than restore 'that lost sense of solid and substantial being', Hegelian philosophy preferred to elaborate its own remote and ideal 'system' and sought to articulate a uniquely logical model of *itself*.

Modern philosophy, that is to say, tends toward self-contemplation; to thinking about thinking. But what revitalizes philosophy and continues to exercise its disturbing presence in the midst of the most arid reflection is nothing other than a renewed sensibility and a renewed encounter with reality. Philosophy is as incapable of utterly divorcing itself from the world as it is of adequately grasping the world. It is just this tension that defines its history, including its trajectory through the development of modern society. In periodically seeking out its roots and restating its task, philosophy becomes aware in ever new ways of the changing reality in which it is implicated and to which it is one kind of response. And it is just this philosophical quest for reality that provides sociology with its most potent subject matter. Rather than reject philosophical knowledge on the grounds that it springs from unrealistic assumptions and is directed towards irrelevant ends, the more fruitful approach is to grasp philosophy as an image pregnant with all the most significant and characteristic features of the times. The issue is not whether Kant, or Hume, or Husserl are 'correct' in a universal sense but, rather, what the insights they offer – insights which bear a genuine, if veiled, relation to their own experience – reveal about the ever changing character of *their* reality and of *our* reality; our world.

Sociology, thus, is not to be viewed as a specialized discipline that either applies the general truths of philosophy, or follows its universal rules of reasoning, in investigating its specific subject matter. Sociology, rather, is the continuation of philosophy by other means. In this regard we can readily understand the intimate but obscure relation between the sociological works of Marx and the preceding philosophical writings of Hegel; or the equally clouded connection between Weber and Nietzsche; or between Durkheim, or Simmel, and Kant.

But need we bother about all this now? Would it not be more instructive, easier, and better founded to investigate society directly? To answer this objection requires a much closer acquaintance with phenomenology. But, in a preliminary way, it can certainly be said 'not necessarily'. No empirical investigation can be complete or exhaustive. Reality, as Max Weber pointed out, is both intensively and extensively infinite. By this he meant not only that, in a practical sense, we would never be able to survey it in its entirety but, more significantly, that any artificially defined and arbitrarily chosen segment within it in practice offers an inexhaustible richness of content (Weber 1975; Oakes 1988). Furthermore, any description involves a particular way of classifying and ordering the immediate reality of experience, so that a whole series of possible 'fields' and 'objects of study' appear, depending on the point of view of the investigation being conducted. The advantage of using philosophical discourse as a privileged source of ethnographic data is that it presents to us, no doubt in rather too neat and orderly a fashion, the 'native categories' of the culture we most want to reach – our own – and through it to clarify the experience from which, we suppose, that culture and those categories themselves arose. Here categories refer, as in ethnography, not only to an intellectual structure but also to the conventions that organize everyday life; the conventions of experience itself.

In short, neither a non-reflexive and dogmatic philosophy, nor a deterministic and equally dogmatic sociology, can any longer command assent within their own self-defining domains of interest, far less successfully annexe neighbouring territories. Sociology and philosophy have to develop in immediate interrelation because each has to become aware of the other as a vital part of their own self-understanding and the continuation of their own projects of grasping reality. The relation of phenomenology and social theory, then, is to be viewed not externally as a partial contact between two fundamentally different academic practices but, rather, internally as an aspect of the many-sided discourse of modern experience. This is a plea not so much on behalf of the interdisciplinary study of modernity – already exemplified in the valuable writings of such diverse scholars as Schwartz (1998), Kwinter (2002), and Starobinski (2003) – as for a fuller and more critical understanding of experience. In our own experience, sociology and philosophy, and the realities to which they refer and in which they are rooted, are not separate entities but aspects of a continuously emerging world. The hidden intimacy that links sociology and philosophy is simply the common world of experience from which they have arisen. But the manner in which each arose has fatally marked their subsequent, largely hostile and mutually suspicious development; the differences can be overcome only through a radical process of reconstruction that is occasioned by an urgent and shared need to grasp more adequately the continually emerging and transforming character of modern life.

The Extradisciplinary

Experience is the common root of philosophy and sociology and each justifies itself to the extent that, prior to any disciplinary considerations, it adequately grasps itself in this foundation. Yet every grasping is, at the same time, a mode of differentiating and distancing; it is a specific perspective on and within experience. The distinction between philosophy and sociology lies in the specific way each distances itself from the world of immediacy; the manner in which each establishes its proper field of investigation. This is not in itself an exclusively intellectual process; it is less a matter of theoretical reflection than it is an aspect of distinctive 'orientations' to and within the world.

Modern philosophy begins in *doubt*; it is a symptom of, and a response to, radical scepticism. Doubt emerges with modern society; it is the philosophic form of the demand for human autonomy that inaugurates the entire development of modernity (Manent 1998). In modernity, human beings claim sovereignty over *their* world, which is the only world open to experience. In this context the equivocal character of all 'exteriority' continually threatens to undermine the self-confidence in which modern culture was established. Philosophical knowledge counteracts this unnerving doubt by bringing into prominence the immediate presence of the conscious subject to itself. Modern philosophy, whatever its specific content, decisively turns towards the human subject and relentlessly develops itself as a form of self-understanding. Sociology, on the other hand, begins in *curiosity*; an orientation that also emerges with modern society itself. Issues immanent in reality itself guide its specific mode of questioning, and humanity and human self-consciousness are included in that reality. It is an exploration of the world that is simultaneously a *self*-exploration. While sociology is untroubled by radical scepticism, it pays for this complacency by plunging human consciousness into the flux of history; for it, there is no privileged experience or aspect of experience that remains outside the ever changing and never wholly known world.

Neither curiosity nor doubt is universal; both emerge as distinctive characteristics of the modern human predicament and are sharply distinguished from the disposition of faith and belief that marked the culture of the premodern west. In the earliest period of modernity, curiosity and doubt, sociology and philosophy, intermingle and condition one another. Montaigne, for example, finds in the ceaseless renewal of both that 'There is no end to our inquiries', that 'It is only our individual weakness which makes us satisfied with what has been discovered by others or by ourselves in this hunt for knowledge' (1991, 1211). The unsettling restlessness of curiosity and doubt, moreover, makes him aware in a new way of his own being and its relation to the world; hence 'I study myself more than any other subject. That is my metaphysics' (1991, 1217). It is also, it might be added, Montaigne's *sociology*; he sought an understanding of his own experience that made sense in terms of the fundamental characteristics of the society in which he lived and from which, in vain, he sought to withdraw. In Montaigne's case it is the realization that this society and this experience are profoundly different from anything that had gone before that is the starting point for both his philosophical reflection and his sociological exploration.

Montaigne's *Essays*, written towards the end of the sixteenth century, are strikingly modern and share with the much later development of phenomenology a determination to grasp in a radical way the continually changing conditions of experience. The kinship that links the earliest and most recent orientations to modernity comes, first of all, from their self-identification as new. Phenomenology, it should be acknowledged from the outset, is a philosophy of modernity; it is filled with the distinctive vitality of the present age. Within sociology, however, and somewhat oddly, it has been viewed with suspicion; misunderstood as a wholly uncritical method of naive description, and utterly lacking in any committed engagement with the world. But phenomenology, as its founder understood its central aims, was much more than a reflection of, or upon, the modern conditions of life. In an important essay, and in language reminiscent of Hegel's magisterial tone, Edmund Husserl makes plain his own view of the fundamental commitments of his philosophical thought:

> The spiritual need of our time has, in fact, become unbearable. Would that it were only theoretical lack of clarity regarding the sense of the 'reality' investigated in the natural and humanistic sciences that disturbed our peace ... Far more than this, it is the most radical vital need that afflicts us, a need that leaves no point of our lives untouched. All life is taking a position, and all taking of position is subject to a must – that of doing justice to validity and invalidity according to alleged norms of absolute validation ... But how is it now, when any and every norm is controverted or empirically falsified and robbed of its ideal validity? Naturalists and historicists misinterpret ideas as facts ... transform all reality, all life, into an incomprehensible, idealess confusion of 'facts'. The superstition of the fact is common to them all. (1981, 193)

Phenomenology, that is to say, is not neutral with respect to the vital issues of the present; it is committed to the world of modernity, to claiming and sustaining the world as a *human* product. The philosophical goal of insight, thus, can be gained only 'if with the radicalism belonging to the essence of genuine philosophical science we accept nothing given in advance, allow nothing traditional to pass as a beginning, nor ourselves to be dazzled by any names however great, but rather seek to attain the beginnings in a free dedication to the problems themselves and to the demands stemming from them' (1981, 195). And if phenomenology is determined to gain an unclouded view of reality it is not, for that reason, to be regarded as a 'foundation' for the social sciences in general or sociology in particular, nor can sociology claim priority as a 'foundation' for phenomenology. Rather, phenomenology and sociology *both* rest on specific circumstances of life grasped in their own way as the essential and characteristic experience of the present.

The Archaic and the Ancient

Bringing sociology and phenomenology together in this way alludes also to a much older understanding of philosophy; one that, in being restored to the centre of intellectual life, makes clear the extent to which each discipline depends for the realization of its projects on the most intimate interrelation with the ideas and perspectives of the other.

Originally, the *social* character of philosophy was self-evident. Philosophy was born as 'love of wisdom', that is as *philia/sophia*. In the ancient world *philia* refers primarily to close interpersonal relations that include, but are not exclusively, kin. Against the trend of recent scholarship that treats these relations in narrow utilitarian terms, the comprehensive study by David Konstan (1997) insists that *philia* should be regarded primarily as freely entered relations of mutual affection. The term (as commonly in Ancient

Greek) also refers to specific body parts and organs, in this instance those regarded as peculiarly 'intimate' – knees, genitals, and chin (1997, 30; Vernant 1991). Rather than say *philia* describes kinship relations or the bonds of close personal friendship, it is perhaps more meaningful to say that *ideally* relations among kin and within the community should be relations of *philia*; that is, relations founded on familiarity, intimacy, and mutual acceptance. The 'love' that is the 'love of wisdom', therefore, is characterized by warmth, familiarity, and openness and is, thus, in some respects quite the opposite of desire (*eros*) that is experienced as a tense, involuntary striving after something distant. Wisdom, equally, is unlike modern knowledge (*episteme*). It is a more inclusive term, embracing practical activities, as well as artistic and technical pursuits; it involves the body in its many-sidedness and not just the art of thinking. It is related to a world that is already familiar; a world lived in and lived through, rather than an obscure reality that confronts us as something strange and remote.

Philosophy in this sense was first of all a summons to the truth of an examined life and not simply a demand for orderly and disciplined thought. It involved a personal commitment and, often, the acceptance of a particular kind of community life (Hadot 1995). Philosophy, thus, is nothing other than an 'orientation', a particular disposition that springs spontaneously from the human heart; it is said to be a response to a primordial state of wonder. Philosophy is this disposition: 'a basic mode of life itself' (Heidegger 2001, 62). Wisdom is the love of wisdom; it is a movement of the soul provoked by wonder. The warmth with which life greets the world is the original genius of Greek philosophy, and phenomenology asks in the most serious way possible whether, for us, and for our world, such a possibility yet exists. Can philosophy even now overcome the strangeness of the modern world?

Sociology, on the other hand, bears the distinction of being an 'ology' and, thus, falls within the constituting order of the *logos*; it is the rationally comprehensible order of society. The Greek term is variously translated as word, speech, discourse, or reason and refers to any process of naming, distinguishing, separating, collecting, and ordering. This does not mean everything in the world is explained or understood, it means just that it is ordered, and that its elements are viewed as belonging together. This coherence is regarded as something that properly belongs to it. But this unity is no longer something friendly; it is 'cold' and aloof; it is withdrawn from the realm of human feeling and turns itself towards us, if it must, with casual indifference. It is not wonderful, however puzzling it may be. The 'love of wisdom' first aroused by wonder at the mystery of things was itself a transition, a magnificent but doomed gesture towards the actuality of change. The plasticity originally imparted by Plato to the *logoi* were gradually fixed and formed into permanent models of realities held to underlie the flux of immediate experience. The *logos* was invoked as the more powerful means of overcoming the fluidity of immediate experience, the flux of things, and reaching a comprehensible world of relations expressed in unambiguous terms. Philosophy allied itself with the authority of the *logos* and developed an understanding of its own role as spokesperson, to articulate the fundamental and unchanging structure of the *logos*.

This was part of a major social transformation in the ancient world; the transition from archaic community to ancient empire. During the period that is sometimes referred to as the 'axial age' (from about 500 to 200 BCE) large-scale and radical change was affecting many aspects of life in unforeseen ways (Voegelin 1956; Eisenstadt 1986; Arnason et al. 2004). The transition from *mythos* to *logos* is not a matter of independent intellectual and conceptual development but should be seen, rather, as a transformation in the consciousness of reality that is part of the large-scale transformation of ancient society; a transformation that involved significant growth in scale and complexity, political centralization and the emergence of new forms of political authority, the development of much more complex market relationships, the division of labour, the use of money, and particularly the growth of cities and the emergence of a ruling class free from the direct exploitation of the land and other economic resources (Thompson 1961; De Ste Croix 1981; Buxton 1999). These dramatic 'tradition-breaking' processes generated a heightened sense of instability and simultaneously created the conditions for the emergence of a general 'philosophical' view of reality as they were suffused with this consciousness.

Philosophy in its oldest form already anticipates this transition and subordinates itself to the *logos* and the task of articulating its immanent structure. Philosophy increasingly falls under the spell of thinking. Wonder gives way to self-conscious mastery of the world through the *logos*. And an eroticized striving of thought to conquer reality and subdue everything to its forceful spirit casts aside the more intimate friendship of wisdom in which philosophy began and in which it found its first fertile stance.

When the *logos* is grasped, thus, as a social form, it becomes clear that, even at the most general level, it is part of the ceaseless transformation of social life. The *logos* has a history, not just in the sense of requiring particular conditions for its birth, but in terms also of its own inner transformation and development. Most significantly in the Christian tradition *logos* becomes the incarnate Word of God and means both creation ('In the beginning was the Word', John 1: 1) and the divine condescension ('the Word was made flesh', John 1: 4). In the *logos* were conjoined the perfect clarity of a rational order and the impenetrable mystery of divine being. Phenomenology, uniquely among modern philosophical movements, retains a strong sense of *both* these domains of meaning. Phenomenology is both rigorous science *and* mystical theology: on the one hand an unrelentingly rational process of describing, through naming, classifying, distinguishing, what is irreducibly present in experience; and, on the other hand, a turning towards and acknowledgement of the ultimately incomprehensible character of phenomena as such.

Philosophy and sociology draw on long traditions and wide-ranging associations. Indeed, it is less easy than at first it might seem to define them in such a way as to keep them apart. Both by turns formalistic and humanistic, their mutual, unacknowledged historical intertwining provides essential insight into the character of the present.

What is proposed here is a general *rapprochement* between philosophy and sociology; a relationship already formed but as yet latent in the development of phenomenology and historical sociology. This suggestion, of course, is fraught with danger. It is surely an act of faith, verging on folly, to suppose that two disciplines which, taken separately, have failed to fulfil their own ambitions might succeed as a joint venture. Yet there is little choice but to trust our intuition and follow the example of creative workers of every sort who step outside the conventional boundaries of disciplinary research.

The aims of the present work, in fact, are modest and do not pretend originality. It is not the radicalism of a new starting point that is proposed but a fresh consideration of established positions; approaches that, viewed somewhat unconventionally, suggest a much broader framework of shared assumptions and insights than is generally acknowledged guides research and reflection in seemingly disparate fields of study. This common ground, it will be argued, is nothing other than the experience of modern life; so that, in different ways, experience and the analysis of experience have been, and continue to be, the essential features of *both* sociology and philosophy.

But sociology and philosophy cannot be merged by *diktat*; there is no secure position outside from which adequately to judge the validity of their approaches or to coordinate their interrelation. What is proposed, rather, is that philosophy be viewed sociologically, and sociology be viewed philosophically. In this way the role of modern experience in each, and the general character of that experience, can be more fully articulated. But there can be no question of carrying through a comprehensive and exhaustive survey along these lines. The following is limited to a single example of what might be termed constructive intertextuality, or cross-reading. The danger of such an approach is both to make the exercise rather too easy by selecting in advance just those aspects of sociology and philosophy where there is a strong supposition of 'agreement', and, subsequently (whatever the result), wildly to overgeneralize from a single case. These dangers may be minimized (though not wholly avoided), by selecting the more difficult cases for consideration. Certainly, as conventionally understood, *phenomenological* philosophy and *historical* sociology are unlikely bedfellows. It does not follow, of course, that, if a positive relation between them is revealed, then a positive relation must or can subsist between philosophy and sociology in general. But, if convincing, it would certainly establish a *prima facie* case in support of such a contention.

The following discussion is divided into two main parts. The first part outlines the historical context of, and major positions within, phenomenology considered as the philosophy of modernity. It also outlines the reception of this philosophy within sociology. It is not intended as a comprehensive introduction or interpretation of Husserl's work, a necessary task already well accomplished (Moran 2000; Sokolowski 2000; Zahavi 2003), but, rather, offers a reading attuned to a specific interest in characterizing contemporary experience. The second part provides, however schematically, a phenomenological sociology of modernity by way of sociological readings of phenomenological investigations, and phenomenological readings of sociological research. The aim of both parts and both approaches is to gain *insight* into the phenomena of modern society.

Part I

Explications

Misapprehension is the primordial phenomenon.
Nietzsche, *Unfashionable Obervations*

1

Astonishment: the Birth and Rebirth of the Phenomenal

> It is a primal state of *amazement* which sets all the creative forces of the soul to work.
>
> Buber, *Moses*

'What gives rise to phenomenological analysis is an unsettling wonder in the presence of things' (Welton 2000, 13). It is to the initiatory power of phenomena themselves that we should turn for an immediately meaningful context in which to view the emergence of phenomenology. And where wonder stands at the beginning of philosophy in the ancient world, what might better be called astonishment at the outpouring of modern phenomena is the particular disposition that inaugurates phenomenology. Wonder should be considered not as something that stands apart from philosophy as an exterior cause of its first tentative probing of reality but, rather, as an inseparable aspect of that movement itself. In a similar way astonishment is part of the phenomenon itself. The phenomenon is, first of all, *phenomenal*; something astonishing. The modern rebirth of wonder, as astonishment, is nothing other than the emergence of reality as phenomenal. In beginning with astonishment (that is by *being* astonished and not merely thinking about astonishment as a concept), we occupy a position anterior to both philosophy and sociology. We begin with the *shock* of modernity.

In the modern period, at the very moment when the world's resistance to the spirit of rationalization seemed finally to have been overcome, wonder once again and in a decisive way broke like a foaming wave over consciousness and bathed reality in a mysterious glow. The modern era, so long regarded as an age of science, of reason, of order, of progress, and as a world in which the *logos* was inscribed in its every particular, bewilderingly sounded with the distant echo of an ancient past. And in the same moment the past seemed to reveal itself in a new light and in its true colours. The rediscovery in the ancient world of the *exstasis* of wonder as well as the calm spirit of detachment owes most to wholly modern sensibilities and the emergence of new psychological insights founded upon them; one thinks especially of the tensions that electrified Nietzsche's philosophical essays on the civilization of Ancient Greece and delivered the culture of modernity from the classicism of Burckhardt and Winkelmann (Nietzsche 1999; Gooding-Williams 2001).

The modern age, in other words, is not only the age of reason; it is, above all, the age of astonishment – the age of the *phenomenal*. The phenomenal appeared and reappeared not only in the recovery of the ancient world but, spectacularly, in the discovery and conquest of distant and exotic lands (Todorov 1984; Greenblatt 1991; 1993; Pagden 1994; Rawson 2001), and, much closer to home, in the exploration of our own experience. And phenomenology as the philosophy of astonishment is nothing other than the general consciousness of the present. Before discussing the key texts of Husserl and other phenomenological philosophers, therefore, it is helpful briefly to consider the modern history of astonishment as their appropriate context.

The Exceptional

Throughout Europe in the early modern period many princely rulers, aristocratic courtiers, scholars, and merchants assembled collections of extraordinary objects. In retrospect these *cabinets de curiosités* and *Wunderkammern* appear to be chaotic repositories, assembled without regard to any coherent principle or common distinguishing features. All manner of natural specimens, artefacts, and artfully produced objects were displayed, or simply stored, by piling one on another in disorderly abundance. Exotic shells, stuffed animals, pictures, rare and arcane books, elaborate clocks, automata, musical instruments from remote parts of the world, dried and preserved plants, amulets, objects charged with magical and medicinal properties, elaborate chests with secret drawers, and much else were juxtaposed and intermingled in a promiscuous riot of marvels. Huge collections were designed to impress important invited guests with the power of their princely custodians and, though rarely open to ordinary people, were housed in buildings of such imposing scale and grandeur as, equally, to amaze the excluded masses. In the popular, superstitious imagination, indeed, the unseen contents of these palaces were scarcely more fantastic than the myriad of objects actually disclosed to their privileged guests. Magnificence became the acknowledged sign of nobility, and nothing was more magnificent than the, actual or imagined, encyclopaedia of *objects* sequestered in the baroque palaces of early modern Europe (Kauffmann 1988, 1993, 1995). The *Kunstkammer* established by Ferdinand I (Holy Roman Emperor, 1548–64) in Vienna, as did the *Studiolo* of the Medici in Florence, aspired to nothing less than total inclusiveness and was said to contain 'specimens of all that could be found in the world' (Kaufmann 1988). And while those and others such as the celebrated collections of Ulisse Aldrovandi in Bologna, and Rudolf II in Prague, surpassed in scale and magnificence the many more modest assemblies that emerged at the same time throughout Europe, all 'aspired to stupefy visitors with wonder' (Daston and Park 1998, 267).

Whether large or small, the carnival of *things* bodied forth the plenitude of being. And, though seemingly monuments to the contingent and arbitrary, these bizarre cornucopia found their unity in the astonishment aroused by the inexplicable presence of exceptional objects. Even the most deranged collectors gradually modified their ambitions; rather than house samples of everything, they preferred to isolate and display only what were *exceptional*. The monstrous jostled the exquisite and the rare; anything 'subverting or straddling the boundaries of familiar categories' qualified for inclusion (Daston and Park 1998, 272). Soon 'only the unique would suffice, the idiosyncratic pushed to the point of incongruity' (Mauriès 2002, 73). The abundance and variety of strange objects, each in their own way peculiar, were drawn together as the contents of an enclosed and secret world; a laboratory for the virtuoso of 'preternatural philosophy' and the aristocratic connoisseur 'so familiar with a multiplicity of extraordinary phenomena that he knew which truly deserved his amazement' (Daston and Park 1998, 167).

At the dawn of the modern era, that is to say, the *phenomenal* emerged as distinctive *objects* of astonishment. This might be viewed as the secularization of ancient wonder. What provoked astonishment was neither the bare existence of things in general nor the unique manifestation of divine power, but the appearance of something bewildering: 'Between the commonplace and the miraculous lay the large and nebulous domain of the marvelous' (1998, 159). And exceptions could appear only because most things, most of the time, readily fell within the range of what was already known, and expected as 'normal' or 'natural' – what conformed to a general rule. The phenomenal object astounded just because it exhibited attributes and properties that lay outside that range and confounded the rule. It occupied a region between the visible and the invisible and in a real sense was an impossible object; something that ought not to exist at all and whose presence, therefore, threw the viewer into a state of confusion (Pomian 1987; Mauriès 2002, 109).

What was astonishing was less the specific peculiarities of unclassifiable objects than *that* such things should exist at all. The origin of the phenomenal object was utterly obscure and induced a questioning stupor. 'How is it possible?', 'How could such a thing come about?', 'What is it?' Most puzzling of all is the certainty that whatever peculiarly marks the phenomenal, it is 'in reality' just another object; one more thing in a world filled with things. Ultimately, the exception is only unusual and, thus, unfamiliar. For *modern* thought and the modern world, however extraordinary and unprecedented something may appear to be, nothing can exist outside nature's monumental regularity. In the sixteenth and early seventeenth centuries, however, this insight was not widely shared and the astonishing was often understood as revealing (though never in an obvious way) the secret working of nature's hidden, occult and, in a sense, 'unnatural' powers (Yates 1964; Eamon 1994; Findlen 1999; Campbell 1999).

Even in the context of Renaissance magic and the animistic cosmology of the 'preternatural philosopher', however, the phenomenal must be distinguished from wonder in the ancient world. It is important to note that in the religious experience of ancient Judaism astonishment was grasped as a manifestation, or breaking through, of the divine: 'The man of early times met the unplanned, unexpected events which transformed the historical situation of his community at a single stroke with a fundamental stirring of all the elements in his being ... The historical wonder is no mere interpretation; it is something actually seen' (Buber 1946, 14). This wonder is captured and sustained in the early saga, the rhythmical form in which is preserved the 'memory of the awe-inspiring Things that had come alive'. This is grasped as a miracle, which is 'nothing but an abiding astonishment'. 'The real miracle means that in the astonishing experience of the event the current system of cause and effect becomes, as it were, transparent and permits a glimpse of the sphere in which a sole power, not restricted by any other, is at work. To live with the miracle means to recognize this power on every given occasion as the affecting one' (1946, 77).

The religious sense of astonishment cannot be rationalized and is distinguished, thus, from the Greek sense of wonder in which philosophy begins. Plato was resting on an already durable tradition when in *Theaetetus* he asserts that it 'is especially the *pathos* [emotion] of a philosopher to be astonished. For there is no other beginning of *philosophia* than this' (1987, 155d). And in his *Metaphysics* Aristotle concurs: 'For through astonishment men have begun to philosophise, both in our time and at the beginning' (A2, 98L b12). But right 'at the beginning' an equivocation emerges. Philosophy is a response to wonder; a response that, on the one hand, recognizes the primitive force of the irrational and, on the other, in this very act of recognition, instigates a process of rationalization that has as its end what Max Weber dubbed the radical 'disenchantment of the world'. Aristotle, thus, characterizes astonishing events, 'that evolve fear and pity', as effects that 'occur above all when things come about contrary to expectation but because of one another' (1996, 6.1). Philosophy is a process of articulating a larger framework of order in which the unpredictable can be accommodated and redefined as a normal and unsurprising event. Philosophy, that is, develops by banishing wonder; but wonder is just the immediate experience of reality most cherished by the philosopher. Philosophy, thus, realizes itself as a process of self-undermining and loss of impulse. Thus, 'the philosophizing and the religious person both wonder at the phenomenon, but the one neutralizes his wonder in ideal knowledge, while the other abides in that wonder; no knowledge, no cognition can weaken his astonishment' (Buber 1946, 75).

Modern astonishment, however, was neither sustained by a religious spirit nor dispelled by philosophy; it occupied, rather, a zone of material ambiguity that, however modest in its scale, resisted the powerful forces of modern rationalization. The overwhelming growth of scientific knowledge, on the one hand, and the continuously developing orderliness and ordinariness of everyday life, on the other, failed wholly to abandon astonishment to the prehistory of modern sentiment. At the very moment when it seemed the world was settling to, and for, unmysterious routine, phenomenal objects reappeared and in frankly astonishing abundance.

This point of transition, itself almost invisible for, indeed, nothing fundamentally had altered in the development of modernity, might in retrospect be fixed at 1851; in the Great Exhibition and in its monumental emblem, the Crystal Palace. Here the new was celebrated in all its variety – yet this variety bodied forth a certain recurrent theme. New materials, including steel and glass, new forms of power, new tools of production all lay behind the variety of artefacts gathered under the temporary pavilions and displayed the new world that industry was creating. This was not just propaganda, or salesmanship; the Exhibition, repeated in major cities throughout Europe and America during the following decades, was most of all a sheer spectacle. Not since the baroque era in early modern Europe, and far surpassing it in scale, had so much effort been lavished on the production of such astonishing effects. But now, rather than dramatize magnificence in order to intimidate and subdue the masses, the Exhibition made public and celebrated the extraordinary diversity of modern products as an open invitation to participate in and realize its promise of abundance. It was as if an entire and entirely new world had appeared overnight; freely available, and within reach of all (Benedict 1983).

At the opening ceremony of the Great Exhibition the Archbishop of Canterbury, who was leading the procession, kept wandering off the prescribed route, drawn first to one side then to another and stopping in front of exhibits to gaze in astonishment (Newsome 1997, 50). A contemporary observer, Samuel Warren, puts it well: 'Who can describe that astonishing spectacle? Lost in a sense of what it is, who can think what it is like? Philosophers and poets alike are agitated, and silent; gaze withersoever they may, all is marvellous and affecting; stirring new thoughts and emotions, and awakening the oldest memories and associations' (1997, xx). And ten years later the *Illustrated Weekly News* observed that 'This is the age of exhibitions ... we have exhibitions of nearly all possible and impossible things' (Hoffenberg 2001, xiii). Above all, the empire was displayed in a congenial light and the display of its benign civilization became a semi-annual event in South Kensington. Here were 'worlds of ritualized and participatory fantasy. Poetry mingled with art. Enchantment reigned: labor in a mine was transformed into a comfortable truck ride; colonial conquest became mosques and minarets' (2001, xix).

The modern world, maturing for over a century in the womb of capitalist enterprises, market institutions, and state organizations, burst forth in an irresistible torrent. What most astonished was the scale and power of modern technology. There was nothing mysterious about steam engines and engineering equipment, but the unprecedented magnitude of forces harnessed and released in a controlled fashion, the tireless repetition of the machine, and the sheer enormity of its productive capacity amazed in a new way. Unlike the marvel of nature or art, here were humanly engineered monsters, reproducible to order and created with a practical purpose in mind. A new and overwhelmingly objective dynamism was unleashed. Modernity, hitherto dispersed in the myriad forms of cultural life, took hold of itself in a novel way, crystallized in the sheer necessity of the world's overpowering abundance of things. The pure materiality of modern life, to which we have become accustomed, and into which we were born as something 'natural', initially appeared as a shattering of all existing, including all modern, assumptions and conceptions about the world and its inherent possibilities.

Exhibitions, of course, suffered the same fate as the early modern marvel; they became progressively less astonishing and, in the end, quite ordinary. By the 1860s and 1870s static museum displays were not enough to gain the attention and admiration of the crowd; motion and noise became essential aspects of the exhibit. Working machinery, and especially early displays of 'self-activating' devices, rekindled interest, offering a utopian vision of production without human labour.

The sheer superabundance of things resulted in deadened senses; the *Illustrated Weekly News* noted that ultimately the visitor 'wearied with the extent and variety of things exhibited: with the endless lumps of coal, the colossal cakes of soap, the thousands of labelled bottles, the colossal engines, and the curious models' (Hoffenberg 2001, 196). Machines were decorated and coloured, covered with banners and ribbons, or draped in tapestries and other conservative historic images. Popular entertainments were added as 'attractions', living ethnological exhibits added an exotic touch, fantasy worlds multiplied and eclipsed the 'real' world of productive machinery and everyday products that had been the central focus of early exhibitions.

Within and outside the exhibition arena, however, the continuing development of modern technology, particularly the development of electrical devices and lighting, renewed modernity's power to astonish (Nye 1992). Above all in the rapid industrialization and urbanization of the United States the 'technological sublime' rose to prominence and furnished ever renewed sources 'of popular wonder and amazement, from the railroad to the atomic bomb and the space program' (Nye 1999, 8–9). In America engineering feats produced effects that so 'entirely filled [the mind] with the object, that it cannot entertain any other'. The skyscraper, the railroad, and the telegraph defied every normal experience of space. And after 1880 'the electrified urban landscape emerged as another avatar of the sublime' (1999, 143). The Philadelphia Centennial Exposition in 1876 displayed a new electrified landscape, a luminous wonderland rather than a display of raw power of heavy machinery. Illumination introduced a new medium of artifice: 'Between 1880 and 1915 electrical engineers found ways to re-present virtually any object with light, so that cultural meanings could be altered as the object was written upon, edited, highlighted, or blacked out. The engineers who developed these effects became showmen' (1999, 145; Cheney 1981). Lighting 'distracted and charmed even the most critical observers' (1999, 149; Schivelbusch 1995). Theodore Dreiser, visiting Chicago Fair, describes how 'a feeling of the true dreamlike beauty of it all came to me' (1999, 148). 'Electricity dematerialized the built environment of the fair, transforming its buildings into enchanting visions, of flowers, blossoms, and other natural forms' (Nye 1999, 150). The social and cultural world of the Exposition and the Fair was a 'liminal' experience, which had an exemplary significance for advanced society, where 'The individual merged into an egalitarian crowd, restricted by few rules' (1999, 204).

The phenomenal was manifest also on a small scale; in the 'ingenious' object. The fountain pen and safety match, as later light bulbs, domestic equipment, and telephone, introduced a more intimate but no less significant scale of astonishment (Briggs 1990). Many of the displays at the Great Exhibition, and those that followed, aimed simply to confound and baffle the sense of what was possible. It was a huge 'celebration of British ingenuity', that featured such baroque absurdities as an 'artificial silver nose, a vase made of mutton fat, the silent alarm bedstead that tipped the sleeper into a cold bath' (Auerbach 1999, 110). The key feature in these later developments, as in the contemporary world of hi-tech 'gizmos', is not the application of massive power, or the inhuman scale of accumulated thingness, but the defiance of nature and what had often been regarded as its insurmountable constraints.

The ingenious device that was also an aid to living was phenomenal and worthy of display as well as use. The voice recorded and transmitted, the astonishing uses of electricity and chemistry promised, towards the end of the nineteenth century, a world of undreamt human powers. In terms of contemporary personal technologies, communicative connection has the same power of astonishing. Here it is the opposite of display, the 'magical' yet known to be wholly explicable, the secret of the black box; the mechanism is concealed, its power supply seems trivial, and the magnitude of its effects seems disproportionate and unrelated to its instigating cause. This was already the case with the prototype of all modern ingenuity; the watch. Since the early seventeenth century clockwork had been the standard mechanical analogy for the 'design' of nature; and the watch personalized and made intimate the key operating system of this phenomenal mechanism.

The astonishing can be distinguished from the wonderful, curious, or mysterious, the unexpected, startling, or strange. The astonishing does not signify an alien or a superior power. It does not manifest presence or disclose transcendence. Nor is it any longer an object of curiosity in the early modern sense; even if never before encountered, the astonishing object conforms to a type and is part of a well-defined system of objects. Mystery no longer clings to the astonishing. The astonishing becomes a difference in scale, in magnitude, in function, in form, in mechanism; its deviation from the normal is simply a result of the ceaseless expansion and adaptation of known techniques. The astonishing is the ephemera of modernity's tireless production of novelties; ultimately, nothing other than the objectification of time itself.

The Phenomenal

The phenomenal is astonishing; the astonishing is phenomenal. It is literally 'unbelievable', the phenomenal *overwhelms*. The astonishing cannot be assimilated to the *logos*. It is *outside* and *other* than the world with which we are, or feel we can become, familiar. It takes up temporary residence in everything that is impressive by virtue of *any* characteristics that make it 'stand out' from a background of unremarkable things and events. In the modern world, where only spatio-temporal objects are dignified as 'real', it is the fate of everything that first of all strikes us as phenomenal eventually to merge with the dull uniformity of the absolutely ordinary. The tension that animates the history of western philosophy, the unresolved tussle of wonder and the *logos*, charts the history of phenomena themselves; their discovery and loss and rediscovery in the process of western rationalization. Nothing stands out for long; the phenomenal is continually on the move, momentarily flaring into life on the horizon of the unexpected. But from another point of view the continual degradation of everything phenomenal, its sinking back into indifference, charges the mundane object-world with the peculiar tension of surprise. Currents of muffled astonishment still run through the dull world of everyday experience and occasionally lighten its surface with flashes of glamour or excitement. But the world is irretrievably transformed. The *phenomenal* theatre of early modernity gives way to a general dynamism of *phenomena*; the exceptional becomes ordinary, and every engagement with reality is suffused with a uniform 'coolness'.

A phenomenon becomes unexceptional; it is simply anything of which we may become conscious or, more precisely, it is the consciousness of a particular something. A vase of flowers, a picture of a vase of flowers, and the memory of either are all examples of phenomena. There is no assumption, explicit or implicit, that the vase of flowers we see and smell is somehow a more 'real' phenomenon than the picture or the memory. As phenomena, everything of which we become conscious 'counts'. A picture or a memory of a vase of flowers does not depend in any simple way upon there being a 'real' vase of flowers of which they are partial copies or representations. And the sense of pleasure, or uneasiness, say, that arises with this looking, remembering, or imagining is also a phenomenon. We may entertain a variety of scientific and other beliefs about the ultimate origin and nature of such perceptions and so on, but these suppositions tell us nothing about phenomena as *phenomena*.

Phenomena, that is to say, should not be confused either with images, or with signs. An image replicates some aspect of a phenomenon and, *because* of this, is taken to represent that phenomenon. Originally an image was a statue, preferably a life-sized replica of aspects of the spatial form and surface appearance of a person. The image bears an immediate resemblance to its model; to be an image at all it has to be recognizable, even where, as in the case of the majority of Greek statues, the original is not a 'real' person at all, but a god. An image must be recognizable to be effective (Ricoeur

1994). Of course, for us, the same statue will be something quite different. *We* do not 'see' an image of a god; we see a work of art, sanctified by tradition and ennobled (or otherwise) by *our* beliefs about the character and significance of classical Greek culture. For us the ancient gods have no reality, but art does. Both the statue and our understanding of what it meant to its original viewers are phenomena for us, but they are no longer essentially linked, and we might well admire the marble form without recognizing it as an image of Apollo. Phenomena, that is to say, are unlike images, ancient and exhausted or newly minted. Phenomena are not 'like' something else. Of course, one phenomenon may be more or less like another phenomenon; but neither is like anything other than a phenomenon. Phenomena are not substitutes for absent non-phenomena.

Signs, on the other hand, represent concepts rather than recall absences. A signifier, by virtue of conventional usage alone, stands for the concept of an object, an event, a feeling, an idea, and so on. There need be no resemblance, or any other form of necessary relation, between the two. The sounds people make when they speak, for example, are not meaningful in themselves, and become so only among a group of language users who share some at least of the same speech conventions. It is the very arbitrariness of the connection between signifier and signified that makes language as we know it possible (Saussure 1986). Of course, the sound of speech is itself a phenomenon or, rather, a complex series of phenomena, as are the meanings understood by these sounds. But the relationship between these two groups of phenomena is, for the phenomenologist, a contingent matter for investigation rather than an issue of what sounds 'really' mean.

Phenomena, that is to say, are neither particular kinds of objects, nor specific forms of meaning. Phenomena cannot be *explained* either in relation to non-phenomenal causes invariantly prior to them or *understood* in relation to subjective meanings they are held to express. Phenomena are immediately present to us; they are nothing other than themselves. Phenomena are in consciousness and only in consciousness; but they are not in the *mind*. It is important to realize that phenomena are not defined simply and arbitrarily as the subject matter of phenomenology, but constitute, in its most general sense, the world in which and through which we live. And phenomenology, therefore, is not defined in terms of its method and procedures, although its mode of inquiry is quite distinctive; it is not another different kind of philosophy, or a specific branch of a more inclusive study, as arithmetic is to mathematics. Phenomenology is the process of exploring and grasping phenomena. It begins and ends in the recognition of reality as constituted exclusively of phenomena. It is not a new way of studying reality but the consciousness of a new reality.

If phenomena are not to be explained through their causes, or understood through their meanings, then how can they be studied at all? How can phenomenology be anything more than a complaint against the established forms of modern discourse that proceed analytically and begin by securing for themselves a vantage point outside and independent of their object of study? It would seem that the very notion of the phenomenal precludes its investigation. There is no place outside and beyond the phenomenal from which we might observe, order, codify, and interpret its ceaseless becoming. We are, in a decisive way, *in* the phenomenal. We cannot become 'detached' from our ongoing activities in the way scholarship in any discipline seems to require. Indeed, it is precisely our own ongoing activities that constitute the fundamental subject matter of phenomenology. Yet it is the principal contention of phenomenology that not only is such a study possible but also only through the study of phenomena can reality properly be grasped.

Even if we were temporarily to grant such a possibility, its results would surely be, at best, of marginal interest. If phenomena 'belong' exclusively to consciousness, then do we not condemn phenomenology to being no more than an introspective psychology, sunk in an interminable game of self-reference? Should we not begin by decisively breaking free of this solipsistic prison and directly exploring the greater world beyond? Again, phenomenology insists that such a break is illusory. Only by grasping phenomena *as* phenomena do we grasp reality. That is to say, consciousness is not what most people have taken it to be. It is not a picture of an absent world contained in the mind of an individual; it *is* the world. Only by seeming to restrict ourselves to the study of phenomena do we, in fact, gain access to the world itself.

The aim of phenomenology is to gain *insight* into the *essential* character of phenomena; that is to say into the essentially phenomenal character of reality. Insight is gained when phenomena are grasped as self-evident. Again, this is not to be confused with *conceptual* clarity (Lonergan 1957), but is a matter of carefully following the interrelationships among phenomena themselves until they are revealed in their simplest possible form. Only phenomena can be grasped as founded in this way, as rooted in themselves; and they can only be grasped this way because reality itself is constituted exclusively as phenomena.

In a determined fashion phenomenology begins by eschewing all those categorical distinctions through which philosophy had previously sought to grasp reality. Radical dualism had characterized western thought since its inception in the ancient world. The very notion of the *logos* seems to require a division between, on the one hand, the changing, unpredictable, ambiguous, and opaque world of human experience and, on the other, a domain of reality that is permanent, well ordered, and transparent. But, in positing such a rationally comprehensible and internally consistent domain, the world of experience is devalued. The realm of ideal forms is grasped as superior; as a higher reality that, in every respect, surpasses the conditions to which our own existence is condemned.

That human reason itself conceives reality in terms of ideal forms demands both a radical separation of the rational and intelligible world from the world of immediate experience and, at the same time, a deep and systematic connection subsisting between these two worlds. The recurrent philosophical problem of modern western society, in a narrower and more technical sense, has been to reconcile the contradictory requirements of intelligibility and sensibility. The tendency to reduce one to the other, so that the ideal is discounted as an illusory appearance, or actual experience is dissolved into a momentary epiphany, has been a recurrent but ultimately rejected temptation that avoids rather than resolves the difficulty. Yet, whether the sensible and the intelligible are two different kinds of reality, or two modes of the same reality, it is difficult to see in what way they can be related or interact. To retain any genuine dualism seems to require a doubling of reality; an extravagant process of mirroring or reflection of the sensible in the intelligible (as representation) and the intelligible in the sensible (as science). All systematic dualisms, thus, become irreducibly different, but equivalent, versions of a singular, 'underlying', and yet more mysterious third reality.

Modernity and Humanity: the Historical Character of Phenomena

The end of feudalism in the west, the expansion of western societies into previously unexplored areas of the world, the re-emergence of centralized authority and the formation of the modern territorial state, the development of trade and markets nationally and internationally; in short, the advent of modern society, in principle and in fact, implied a reunification of being under the banner of humanity. A new, secular spirit turned towards the reality of this world as an inexhaustible and neglected treasury. The Renaissance was by no means only a revival of classical learning and a new and vigorous departure in the arts; it proclaimed an original and vital reality (Bouwsma 2000; Manent 1998; Cooper 2002). Humanity, hitherto a degraded and utterly dependent being, roused itself to a declaration of autonomy. Human beings, after all, were not the least of God's creatures, and if they had misused the immeasurably valuable gift of freedom, spoiling themselves and their world, it was the creative use of this very gift that promised most for the possibility of redemption. Human beings now claimed the *dignity* of self-movement and wilful action (Kristeller 1972; 1979, 173–5; Schneewind 1998). In a bold and decisive way, and unaware of the full implications, which continue to work themselves out in the struggles of the contemporary world, the most adventurous spirits of the new age made a practical and theoretical declaration of autonomy (Koselleck 2000; 2004; Blumenberg 1985; Todorov 2002; Lambropoulos 1993).

No longer turned in helpless longing towards the divine, human thought and activity sank themselves in the immediate world of their own experience. But in separating itself from God or, rather, in finally accepting God's abandonment of His creatures to their own freedom, humanity opened its eyes to a strange and remote world. Hitherto, absolute dependence upon superior forms of being for the very possibility of their own lowly existence had made humanity intimate with the created world; a community of impermanence and imperfection, of decay, mortality, and the exhausting and degrading necessity of regeneration (Gurevich 1985; Le Goff 1988; Kleinschmidt 2000). Humanity and nature were one in abjection; their shared wretchedness was the defining aspect of an immediate participation in the world. The natural world offered itself as an emblematic code; a tapestry of symbols through which, as if they were not already made sufficiently aware of their situation, human beings confirmed the infinite distance between themselves and God (Mâle 1958). Nature was both a book and a mirror. In the encyclopaedias of the fourteenth century such as Vincent of Beauvais's *The Mirror of Nature*, creation was grasped as 'a vast reservoir of symbols' (Le Goff 1990, 405; Gurevich 1985, 61). The immediate empirical world was understood to exist both as a part of creation and, at the same time, as an abbreviated form of the totality of that creation. A symbol shares in the substance of the reality it symbolizes; as the Lord's Prayer, for example, is a symbol, or brief statement, of the Christian faith. The empirical world, thus, was understood as the symbol of the entire work of creation and the divine will that had brought it into existence. Indeed, every aspect and discrete entity within the natural world similarly bodied forth an image of this larger and more inclusive reality.

The defiant act of self-assertion in which modernity commenced its troubled history had the immediate effect, not only of confining God to a remote and uninteresting region outside space, but also of disentangling the human from the natural. The self-consciousness of breaking with the past, with traditions, and inaugurating a new era of human history, meant that the world of sensuous appearances took on a new substantiality. Nature became a vast repository of objects, of things; self-sufficient material bodies that, *because* they could be seen and touched, were deemed to have a reality of their own. The historic abyss between God and His creation was reconfigured as the difference between humanity and nature. And in recognizing sensuous objects as fully real, humanity cut itself off from immediate participation in creation. Nature became something *outside* us; something, however, to which we were joined and, in a limited sense, to which we still belonged. Human beings, therefore, were confronted by an objective reality about which they could, in principle, gain knowledge. Knowledge of nature was both possible and necessary as a consequence of the rejection or, what amounted to the same thing, the recognition of the absolute transcendence of God. The grammar of subject–predicate gave way to the harder logic of subject–object and a conception of the world as composed of dead matter.

The natural world, thus, became the supreme object of curiosity, and was humanized by a process of intellectual and aesthetic, as well as political, colonization. Nature was collected, arranged, classified, ordered, and represented in a dramatic explosion of human knowledge, that began in earnest during the latter part of the sixteenth century (Jardine et al. 1996; Reiss 1997). This entire process was begun as a demonstration of the self-willed character of humanity and its power to control and explain everything outside itself. Baroque science, wrenching nature free of God's ordinances, imposed upon the newly discovered reality of material things; an exemplary discipline.

Yet, just as absolutism could not, in the end, guarantee the order of a society through the sheer imposition of a commanding will, so nature also rebelled and, retreating deeper into the recesses of the purely objective, hid from the enquiring mind. The sheer materiality of things defeated human understanding. Matter had simply to be accepted as the given condition of reality. And herein lay a difficulty. Matter could be known through the senses, as phenomena; but *as* phenomena existed for us only in images or representations of a reality to which we had no immediate access. The recalcitrant dualism of the western tradition reasserted itself even before the principle of human autonomy and the independence and coherence of nature had properly been elaborated. Abjection had been traded for ignorance; the austere otherness of God was rediscovered at the heart of the new world. Behind, within, or beneath (but at least not above) the alluring appearance of things, reality had taken up a new position and made itself invisible. It was not that we could not know nature but, rather, that we could *only* know it. That is, we could grasp it, sensuously as well as intellectually, exclusively through the medium of *representations*; mental images that, unlike their ancient counterpart, did not carry any guarantee of likeness to the 'real' matter of 'real' objects. Ultimately, matter was as transcendentally hidden as God had been and, worse, unreceptive of human hopes or fears, offered nothing in the way of irrational comfort.

Matter was dead; a corpse rather than a body, but a corpse that could not be disposed of and, obtrusively lying in state, could neither be thought nor thought away. Reduced to its so-called primary qualities of mass, shape, and extension, matter provoked and scandalized those who had sought, through this reduction to its fundamental properties, to gain access to reality that otherwise concealed itself in sensuous forms. Most fundamentally of all, matter proved to be *impenetrable*. And just as the theologically inspired had once sought ever higher rungs of a ladder that never quite reached to God, so the physical scientists sought ever smaller quantities of matter, ever more refined methods of measuring, analysing, and subdividing without ever quite reaching the simple, bare substance that they craved. The solution, such as it was, consisted in a programme of abstraction. The elemental and impenetrable bodies of nature were grasped as purely geometric points of an ideal space. Matter could then be manipulated at will, and turned into the very stuff of thought (Garber 1992). At the very moment that matter gained its own reality, it all at once lost its substance and became a ghostly presence haunting the rational constructions of scientific theory. In the mature development of modernity, that is to say, phenomena were regarded as representations of an undisclosed reality rather than semblances of 'real' objects; it could not be assumed that they were 'like' their ultimate causes.

The initial determination to break with dualism and deal directly with one world, the only real world, proved fertile of unsuspected obstacle and contradictions. Kant felt compelled to reintroduce in a formal way the difference phenomena themselves had seemingly abolished. The phenomenal was nothing other than appearances grasped immediately as sensuous intuitions; but 'All our representations are in fact related to some object through the understanding, and, since appearances are nothing but representations, the understanding thus relates them to a *something*, as the object of sensible intuition' (1997, 347–8). Phenomena were not given to us directly; they only became phenomena for us in being experienced, and experience itself was possible only in terms of the *a priori* categories of the understanding. All phenomena appeared, therefore, as spatio-temporal objects or, although Kant did not accord this the same logical status, as modifications of the inner feeling of the subject. The categories are free of any specific empirical content 'but serve only to determine the transcendental object (the concept of something in general) through that which is given in sensibility, in order thereby to cognize appearances empirically under concepts of objects' (1997, 348). Phenomena were not the sole reality; the fact that we grasped them as things presupposed the understanding was not itself a phenomenon. The understanding, united with immediate sense data, constituted the world in terms of appearances. This was a serious blow to any simple empiricism, but what more seriously undermined the aspirations of a phenomenal account of the world was the limitations that the understanding itself placed upon such a project: 'Sensibility and its field, namely that of appearances, are themselves limited by the understanding, in that they do not pertain to things in themselves, but only to the way in which, on account of our subjective constitution, things appear to us … from this arises the concept of *noumenon*' (1997, 348). The understanding recognized that, although *for us* all experience took the form of sensible intuitions, this did not mean that things could not also be thought as altogether outside experience. This had the awkward implication that they could not be thought at all. Noumena were not *other objects* of which we were temporarily ignorant and might some day come to know (although many read Kant to mean just that); they were radically beyond experience, in fact the 'boundary concept' of experience itself.

One form of presence, however, *was* immediately knowable, and graspable in its fullness, namely the self-constituting activity of the human *subject*. The phenomenal form of selfhood, the self-aware human subject in which and before which all other phenomena made their appearance, was not itself an object. The self was not outside and over against us, but was simply the observing and acting subject that saw and felt the alien objectivity of all those estranged forms. And as there was no gap between the self and itself, we did not require knowledge of the self in the way we required knowledge of the world in order to act. The effortless self-certainty of the self, fully in possession of itself, was the real foundation of all modern reality. The self was the primary phenomenon, the possession of which made possible the continually appearing world.

Thus, in categorically dividing reality into two different substances, object and subject, Descartes had really introduced an elementary principle of subjectivity into modern thought (Judovitz 1988). Certainty was restricted to self-knowledge, which was, properly speaking, not knowledge of something but immediate self-awareness and the bare sense of our present existence. All objects lay beyond the self and were known only through possibly deceptive representations.

The seemingly self-evident character of the self and the principle of subjectivity that it founded, however, proved to be as elusive and enigmatic a phenomenon as the external object. The self was as changeable and unstable as any other phenomenon. Not all Descartes's contemporaries shared his founding self-confidence. Michel de Montaigne at the end of the sixteenth century, for example, already wondered at the changing quality of his own selfhood and wrote his incomparable *Essays* as a series of 'trials' in self-discovery. 'I am the subject of my book,' he claimed; yet every essay provided him with a fresh start, a new and slightly altered persona. At the same time Miguel de Cervantes, in creating the first great European novel, provided in Don Quixote a figure of chaotic instability, as deluded about himself as he was about the world of objects. Just as the new sciences sought to uncover a coherent and fixed reality behind objective, changing appearances, so a distinctively modern psychology developed through the task of revealing the consistent, authentic subject that was concealed in the ever changing presentations of the self. And just as the natural scientist burrowed inwards and downwards in the pursuit of indivisible and incorruptible matter, so the psychologist looked inward in the expectation of discovering the fixed and well-formed structure that was the real foundation of selfhood. But modern selfhood proved to be as intensively inexhaustible as modern space was externally infinite. Blaise Pascal, a gifted mathematician and physical scientist as well as a major religious writer and sensitive psychologist of the modern human condition, recognized that the double infinity of object and subject was the inescapable implication of the postulate of human autonomy. The subject was as remote and unknown as the object; neither could be touched or grasped other than in frustratingly superficial forms of everyday experience.

Just as the natural sciences invested the mathematical point with real presence, so the authentic self was invoked as the empty freedom of the *moment*, the point in time in which self and ego were conjoined. Time compressed to the moment, like space shrunk to the point, offered itself as a representation filled with reality, a completely undifferentiated unity from which, at once losing touch with this numinous essence, phenomena sprang as mere appearances. The search for reality was an attempt to trace a path back through the labyrinth of superficial forms to the originating singularity in which reality lay coiled; the plenitude of a self-positing 'I'.

In acknowledging the *unreality* of all phenomena as their starting point, however, both rational, objective sciences of the object, and depth psychologies of the subject, sought imaginatively to *replace* all recognizable experience of the world with an order of being of which we must remain unconscious. The superficial was given weight by association with the incomprehensible, and if it did not, it remained a mere appearance. Human consciousness, which was the instrument and medium of human autonomy, seemed bent on self-denigration and the inevitable undermining of its own historic project.

As systematic philosophical positions, empiricism and idealism, which found their starting point in the exclusive reality respectively of object and subject, became ever less convincing. The seventeenth-century mechanical philosophy persisted, as materialism, particularly in France, then more generally as positivism. Philosophically discredited in different ways by Hume and Kant it nonetheless survived in the reductionism of later-nineteenth- and twentieth-century psychology. And idealism, too, sustained itself by retreating into dogmatism. However, by the second half of the nineteenth century systematic philosophy was itself largely discredited as a result of the impasse separately reached in both the major traditions of modern thought, and equally by their failure to reconcile or synthesize their differences in a creative and convincing way. In the meantime serious students of both the natural and the human sciences continued to develop their own insights, paying scant regard to the more general implications of their own work or its connection with developments in other fields. By the end of the nineteenth century a general scepticism, increasingly narrow specialization, and an easy relativism were pervasive characteristics of a culture that continued to pay lip service to the originating humanism of the Renaissance and its principled renewal in the Enlightenment.

Subject and object, the characteristically modern division of reality into two kinds of substance that both provoked and assuaged the ancient metaphysical quest for being, were reunited in the rebirth of the phenomenal. And if they were not yet wholly reintegrated into the seamless manifold of events it was at least admitted that all phenomena were both subjective and objective. What, ultimately, had driven the modern philosophical programme was not so much unsettling epistemological questions about the status of our knowledge of external reality, or uneasiness over the possibilities of selfhood, as it was a response to the longing for reality as a coherent and transparent unity. This unity, as Kant recognized, if it could be reclaimed at all, could only be grasped in an act of pure intellectual intuition, divested of all phenomenal forms.

Picturing Phenomena

Was human experience trapped in an endless process of reflection? If phenomena were representations, they could be nothing other than representations of other phenomena; that is of other representations. There was no way out of the hall of mirrors that human beings had closed around themselves. There was no access to noumena, yet we could not help but posit the existence of the noumenal and place there everything that, in fact, we took to be 'most real'. But, just as these disquieting thoughts came to the centre of philosophical reflection, the process of representation itself underwent a fundamental transformation. Modernity had first become conscious of itself and its difference from the past in art. In art, the process of representation itself became visible, and the autonomous world of human being found its immediate correlate in the process of *picturing* reality. Where previous artistic traditions had presented symbols of other symbols of the sacred order (Belting 1994), Renaissance painting developed conventions of naturalism through which to depict the three-dimensional structure of the human world. The development of perspective techniques and the use of shadow and modelling of figures enabled the artist to depict scenes that appeared to be self-contained realities. The viewer, taking the place of the artist, gained a privileged position from which to overlook an incident, precisely located in space, as if seeing it actually about to unfold. Painting became a recording device through which we could see again and examine in realistic detail a moment from the past. The picture drew back the curtain or opened the shutters of a window through which we were offered a view wrenched from the destructive flow of time. In a formal sense it was the annihilation of time that brought art and science into close alliance; art was a way of accurately describing a specific segment of the real world, and science was an art of visualizing that reality reduced to its essential processes and inter-relations (White 1961; Damisch 1995; Kemp 1992; Alpers 1983).

The autonomous, framed scene was an emblem of modernity. The picture was a pure object viewed by a pure subject, and represented with dreamlike precision a world in which this relation itself was replicated. The enabling assumption of this entire movement was the illusion of natural-ism: that the picture was a picture of something 'real', that is to say some-thing independent of the process of representation itself. Indeed, the distinction between subject matter and form of representation encouraged a conspicuous ontological playfulness to emerge in modern painting. During the early Italian Renaissance *trompe-l'œil* techniques had been exploited in rendering architectural detail with heightened illusionism. But many artists had deliberately transgressed the rules of perspective and the adoption of a singular 'vanishing point' to create realistic representations of impossi-ble spatial relations, or experimented, as had Paolo Uccello, with extreme perspectives of an arbitrary sort. Such deviations from 'normal' viewing brought into focus, and made the significant subject matter of the picture, the process of representation rather than the character of depicted objects. The process of picture making, in fact, became a favourite subject matter, as did the incorporation into the finished painting of other pictured scenes, views through half-open doors, and reflected images in mirrors and polished surfaces (Stoichita 1997).

In the sudden appearance of still-life painting around 1600, in particular, illusionism became a major preoccupation. And later in the seventeenth century artists such as Samuel van Hoogstraten aimed momentarily to deceive the viewer into taking the picture of everyday objects or interiors for actual objects in real space. After Caravaggio's miraculous *Basket of Fruit*

(1595) and Jan Breughel's paintings of flowers for Cardinal Borromeo (1606), which were deliberately hung unframed and merged with the background wall, success in deception became a way of demonstrating technical prowess as a painter (Ebert-Schifferer 1998).

Visual likeness was taken to be a 'natural' means of representing an absent object. Of course the phenomenal object in its actuality was *also* the representation of unreachable noumena, albeit it a representation that was a pure, uninterpretable sign. Towards the end of the nineteenth century, however, a type of painting emerged that, rather than representing objects, reflected the process of seeing. Vision became the *topos*, rather than the modality, of painting. And, consequently, rather than represent the presence of an absent object, the painting reproduced the visual image that *was* the phenomenon. The painting, in fact, became its own phenomenon; something to be looked at, rather than something to remind the viewer of what was not there. The painting of a vase of flowers became just that and not an impoverished duplicate of a 'real' vase of flowers. This, of course, had always been the case, but artists now took advantage of a clearer consciousness of their own task as creators of phenomena.

After Manet's call to 'sincerity' in painting, many artists consciously sought to depict visual *impressions* rather than objects; 'The unavoidable effect of this sincerity, and of the impressionists' attitude in general, was to minimize the importance of subject matter, or altogether negate it' (Barasch 2000, 50). Impressionists were painters for whom the fleeting sensual impression was the reality. As a consequence their paintings were criticized as formless and incoherent. Yet the major works of Monet, for example, hinted at the emergence of a new and rich subject matter. In painting an entire series of haystacks depicted in different light conditions depending on the time of day, or the vast wall of Rheims Cathedral, he threw the viewer into a confused state from which there emerged not so much a momentary, chance impression as a pure experience of seeing; the process of looking, and not the impression of the external object, became the real subject of the picture. This became even more evident in his vast canvases of water lilies. Outrunning the immediate visual field the viewer was overwhelmed by the sheer extension of the depicted scene. And, dissolved into reflections, orientations of up and down were lost in reflected clouds that might lie beneath water or fill a huge web-strewn sky. Again coherence returned only in the emerging elemental sense of looking, an awareness of actually seeing, rather than recognizing the familiar, in which the subject gained a new relationship to the world.

Cézanne, however, remained 'a painter of objects' (Gowing 1977, 55), and only briefly associated himself with the new impressionist school. In his later years and in a more decisive way, he developed a technique and method of his own and, more importantly, a valid conception of his own work as a genuinely phenomenological, rather than an impressionistic, art (Merleau-Ponty 1974, 280–311). Once the artist had achieved the condition of purified seeing, the world itself was renewed and filled with fresh content. The 'primary quality' of this richness was colour. Figures, objects, and landscape forms 'increasingly merge into the flux of color' (Gowing 1977, 55). Colour was no longer a 'merely' subjective and secondary experience of objects but constituted the essential content of the painted form; and the painted form, like any other reality, existed as a phenomenon. We did not 'see' forms directly through line but, rather, grasped them as relations among colours; 'There is no such thing as line or modeling, there are only contrasts,' Cézanne asserted. The aim of his painting was to 'realize our sensations in an aesthetic form' (Gowing 977, 62); that is not to reproduce the object or the sensations the object in some way produces in us, but to recreate, in the medium of painting, the process of vision in which the object becomes real for us. In exploring the limits of painting, the artist was engaging with and creating phenomena; touching and testing reality itself.

Cézanne is the Kant, if not the Husserl, of painting; reacting against the pure empiricism of the impressionists and the idealism of classical forms. Colour is used not mimetically but in terms of its already given harmonic relations. Paintings, successful paintings, were realized sensation, a phrase that Husserl himself was to employ in relation to the overwhelming sense of exteriority that characterized our perception of objects. The picture was neither a representation nor a copy of the object, but the realization of the painting's own phenomenal possibilities.

To this end it is necessary to study the work of other artists: 'The Louvre is the book in which we must learn to read,' Cézanne remarks in a letter to Émile Bernard, but at once adds a warning that 'We must not, however, be satisfied with retaining the beautiful formulas of our illustrious predecessors' (Cézanne 1995, 240). In order to develop valid ways of seeing the phenomenal world and perfect the means of depicting this process itself, it is essential that the artists use the history of painting to free themselves from conventional forms of vision that interpose and reproduce 'formulas' rather than genuine vision. His aim simply is 'the realization of that part of nature, which, coming into our line of vision, gives us the picture ... we must render the image of what we see, forgetting everything that existed before us' (Cézanne 1995, 241). The process of freeing oneself from conventionalized objects is slow and difficult, and the task of rendering the resulting sensations is never wholly satisfactory. In a letter to his son, Paul, he remarks that 'as a painter I am becoming more clear-sighted before nature, but that with me the realization of my sensations is always painful. I cannot attain the intensity that is unfolded before my senses. I have not the magnificent richness of colouring that animates nature' (Cézanne 1995, 244). Yet painting has the advantage over writing that it forces concreteness upon the process of representation: 'The man of letters expresses himself in abstractions whereas a painter, by means of drawing and colour, gives concrete form to his sensations and perceptions' (Harrison and Wood 1998, 38).

Forms emerge on the canvas in the overwhelming conviction of their own reality. In a way that radically breaks from any conception of imitation, the picture realizes sensations according to its own logic and through its own materials. Without resorting to illusionism, this results in monumental objects: 'the still life takes on the character of an indoor landscape' (Gowing 1977, 64). His apples and peaches are little worlds; palpably weighty. These are not ideal forms, the abstract body-in-space depicted in the early modern still life by Juan Cotán, or ideal collections of precious items arranged with scientific precision, or conspicuous displays of wealth, as brought to prominence in seventeenth-century Dutch still-life painting (Bryson 1990); they are as indifferent to the viewer as are the objects of the real world but, as realized sensations, are endowed with essential and unrepresentable qualities that capture and hold our interest.

The movement from nineteenth-century realism or naturalism through impressionism to Cézanne's determined search for the reality of visual phenomena took place against a general background of increasing mechanization of production, growing urbanization and the emergence of new forms of leisure and recreation. Cézanne deliberately withdrew from the hectic life of Paris, which had provided the 'painter of modern life' with both the subject matter and the blurring imprecision of impressionism. Impressionism is modern reality experienced in the immediate chaos of reckless movement. Impressionism is fully absorbed in its subject matter; it is vitally interested in the activities, events and occasions that, even as they are being represented, are being replaced by some new and equally valid experience.

But modern reality revealed itself fully only to the observer at some distance from it; it was possible only after an initial rejection not only of the hypostasized object but of the spontaneous impression. Seeing is not just registering impressions, it is, in an older and richer sense, vision: 'we must render the image what we see, forgetting everything that existed before us' (Harrison and Wood 1998, 39). Impressions are so many reminders of just what we think exists *before* us. Only when we have forgotten in a more radical sense can we see again the fullness of phenomena. Cézanne's painting is important here because it so perfectly illustrates the inexhaustible richness of a reality that is now fully constituted *as* phenomena. The plenitude of being that had hidden itself in the remoteness of things now flowed into and filled the phenomenal forms that previously had existed only to symbolize or signify an ineffable reality. The, superficially paradoxical, result was that the phenomenal, the very notion of which had implied simplicity and clarity, became veiled, contradictory and obscure. Like Cézanne's apples, phenomena generally became heavy with reality. The work of the painter, as of the philosopher, is to lay bare the reality that now resides in phenomena themselves. This is a difficult and lengthy process that calls on all the resources of the observer: 'I progress very slowly, for nature reveals herself to me in very complex ways; and the progress needed is endless. One must look at the model and feel very exactly; and also express oneself distinctly and with force' (Harrison and Wood 1998, 37).

2

Insight: Edmund Husserl's Clarification of Experience

> Perception does not consist in staring blankly at something lodged in consciousness, inserted there by some strange wonder as if something were first there and then consciousness would somehow embrace it ... It is an accomplishment that must be new for every novel object.
>
> Husserl, *Ideas Pertaining to a Pure Phenomenology and to a Phenomenological Philosophy: First Book*

> If phenomena have no nature, they still have an essence.
>
> Husserl, 'Philosophy as a Rigorous Science'

> An immense reality appears in self-consciousness.
>
> Dilthey, *Introduction to the Human Sciences*

Prior to the writings of Edmund Husserl the term 'phenomenology' was occasionally used without implying by it a well-defined and comprehensive philosophical position or project. Husserl himself viewed the emergence of modern thought in the writing of Descartes as the phenomenological insight that initiated his own radical reflection, and later linked his mature work to the spirit of Kant's critical method. Of course, major figures cannot simply be reduced to playing the role of precursors, and Husserl's reading of Descartes and Kant is just one interpretation of works that, equally, are claimed as justifying quite different positions. Modern empiricism *and* idealism also trace their thought to the original philosophies of Descartes and Kant. Thus while, in retrospect, phenomenology may plausibly be traced to the Cartesian *cogito*, and viewed as firmly established in Kant's restriction of philosophical knowledge to the elucidation of *possible experience*, in Husserl's immediate background that tradition was understood exclusively within an epistemological framework. The revival of Kantianism, thus, which was prominent at the time of Husserl's early career, had taken the form of radical positivism. The Kantian categories were viewed objectively and naturalistically as exterior facts that condition experience and, in some versions, determine its content (Köhnke 1991). And the neo-Kantian positivism in which Husserl was educated was itself a reaction against the earlier idealist interpretation of the *Critiques* found in the influential writings of Fichte, Hegel, and Schelling.

However, notwithstanding the importance of his own interpretation of its philosophical antecedents, and the immense influence (in a different tradition) of Hegel's *Phenomenology of Spirit*, as well as the independent emergence of original and significant phenomenological insights in the work of Brentano, Meinong, and Twardowski, it is the development of Husserl's thought that articulates all the essential characteristics of phenomenology as it was to develop throughout the twentieth century (Spiegelberg 1976; De Boer 1978; Moran 2000; Welton 2000).

Husserl's philosophy neither begins nor is established in the drama of a confrontation between truth and error, doubt and certainty, right and wrong, good and evil. It begins, rather, in the midst of things; in and with actual experience. The radicalism of Husserl's philosophy does not consist in an explicit (and thus easily rejected) principle, axiom, or proposition but is expressed, rather, in the arbitrariness of its starting point, with what first happens to appear, and, even more, in its tireless determination to characterize that appearance. His is a philosophy that eschews system-building in favour of following experience itself with its ceaseless shifts in modality, changes of direction, and transient moods. Its aim is to 'clarify' and 'illuminate' experience rather than further to obscure it by imposing upon it an explanation, or imputing to it a meaning, that have their sources in extraneous considerations. To grasp the distinctive character and significance of phenomenology, therefore, it is helpful to adopt Husserl's own method and 'follow the things themselves'; that is, briefly, to recapitulate the formation and development of his thought.

The Ambiguities of Experience

Husserl seizes experience as the essential subject matter of philosophy; the task of philosophy is to gain insight into experience. This means, above all, that philosophy must not go 'beyond' experience; it must steadfastly reject all approaches that stray beyond consciousness and, rather than grasp phenomena *as* phenomena, reduce them to elementary sensations or replace them with empty concepts. Husserl reacted vigorously against both empiricist and idealist tendencies in modern thought, and rejected both. The notion of insight is central to a wide range of developments in modern thought (Lonergan 1957), but in his mature work Husserl contrasts phenomenological insight with other kinds of intellectual understanding. It is neither concrete description nor abstract reasoning but a particular way of 'viewing' phenomena.

Psychology and logic

Husserl's thought begins in a conventional way by considering epistemological issues conceived at the time to be fundamental to the mainstream of modern philosophy. Initially, it was in relation to the empiricist tradition and, more particularly, as a critical response to the growing dominance of 'psychologism' in the study of logic that he formulated his position. Later commentators have sometimes accused Husserl of 'idealism' on the basis of his earlier work, but it is important to recognize both the original features of his critique that point beyond the framework of conventional epistemological positions, and his explicit and equally sophisticated arguments against idealism (Sokolowski 2000; Depraz and Zahavi 1998; Smith and Smith 1995). There is more than a historical issue here. The context of Husserl's early work remains relevant to any discussion of the relation between phenomenology and sociology because much contemporary sociology may reasonably be construed as a late variant of psychologism.

For Husserl the leading example of psychologism was to be found in the work of John Stuart Mill, particularly in his *System of Logic* (first published in 1835). Mill equates philosophy with epistemology, and identifies epistemology with logic. For him, as all knowledge must be derived from experience, it followed that logic must ultimately be considered an empirical science. He argues that as 'all knowledge consists of generalizations from experience' and experience is derived from sensation alone, then, 'Sensation, and the mind's consciousness of its own acts, are not only the exclusive sources, but the sole materials of our knowledge.' Nothing 'can be the object of our knowledge except our experience, and what can be inferred from our experience by the analysis of experience itself' (Mill 1973, xxii). Mill was representative of a position Husserl was later to define with admirable brevity: '*Psychologism* is characterized by the thesis that the theoretical foundations of logic lie in psychology' (1981, 146).

Mill insists that what is immediately available to us as experience is indubitable: 'whatever is known by consciousness, is known beyond possibility of question. What one sees or feels, whether bodily or mentally, one cannot but be sure that one sees or feels' (1973, 7). The doubt that feeds modern scepticism does not infect immediacy, but is relevant only to the inferences, frequently almost instantaneous, that we make from it. We confuse sensations with perceptions and perceptions with deductions. Thus:

> what is perceived by the eye, is at most nothing more than variously coloured surfaces; that when we fancy we see distance, all we really see is certain variations of apparent size and degrees of faintness of colour; that our estimate of the object's distance from us is the result partly of rapid inference from the muscular sensations accompanying the adjustment of the focal distance of the eye to objects unequally remote from us, and partly of a comparison (made with so much rapidity that we are unconscious of making it) between the size or colour of similar objects as they appeared when close to hand, or when their degree of remoteness was known by other means. The perception of distance by the eye, which seems so like an intuition, is thus, in reality, an inference grounded on experience. (1973, 7–8)

Logical relations are simply empirical generalizations borne out by experience. What appears as deductive reasoning resting on pure relations among concepts is, rather, to be understood as general propositions abstracted from the observation of similarity, difference, succession and so on: 'The successive general propositions are not steps in the reasoning, are not intermediate links in the chain of inference, between the particulars observed and those to which we are to apply the observation ... they are mere formulae for inferring particulars from particulars' (1973, 212).

The apparently 'pure' system of mathematical truth should be regarded as nothing other than a series of empirical generalizations rooted in direct observation; the axioms of geometry, for example, are founded as 'experimental truths; generalizations from observation' (1973, 231). Geometry appears to be intuitive and deductive only because there are few original observations required to establish its fundamental 'propositions'. The peculiar 'necessity' of mathematical proof 'is an illusion; in order to sustain which, it is necessary to suppose that those truths relate to, and express the properties of, purely imaginary objects' (1973, 224). However, 'There exist no points without magnitude; no lines without breadth, none perfectly straight; no circle with all their radii exactly equal, no squares with all their angles perfectly right' (1973, 225). The unrealistic assumptions of geometry suppress small irregularities and differences in actual forms and idealize points and lines as the *minima* of actual experience.

Psychologism was a modern version of empiricism that confined philosophy and the sciences strictly within the field of experience but, importantly, did not take experience at face value. Any deeper knowledge of reality depended upon a critical analysis of consciousness and its resolution into elementary and simple units. Thus, though psychologism was fiercely opposed to all idealism and any reference to innate ideas or the categorical structure of the mind independent of the contingent content of actual experience, that experience (what we happened to find in our mind) was the starting point for a philosophical analysis that would ultimately provide foundational knowledge of reality. From any arbitrarily chosen, empirical starting point, analysis would lead into the unfamiliar world of raw sensations and their modes of combination which were the elements of *both* empirical experience *and* logical thought.

The only alternative to this reductive programme seemed to be a continuing reliance on the doctrine of innate ideas. Here, rather than treat all general propositions as, implicit or explicit, empirical generalizations, they were viewed as abstract concepts that referred directly to ideal forms lodged in the mind. The certainty with which we grasp, for example, mathematical truths rests on an intuition of forms and their interrelations given directly to the mind. Indeed, the formed character of the perceptual world is not a consequence of, largely unconscious, processes of induction, smoothing, and classifying the raw data of sensuousness but, rather, the application of innate, abstract ideas to the immediate flux of impressions.

Both modern positions took their point of departure in Descartes and in their opposition revealed the instability of his dualistic conception of reality. He had defined reality in terms of two distinct *substances*. The radical character of this differentiation precluded any genuine interaction between the two. Dualism, thus, gave way to two versions of monism, one empirical and particular (for which the possibility of mind posed a fundamental problem) and the other abstract and ideal (for which empirical actuality remained unintelligible).

Of course Husserl was not alone in criticizing simplistic and extreme versions of such views. In fact new and sophisticated psychological research, as well as systematic considerations, had rendered either position untenable. In the varied studies and reflections of, among others, Lotze, Sigwart, Lipps, Windelband, Meinong, Volkelt, and including one of Husserl's teachers, Franz Brentano, the framework of philosophical discourse had already been irreversibly transformed.

Sigwart, for example, drawing on newer psychological studies, raised the issue of logic in a non-sceptical framework. It was not so much doubt as certainty that prompted critical reflection. The world of thought was something to be considered *sui generis* and grasped in its own terms rather than analysed into elements and units that could not themselves be experienced. The real issues of logic are concerned with questions that arise only in relation to the actually experienced level of conscious thought, amongst which Sigwart draws attention to its irresistible flow: 'the involuntary production of thoughts continues throughout our whole life. It is absolutely impossible, when conscious and awake, to check the inner activity which is necessarily excited by the most varied motives to form a constant succession of ideas which it combines in different ways, and thus, without any intervention on our part, maintains an inner world of thoughts present before us' (Sigwart 1895, 2). Sigwart's approach, like several similar attempts at the same period, forced together the polarities of philosophical discourse rather than provide it with a fresh point of departure. By the latter part of the nineteenth century an uneasy truce rather than a resolution of conflict resulted from such contributions.

Number

As a student Husserl had studied mathematics as well as philosophy and his first philosophical work was on the foundations of arithmetic. Though a 'pre-phenomenological' work that he was later to regard as seriously flawed, it raised issues central to the impasse between psychologism and idealism; considerations that led directly to the development of important transitional works later published as *Logical Investigations* (Willard, in Husserl 2003).

The analysis of number he contended was the unavoidable starting point for any philosophical clarification of mathematics and 'the means which it employs to this end belong to psychology' (Husserl 1981, 95). Far from criticizing psychologism at this point he here claims that 'not only is psychology indispensable for the analysis of the concept of number, but rather this analysis even *belongs within* psychology' (1981, 95). He goes on at once to claim a more general validity for such a starting point and asks rhetorically 'how otherwise could it [philosophy] attain insight into the internal structure of that fantastically interwoven tissue of thought which constitutes the substance of our thought-life? The understanding of the first and most simple modes of composition of representations is the key to the understanding of those higher levels of complication with which our consciousness constantly operates as with seamless and fixed formations' (1981, 95).

Husserl's approach, however, is quite distinct from that of Mill and others who saw in number nothing other than a generalization based on perceptual unities. Rather than begin with the *concept* of unity, of oneness, and trace its origin to the perception of singular objects, Husserl interestingly begins with totalities and arrives at the concept of unity by a process of differentiation: 'the concrete phenomena which form the basis for the abstraction of these concepts are ... totalities of determinate objects. But we also add that these totalities are completely *arbitrary* and optional. In the formation of concrete totalities there is in fact no limitation whatever upon what particular contents are to be included' (1981, 97).

The general concept of number emerges through a process of suppressing everything variable that distinguishes the members of such totalities. Husserl initially sees this also as a psychological issue; it is a problem of *attention*. We attend selectively to specific characteristics of objects and in conceiving number we attend exclusively to the object as a member of a specific set of objects: 'What is then present when we speak of a totality of certain objects? Nothing further than the co-presence of these objects in our consciousness' (1981, 99). What makes individual objects members of a set depends 'only in their belonging to the consciousness which encompasses them'. Enumeration requires a 'special act of noticing'.

Husserl's work immediately drew strong criticism from Gottlob Frege, whose own, idealist understanding of arithmetic was also published in the 1890s. In fact, he accused Husserl of psychologism, a view the author himself later accepted. Recent interest in Husserl's early work, however, has stressed the equivocal positions of both Husserl and Frege on fundamental issues (Husserl 2003; Frege 1953; Mohanty 1982).

Intentionality and certainty

Husserl's early work is consistent with that of his teacher, Franz Brentano, whose influential *Psychology from an Empirical Standpoint* made a deep impression on his developing student. 'My psychological standpoint is empirical,' writes Brentano, but at once continues 'yet I share with other thinkers the conviction that this is entirely compatible with a certain ideal point of view' (1973, xxvii; De Boer 1978; Kockelmans 1994). While 'neither sense perception nor inner experience reveal substances to us', the latter is distinguished by 'clear knowledge and complete certainty which is provided by immediate insight' (1973, 10). The phenomena of 'inner perception' are 'true in themselves. As they appear to be, so they are in reality' (1973, 20), but these phenomena are not to be confused with 'observations'. We cannot detach ourselves from our own inner experience to observe, as if from some other position, the images that arise in consciousness: 'we can never focus our *attention* upon the object of inner perception' (1973, 30).

Inner experience is composed both of perceptions and of intuitions; this much was the common heritage of modern logic as well as psychology from the time of Locke and had received its definitive elaboration in the writings of Kant, but Brentano emphasized in a new way both their identity and their difference as *acts* of consciousness.

Brentano claims the doubtful parentage of scholastic philosophy for his notion of intentionality: 'Every mental phenomenon is characterized by what the Scholastics of the Middle Ages called the intentional (or mental) inexistence of an object' (1973, 88). However, the context of premodern discussions of the 'intension' and 'remission' of qualities is so distinct from modern philosophical issues as to make any comparison misleading (Lindberg 1992, 281–315). Brentano's notion of intentionality is that consciousness is always 'consciousness of something', that is, it is always particular. But this 'objectivity' is not dependent on the extraneous presence of an actual object outside consciousness, and may be considered independently of questions of the status of conscious acts as truthful, valid, illusory, erroneous, and so on. Furthermore, each act of consciousness gives rise to a related and particular modality of consciousness. 'Every mental phenomenon includes something as object within itself, although they do not all do so in the same way. In presentation something is presented, in judgement something is affirmed or denied, in love loved, in hate hated … and so on', there is always and in a distinctively appropriate manner a 'fusion of consciousness and the object of consciousness' (1973, 139).

The direction of Husserl's thought, however, quickly led away from issues that could be explored through a further development of Brentano's approach. In a series of rich but still inconclusive studies, he raised fundamental questions about any sort of relation within consciousness; these issues he had already recognized lay at the heart of 'a very dark chapter of descriptive psychology' (1970b, vol. 1, 112), and their further consideration would result in the outright rejection of *both* psychologism and idealism rather than the continuing elaboration of any proposed and unstable compromise.

Psychologism was finally confronted and decisively rejected in Husserl's *Logical Investigations* and this work is often read exclusively within the context of his attack on that position. Husserl, certainly, set out from a polemical standpoint in relation to 'the prevailing assumption that psychology was the science from which logic in general, and the logic of deductive sciences, had to hope for philosophical clarification' (1970b, vol. 1, 2). And throughout he elaborated more rigorously and with greater precision than elsewhere reasons for the outright rejection of such a claim. But his ambitions grew well beyond this important negative task. In a positive sense his investigations were a patient 'working of oneself into ever new logical and phenomenological insight' (1970b, vol. 1, 5).

His starting point, in fact, lies in an observation unremarked within the literature of psychologism. 'The field of science is an objectively closed unity,' claims Husserl, 'we cannot arbitrarily delimit fields where and as we like' (1970b, vol. 1, 12). The sciences, that is to say, render an account of a world that *already exists* and is formed into structures independent of *its* intellectual efforts. Equally, this preconstituted reality cannot be grasped as the extension of any merely psychological content within consciousness: 'The realm of truth is objectively articulated into fields: researchers must orient themselves to these objective unities' (1970b, vol. 1, 15). We might be tempted here to use psychological evidence against psychologism; the scientist has no sense of freedom in relation to his or her chosen *field* of investigation. It is simply *there*. Husserl, thus, immediately arrives at an important statement that foreshadows much in the subsequent development of his new phenomenological perspective: 'Science neither wishes nor dares to become a field for architectonic play. The system peculiar to science, i.e. to true and correct science, is not our own invention, but is present in things, where we simply find or describe it' (1970b, vol. 1, 18).

The compelling sense in which the world is given to us, as well as the scientist, as a preconstituted structure remains unacknowledged, far less clarified, in both psychologism and idealism. Equally, the compelling character of scientific truth, which, beyond the validity of any particular explanation of events, reveals a 'systematic coherence in the theoretical sense' (1970b, vol. 1, 18), requires clarification – clarification that can come only from a radically new approach.

Husserl simply pushes aside the modern preoccupation with scepticism; this is not and can never be a fundamental issue for philosophy. Rather, the peculiar certainty of scientific truth and what might be termed trust in the world it explicates sets in train a process of clarification that breaks free of the narrow epistemological concerns of modern philosophy. Both in a scientific and in a more everyday sense 'The most perfect "mark" of correctness is inward evidence, it counts as an immediate intuition of truth itself ... Ultimately, therefore, all genuine, and, in particular, all scientific knowledge, rests on inner evidence: as far as such evidence extends, the concept of knowledge extends also' (1970, vol. 1, 17–18). This 'intuition' is not itself founded upon some particular empirical content of consciousness, nor is it an idea, concept, or category immanent to the mind; rather, it is the self-evidence of a living being, the immediate consciousness of an existing subject. Only that which flows directly from the self-evidence of the living person carries with it the inner sense of absolute certainty.

Husserl claims that we have in relation to the laws of logic just this character of unshakeable conviction: 'We have insight into, not merely the probability, but the truth of the logical laws' (1970b, vol. 1, 48). Scientific truth now seems less extensive and general; so-called laws of nature 'only hold as ideal possibilities' but logic, like arithmetic, escapes the imprecision and doubt that attaches to all possibility and 'free from all existential content ... [is] established by *insight*' (1970b, vol. 1, 53).

This does not mean that logical truth exists somehow in an ideal world outside experience: 'All knowledge "begins with experience" but it does not therefore "arise" from experience' (1970b, vol. 1, 55). What Husserl seems to mean here is that where scientific knowledge 'arises' inductively from individual experiences, 'truth' is directly experienced in the same manner that we experience ourselves as living subjects:

> Inner evidence is no accessory feeling, either casually attached, or attached by natural necessity, to certain judgments ... The situation is not at all like the way in which we like to conceive of the connection between sensations and the feelings which relate to them: two persons, we think, have the same sensations, but are differently affected by their feelings. Inner evidence is rather nothing but the 'experience' of truth. (1970b, vol. 1, 130)

The *Logical Investigations* or, rather, the programmatic statement that precedes them, might itself be said to stand in need of clarification. While many of the sharp criticisms of psychologism certainly hit their mark it was not at all clear how 'self-evidence' was connected to the truth of logic or arithmetic. The primitive experience of self-presence seemed quite distinct from any experience of truth we might encounter in logic. What, above all, that stands in need of clarification is just the notion of experience, the term that remained the dark centre of the entire development of modernity.

Experience is always conscious, but not all consciousness is constituted *as* experience. We can imagine, for example, a 'consciousness prior to all experience' and this may be indistinguishable from the *sensations* we ordinarily experience:

> But it will intuit no things, and no events pertaining to things, it will perceive no trees and no houses, no flight of birds nor any barking dogs. One is at once tempted to express the situation by saying that its sensations *mean* nothing to such a consciousness, that they do not *count as signs* of the properties of an object, that their combination does not count as a sign of the object itself. They are merely lived through, without an objectifying *interpretation* derived from experience. (1970b, vol. 1, 309)

Normally, however, these meanings accompany sensations in an effortless flow of objectifying interpretations, so that 'we live entirely in the consciousness of meaning, of understanding' (1970b, vol. 1, 304).

It is just in the effortless character of this union that the world appears to us as already formed, and because of this, 'Dazed by the confusion between object and mental content, one forgets that the objects of which we are "conscious", are not simply *in* consciousness as in a box, so that they can merely be found in it and snatched at in it; but that they are first *constituted* as being what they are for us, and as what they count as for us, in varying forms of objective intuition' (1970b, vol. 1, 275). Truth confronts us in its absolute validity but, at the same time, we enter into the construction of this truth as form creating subjects. We are not passive spectators of a preformed and ultimately impenetrable world of objects; nor are we the spiritual demiurge creating the world afresh each moment from within ourselves. Experience and consciousness, consequently, cannot readily be grasped as an undifferentiated and simple unity.

While consciousness is always consciousness of *something*, the self-constituting subject cannot become an object to itself:

> The *popular* meaning of 'experience' is to 'have' outer events and acts of perception. But this 'having' furnishes an instance of the quite different 'experiencing' in the sense of phenomenology. This merely means that certain contents help to constitute a unity of consciousness, enter into the phenomenologically unified stream of consciousness of an empirical ego. This itself is a real whole, in reality made up of manifold parts, each of which may be said to be 'experienced' ... there is no difference between the experience or conscious content and the experience itself. (1970b, vol. 2, 85)

That is to say, while experience is, indeed, 'all of a piece' it may be distinguished in its fundamental modes through acts of reflection that temporarily isolate particular aspects of consciousness and view them from different perspectives. These reflective acts are simultaneously *also* experiences that enter into the unity of consciousness. The self-evidence upon which all truth rests is, at the same time, the normal experience of some particular content. The 'pure' self-presence cannot appear to itself as an object, separate from, and outside, any concrete experience of the world but is, rather, immanent in all the empirically particular acts of consciousness. What Husserl at this point calls the 'phenomenologically reduced ego' is in a practical sense indistinguishable from the ordinary stream of consciousness; it is 'nothing peculiar, floating above any experience: it is simply identical with their own interconnected unity' (1970b, vol. 2, 86).

The study of logic opened the way to a broader understanding of experience as its central issue and, as he later expressed the important insight, 'experience is not an opening through which a world, existing prior to all experience, shines into a room of consciousness; it is not a mere taking of something alien to consciousness into consciousness' (1969, 232).

Towards a Science of Phenomena

The problem of logic could only be clarified through a more comprehensive and radical understanding of human experience in general. Logic is not a technical discipline; rather, in the intellectual context of *fin de siècle* European culture, it is an opening through which the philosopher glimpses a vast and unexplored world. At the very point at which the entire unfolding of modern thought should reach completion and shut off, finally and completely, the obscurity of a distant and confused past in which humanity could not yet assert its own identity, the uninterrupted development of knowledge was halted and turned back on itself. Husserl viewed his work and the task of philosophy as committed to the removal of this obstacle and, breaking through the impasse of logic, the delineation of as yet critically unexplored regions of human experience.

Essences

In a significant essay on 'Philosophy as a Rigorous Science' for the prestigious journal *Logos* (1911), Husserl expresses himself boldly and with a new confidence, placing his thought in a broader historical framework of

European humanism. Philosophy in the recent period, he declares, 'has followed from the Renaissance up to the present an essentially unitary line of development', a development that expresses 'humanity's indispensable demand for pure and absolute knowledge (and what is inseparably one with that, its demand for pure and absolute valuing and willing)' (1981, 166).

The purification of knowledge is just the aim of Husserl's new phenomenological philosophy. And pure knowledge is simply insight into pure phenomena. Calling for a 'rigorous science' of philosophy Husserl in fact contrasts his emerging programme of phenomenological research with the established procedures of the natural sciences. Thus, while 'All natural science is naïve in regard to its point of departure' such that, for it, 'Nature is simply *there* to be investigated' (1981, 171), the new philosophy deals with pure phenomena as they are given prior to any meaningful scientific, or any other, interpretation. A phenomenon lacks the very characteristics that opens experienced objects to investigation by the methods of the natural sciences: 'A phenomenon, then, is no "substantial" unity; it has no "real properties", it has no real parts, no real changes, and no causality ... a "phenomenon", comes and goes; it retains no enduring, identical being that would be objectively determinable as such in the sense of natural science' (1981, 180).

Unsurprisingly Husserl remarks that 'We do not easily overcome the inborn habit of living and thinking according to the naturalistic attitude' (1981, 181). At this point we might be forgiven for concluding that the new philosophy has been still-born; that it amounts to a version of negative theology in which reality is dissolved into an utterly formless and indeterminate flux. However, he persists, 'if phenomena have no nature, they still have an essence, which can be grasped and adequately determined in an immediate seeing' (1981, 181). And, as if anticipating the suspicion of the sociologist for whom all talk of 'essence' betrays a hidden and prejudicial interest, he insists that 'Intuiting essences conceals no more difficulties or "mystical" secrets than does perception' (1981, 181).

At this point he does not elaborate on the specific character of 'essential intuition' – how it is to be achieved, or what it might reveal. Two years later, however, he published a full-length exposition of his phenomenology in which those and related issues were examined in detail.

Reduction/expansion

In fact, the 1913 publication of *Ideas Pertaining to a Pure Phenomenology and to a Phenomenological Philosophy* was the first volume of a general work, the continuation of which remained unpublished and incomplete at his death in 1939. It remained the fundamental statement of his approach and, rather than make public the extraordinarily rich developments of his thought, recorded in voluminous notebooks that, meticulously edited, continue to yield unexpected and valuable material, he devoted his further publications primarily to ever renewed efforts to present, in a shorter and more accessible form, a lucid general introduction to its fundamental themes and methods.

Husserl begins with a sharp differentiation between *empirical* sciences, which 'posit something real *individually*', and *eidetic* sciences that deal with essences. All empirical facts are contingent, while an essence is given necessarily. A tone, for example, is essentially given as a sound-act and, simultaneously, appears as a particular, contingent, note. While, as a note, it might have been or become different to the one that in fact it is, as a tone it cannot be otherwise. Thus, the *'unrestricted universality of natural laws* must not be mistaken for *eidetic universality'* (1982, 15).

Intuition of essence rests on the 'free possibility' of directing our regard and forming in consciousness a variety of examples. The peculiarity of the *eidos* is that, while it is always present in empirical data and can be exemplified through such data, it may, equally, become evident in phantasy. Generally, indeed, we can more readily seize essences in relation to 'imaginary' objects. The eidetic sciences, that is to say, are free of experience in the specific sense of the direct apprehension of a formed and meaningful world filled with empirical objects.

To grasp essences is an immediate 'seeing in the universal sense as an originally presentive consciousness of any kind whatever' (1982, 36). Phenomenology is nothing other than a 'return to the phenomena themselves', in acts of essential seeing. Phenomena themselves, as distinct from their conceptualization, explanation, or description, are *'prior to all* standpoints' (1982, 38). This means not only setting aside the enshrouding objectivity of natural consciousness but, equally, resisting the temptation of conceiving phenomena as *a priori* forms or categories. Rigorous phenomenology, that is to say, is incompatible with any version of Platonism as well as any residual tendency towards psychologism. The error of idealism is 'to set up ideas or essences as objects and ascribe to them, as to other objects, actual (variable) being' (1982, 40). Essential seeing is neither a perceptual nor an imaginative act, but a seeing through *any* experiential act. Phenomena do not stand behind, above, or beneath the immediate contents of consciousness but exist and come to appearance only in and through such content.

The method of phenomenology is, then, a peculiar way of seeing or viewing, rather than a matter of taking a position or adopting a perspective. This special way of regarding lays aside our normal, practical or theoretical, *interest* in the world as an actually existing set of objects and events. What Husserl variously calls the phenomenological reduction, or *epoché*, obliges us to surrender our normal waking 'grip' on reality and progressively suspend all *positing* acts of consciousness. Put simply, our ordinary acceptance of the world as 'real' in the sense that it exists, just as it seems, outside and independently of us, is held temporarily in abeyance. This is not a sceptical position; we do not for a moment doubt the existence of the world. But, rather than orient ourselves to that world in terms of current practical or theoretical interest in *it*, its particularity, we regard it as just one of a series of possibilities. This is less an imaginative flight from reality, than a process of stripping reality of the contingencies through which, alone, it appears to us. The phenomenological reduction is 'the methodic step by which one returns to the origin of our knowledge, of which our superficial everyday thinking has lost sight' (Kockelmans 1994, 14). This involves a two-stage process: first 'the systematic and radical inhibition, or *epoché*, of every objectifying, positing act in every concrete experience' and then 'the recognition, comprehension, and description of the very essence of that which no longer appears as an object but only as a "unity of meaning"' (1994, 43).

In fact, and in a manner similar to Hobbes, Husserl claims this process is less difficult than one might imagine it to be, that 'No limits check us in the process of conceiving the destruction of the Objectivity of something physical' (1982, 105). Of course this is no actual destruction, but a temporary withdrawal of the sense of actuality that normally qualifies existence. *That* sense of immediate givenness is placed on one side. This means 'bracketing' nature, history, society, and any other similarly objectified structures; thus, for example, 'a transcendental investigation of consciousness cannot signify an investigation of nature and cannot presuppose the latter as a premise because nature is as a matter of essential necessity parenthesized in the transcendental attitude' (1982, 115). This is quite a different orientation to that of scientific 'detachment'. The latter not only posits the reality outside consciousness of the specific object of investigation, it does so through a particular act of attention. The phenomenological reduction, on the other hand, can be thought of as involving a 'suspension of attention' (Crary 2001).

In a striking passage from a later presentation of his ideas Husserl describes the process of essential viewing as follows:

Let us make this clear to ourselves, and then fruitful to our method. Starting from this table-perception as an example, we vary the perceptual object, table, with a completely free optionalness, yet in such a manner that we keep perception fixed as perception of something, no matter what. Perhaps we begin by fictively changing the shape or the color of the object quite arbitrarily, keeping identical only its perceptual appearing. In other words: Abstaining from acceptance of its being, we change the fact of this perception into a pure possibility, one among other quite 'optional' pure possibilities – but possibilities that are possible perceptions. We, so to speak, shift the actual perception into the realm of non-actualities, the realm of the as-if, which supplies us with 'pure' possibilities, pure of everything that restricts to this fact or to any fact whatever. As regards the latter point, we keep the aforesaid possibilities, not as restricted even to the co-posited de facto ego, but just as completely free 'imaginableness' of phantasy. Accordingly from the very start we might have taken as our initial example a phantasying ourselves into a perceiving, with no relation to the rest of our de facto life. Perception, the universal type thus acquired, floats in the air, so to speak – in the atmosphere of pure phantasiableness. Thus removed from all factualness, it has become the pure *'eidos'* perception, whose *'ideal'* extension is made up of all ideally possible perceptions, as purely phantasiable processes. Analyses of perception are then *'essential'* or *'eidetic'* analyses. All that we have set forth concerning syntheses belonging to the type, perception, concerning horizons of potentiality, and so forth, holds good, as can easily be seen *'essentially'* for everything formable in this free variation, accordingly for all imaginable perceptions without exception – in other words: with absolute 'essential *universality*', and with '*essential necessity*' for every particular case selected, hence for every de facto perception, since every *fact can be thought of merely as exemplifying a pure possibility*. (1967, 70)

Essential seeing is still a 'presentive act', analogous to perceiving. Eidetic viewing is never detached from the individuated and formed object of ordinary perception. Furthermore, as *eidos*, it is singular. Essential regarding is a way of looking in which the act of viewing, rather than the specific characteristics of the object viewed, come into prominence. In the classical modern formulations the act of viewing, the living *cogito*, loses itself in the object. What characterizes essential viewing is just that the object, in a special sense, is subordinated to the *cogito*. Thus, in addition to the essence of the object, the essence of the *cogito* comes to consciousness. As phenomenologists we 'become disinterested bystanders watching our own conscious life' (Kockelmans 1994, 121) rather than self-conscious subjects exploring the world.

Husserl finds a clue to the historical origin of his methodical approach in the familiar example of Euclidean geometry, rather than in the theme of his own early work on modern arithmetical logic. The compelling character of geometric proof, the sense in which it carries absolute conviction, has its origin in the *arbitrariness* of its constructions, rather than in its simplified empirical content. The student is asked to draw *any* triangle, *any* circle, *any* square, and so on. Then, a demonstration of the specific properties of the figure (in the case of triangle, for example, that the sum of its internal angles is two right angles) is immediately grasped as true of *any* triangle, *any* circle, *any* square and, thus, of *all* triangles, *all* circles, or *all* squares. In any act of reflective regarding the empirically given starting point is considered, equally, as something arbitrary. Though wholly the outcome of a process of natural necessity, the empirically existent object is relativized as a 'possible' object, that is, an object that might just as well have been otherwise. Any everyday sensuous object, for example an orange, may be viewed eidetically by setting aside its specific spatio-temporal determinations; viewed as *any* orange its essential qualities become prominent. The peculiar *qualities* of orangeness, for example, as distinct from 'appleness' or 'plumness', become the sole object of regard. In this process the original orange is 'in parenthesis' but remains intact and just as it is; it is neither broken down into simple analytic units (rind, pith, flesh, seeds etc.), nor included within an abstract classification ('citrus fruit', 'imported food stuff', 'healthy breakfasts' and so on).

Husserl presented his phenomenology in the context of modern philosophical positions and disputes; he began and to a large extent concentrated, as had Brentano, on the clarification of perceptual acts as the central focus of presentation. But he also stressed, and from the outset, that perceptual acts continually give way to, and in innumerable ways are interlaced with, other qualitatively distinctive acts. The perceptual field undergoes continual modulation into remembering, imagining, willing, feeling, judging, dreaming and so on, each characterized by its own essential quality and structure of presentive acts. These 'regional ontologies' spontaneously emerge and, so to speak, occupy consciousness and fill it with its variously shaded contents; disclosing their own inner, effortlessly expanding horizons, their own inner perspectives and forms of objectification. The characteristic inner sense of subjectivity undergoes changes in its modality; it shifts from the perceiving state to the recollecting state, the willing state, and so on. Many such variations have the sense of an irresistible spontaneity. While some regions open themselves to deliberative acts ('at will'), such as aspects of remembering, primarily (and primally) they simply appear within us; an unexplained and usually unremarked characteristic of reality. Like perceptual objects, the ontological richness of consciousness has the character of 'givenness' and, like perceptual objects, is only partially under our control. We cannot 'deliberately' love, feel anger or joy, or dream, or become depressed; these are modalities of consciousness that sweep over us and through us.

Ontological variation is also a way to the phenomenological reduction. There is a sense in which the *experience* of such variation turns the subject back upon itself. In these shifts, as well as grasping ever new contents of consciousness, we become aware of the characteristic 'act quality' specific to each mode of grasping; we become aware of the essential character of willing as willing, loving as loving, judging as judging, and so on. Ontological variation is a spontaneous prompt to essential seeing. Each ontological region is distinguished by a characteristic and 'given' mode of presentation, and correlatively of grasping, its objects. The immediate obviousness of these differences, their unanalysable givenness, does not require verification and does not call for explanation.

Husserl frequently stresses the complex interplay among appearances within continuously shifting horizons of experience and modalities of presentation. In particular he draws attention to the creative activity through which experience is constituted and the continuous process of anticipation this involves. Variations in perceptual images, and in every other ontological field, are inexplicably also open to a specific and absolutely free transformation into 'phantoms'. The perceptual image may be imagined nearer or farther away, differently coloured, inverted, turned around, utterly destroyed and reconstructed. Equally an intention may be imagined otherwise, as intending something else, as succeeding, or failing, and so on. Any objectivity given in its own way may be seized imaginatively and transformed without regard to its original appearing context or the natural and psychological 'laws' that govern such appearances. We can, and often do, imagine that we can fly, that it is already tomorrow, or that we have been transformed into a giant insect.

Phenomenological reduction, crucially, does not result in a mere emptying of consciousness of its content. Husserl asks pointedly of the *epoché*, '*What can remain, if the whole world, including ourselves with all its cogitare, is excluded?*' (1982, 63). In fact this is the prelude to '*the acquisition of a new region of being never before delimited in its own peculiarity*' (1982, 63); the phenomenological reduction, or the 'eidetic transformation' of an object, brings into view 'a multitude of possible worlds and surrounding worlds' (1982, 106). For Husserl, as for Weber, reality is extensively and intensively infinite. Even prior to the opening up of new potential worlds through the reduction, consciousness ceaselessly probes the world without finding any limitation. The process of probing is both active awaking and, often, a more soporific sensing of vague objectivities. In an important passage Husserl characterizes the world viewed eidetically and adumbrates its rich development:

> But not even with the domain of this intuitionally clear or obscure, distinct or indistinct, *co-present* – which makes up a constant halo around the field of actual perception – is the world exhausted which is 'on hand' for me in the manner peculiar to consciousness at every waking moment. On the contrary, in the fixed order of its being, it reaches into the unlimited. What is now perceived and what is more or less clearly co-present and determinate ... are penetrated and surrounded by an *obscurely attended to horizon of indeterminate actuality*. (1982, 52)

Ego/body

The intellectual trajectory of Husserl's project, radical and original as it was, had nonetheless located itself within a discourse that remained recognizably philosophical. The phenomenological reduction, however, seemed to step beyond the boundaries of philosophical discourse and his own self-imposed limitation to a discourse of consciousness. In *Cartesian Meditations* he poses the issue in a sharp way:

> At first, to be sure, the possibility of a pure phenomenology seems highly questionable, since the realm of phenomena of consciousness is so truly the realm of Heraclitean flux. It would in fact be hopeless to attempt to proceed here with such methods of concept and judgment formation as are standard in the Objective sciences ... Processes of consciousness ... have no ultimate elements and relationships, fit for subsumption under the idea of objects determinable by fixed concepts and therefore such that, in their case, it would be rational to set ourselves the task of an approximative determination guided by fixed concepts. (1967, 49)

The phenomenological reduction would seem to lead either to utter emptiness or to a complete dissolution of the ego into a chaotic multiplicity. In essential viewing the given character of objects, as objects and as distinct from the particular and ultimately arbitrary empirical shroud through which they appear, come into prominence. This applies not only to perceptual objects but, equally, to the objectivities of willing, feeling, judging, and so on. Essential viewing, that is to say, is oriented to reality exclusively in terms of the founding character of such objectivities as such. At the same time this process brings into focus the continuous stream of existing being which is the *cogito* of consciousness and the effortless 'self-evidence' in which all fundamental insight is given. Ontological variation, spontaneously and in the free variation of imaginatively manipulated experience, makes available to reflection in a more general way the essential character of consciousness as a continuous streaming. In a peculiar way subjectivity always has before it the possibility of self-reflection. And in this process the essential character of subjectivity is discernible.

The ego may appear to us as an object, an object of thought, of will, of feeling, and so on, and in this sense it is given in just the way other objectivities within these domains are given. Within the natural attitude of normal experience, for example, the empirical ego emerges as a particular bundle of characteristics that belong together by virtue of some presumed inner relationship. Just as the natural object stands out from its background and gathers together within strict spatial limits a multiplicity of empirical characteristics, so the ego locates psychically a whole series of different but typical experiences. The ego is nothing other than the temporal unity of these experiences. At the same time this empirical continuity, as an object of thought, is conceptualized as an inner identity or soul. Husserl insists that, even for the natural attitude, such a conceptualization is misleading: 'The ego is not a box containing egoless lived-experience ... We do not find it like a part, as something in the lived-experience or literally on it' (1982, 17), but it exists wholly in the directional flow of consciousness, 'the unity of the stream of lived experience' (1982, 18).

The empirical ego is reflected in the natural objects it finds in the world and which furnish the content of its experience. Husserl describes this in a dramatic manner that recalls ancient theories of perception: 'the Ego directs itself in every case to the Object, but in a more particular sense at times an Ego-ray, launched from the pure Ego, goes out toward the Object, and, as it were, counter-rays, issue from the Object and come back to the Ego' (1989, 104). The empirical ego, of course, has no greater claim on reality than any other empirical object. The Humean critique, taken up in William James's descriptive psychology, is a compelling demonstration of its ultimate arbitrariness; the 'self' dissolves into a series of actually unconnected accidents. Nor can this critique readily be overcome by positing some 'other' self, located more deeply in the soul, as the unifying agency of disparate experiences; this would be no more convincing than the appeal to unfounded concepts of 'atoms' to account for our *experience* of the physicality of natural objects. The episodic character of the empirical ego, its 'stepping forth' and returning from activity, punctuates the pure stream of lived experience and structures our recollection with its characteristic phasic tensions.

As distinct from the inherent instability of the empirical ego, in the process of eidetic viewing, in the free variation of phantasy, and in the ontological shifts among diverse modes of appearing, the essential subjectivity of a pure ego becomes evident. The pure ego is identical, not with itself ideally or empirically, but with the streaming character of consciousness. The pure ego is given absolutely: 'As pure Ego it does not harbor any hidden inner richness; it is absolutely simple and lies there absolutely clear' (1989, 111). It does not stand out and apart from the ceaseless variety of experience but is wholly absorbed in 'the infinity of experiences in which I come to know myself under ever new aspects, according to ever new properties, and in an ever more perfect way' (1989, 111). It must be remembered here that 'experience' is understood in its phenomenologically reduced essence, and not in terms of a natural attitude. The pure ego is 'the identical subject functioning in all acts of the same stream of consciousness; it is the center whence all conscious life emits rays and receives them ... all the multi-formed particularities of intentional relatedness to Objects ... have their necessary *terminus a quo* in the Ego-pole, from whence they irradiate' (1989, 112). And the ego is the *terminus ad quem* to which returning rays stream as constituted objects. The pure ego, however, like any essence, is given essentially and is, therefore, *'incapable of and in no need of constitution through "manifolds"'* (1989, 118). The pure ego becomes enshrouded in the limitations of empirical actuality.

A radical dislocation of empirical ego and pure ego is, thus, conceivable. Indeed, given the unrealistic constraints of any natural attitude, such a rupture is unavoidable. 'In principle it is always possible,' Husserl therefore claims, 'that I, this person, am not at all ... it could turn out, in future experiences, not to be. On the other hand, in order to know that the pure Ego is and what it is, no ever so great accumulation of self-experiences can profit me more than a single experience of one sole and simple cogito' (1989, 111).

It is in the body, the living being of the subject, that both pure and empirical egos were lodged, not as concepts, or images, but as living reality. Husserl is at pains to avoid the difficulties of Cartesian dualism by treating the *living* body as an indivisible unity. Descartes had radically separated the self as pure living ego from the world of objects, such that the self-evidence of the living presence of the subject could never serve as an adequate foundation for philosophical truth. But for Husserl, the world and the ego belong together in the body, which is *both* a given object and a phenomenologically pure essence.

The distinctive character of the body is, first of all, as a field of localization. It is the given spatio-temporal point of reference that necessarily structures space and the relationship of objects to each other. The body is and has an ego with 'the unique distinction of bearing in itself the *zero point* of all orientations' (1989, 166). All objects appear in relation to this zero point. 'I have all things over and against me: they are all "there" – with the exception of one and only one, namely the Body, which is always "here"' (1989, 166).

Just as objects do not lie in consciousness as things in a box, so the ego is not in the body but, rather, is essentially embodied. And, equally, the body is an ensouled object and not a thing. The body, that is to say, is living and continually manifests itself as living being. Yet the body is localized and does appear always as a distinctive and non-arbitrary structure. In fact the body is uniquely an *essential* object, the meeting ground of the pure streaming ego and the objectifications of the empirical ego. And just because of this the body, in its primal givenness, remains incomplete: 'The same Body which serves me as a means for all my perceptions obstructs me in the perception of it itself and is a remarkably imperfectly constituted thing' (1989, 167). We cannot voluntarily alter our orientation to the body, we cannot distance ourselves from it.

'In the concrete perception, the Body is there as a new sort of unity of apprehension. It is constituted as an Objectivity in its own right' (1989, 163). We experience this unity directly, even though we cannot adopt a 'position' in relation to it, and have imperfect knowledge of its constitution: 'If, despite all this, we apprehend the Body as a real thing, it is because we find it integrated into the causal nexus of material nature' (1989, 167). Above all it is a unity that responds 'spontaneously' and 'freely' to the will of the ego. The body is constituted 'objectively' and simultaneously as nature and as spirit.

Problems of Intersubjectivity

Towards the end of the second book of *Ideas* the rupture between the empirical ego and pure ego, between the natural and transcendental attitude, raises itself in ever more intractable forms. Embodiment, certainly, points directly to the living unity of both empirical and transcendental objects. The body cannot here be taken as a contingent and exterior 'fact' of some kind in which is miraculously reconstituted as a unity that reflection had insisted upon tearing apart; the body is both an incompletely constituted and continually emerging object, and a pre-given and always available subject. The *essential* givenness of the body – its self-appearance as its own essence rather than shrouded in contingency – is just the reason why it can never appear as a complete and unified object and only partially emerges from the restless flux of duration. Both as ego and as object the body is familiar with itself from the beginning, it does not *require* self-knowledge because there is no distance between itself and its world.

Husserl's sustained and radical attack on the epistemological problem of modernity dissolves, and dissolves in, the body. And it is just at this point that his thought becomes charged with a fresh endeavour. The relentless investigation of consciousness that had begun, however critically, within the sphere of the individual subject finally breaks free of philosophical assumptions (and practical conventions), inextricably bound up with the entire project of modernity. In retrospect it was clear that the phenomenological reduction moved reflection outside the boundaries of any individuated consciousness and, equally, that the pure ego was, in a strict sense, 'egoless' from an empirical standpoint. The transcendental reduction was immanent in the phenomenological project from the start. Now the body, which was the localization of all transcendental realities in so far as they come to appearance at all, also proved to be imperfectly individuated. The strong self of self-presence, which we unthinkingly locate in the body as its individuated subjective companion, turns out to be an intersubjective reality or, better perhaps, a collective subjectivity.

The Transcendental and the Interactive subject

Towards the end of the second book of *Ideas* Husserl remarks that 'This world of things is, at the lowest level, intersubjective material nature as common field of actual and possible experience of individual spirits, solitary ones and ones in community of experience. All individual bodies have their place on this level' (1989, 207). That the world is 'there', a shared experience, means, given the intentional structure of consciousness, that the body and pure ego, equally, are shared. The phenomenological reduction does not lead from a socialized 'natural attitude' back towards ever more private, inward, individuated, and incommunicable quasi-experiences (which is the Romantic path to authenticity); quite the reverse, the natural attitude which is a function of theoretical and practical dogmatism gives way to an intersubjective fluidity.

In some respects the *Cartesian Mediations*, published in 1929, in which Husserl once again set out an 'introduction' to phenomenology, seems to be a step back from the radical implications of these insights. In returning once again to Descartes, Husserl seems to restrict himself to another investigation of an individually conceived consciousness. But the focus of the discussion has decisively shifted from a consideration of doubt and the epistemological relation to the world, to a more complete embrace of the transcendental ego, as the source of all reality; the transcendental-phenomenological *epoché*, far from stripping reality of substantiality, reveals, rather, the true source of its being for us:

> The Objective world, the world that exists for me, that always has and always will exist for me, the only world that ever can exist for me – this world, with all its Objects, I said, derives its whole sense and its existential status, which it has for me, from me myself, *from me as the transcendental Ego*, the Ego who comes to the fore only with transcendental-phenomenological *epoché*. (1967, 26)

But the transcendental ego, prior to all experience, is not an individuated form of subjectivity and must be grasped rather as the most general level of intentional consciousness. Thus 'the *epoché* can also be said to be the radical and universal method by which I apprehend myself purely' (1967, 20–1). And in this essential seizing of the ego, every particular mark of individual existence falls away into the pure stream of living.

Husserl stresses once again that consciousness does not grasp something outside itself and other than itself, but constitutes itself in and through the experience of objectivities: 'The "object" of consciousness, the object as having identity "with itself" during the flowing subjective process, does not come into the process from the outside; on the contrary, it is included as a sense in the subjective process itself – and thus as an "*intentional effect*" *produced by* the synthesis of consciousness' (1967, 42).

It is the remarkable character of consciousness that, on the one hand, every 'given' content may be imaginatively manipulated and altered in any particular detail and, on the other hand, imaginative manipulation is itself bound by the ontological structure of consciousness. We are free to imagine what we will, but not just as we please; an imagined perception still appears as a 'quasi-perception', as a partially disclosed object within a field, and so on. In Husserl's earlier attack on psychologism and idealism, essential viewing emerged as a decisive rupture with the normal experience of the world, but now all grasping of empirical reality (all perceiving, willing, feeling, and so on), is placed within the constituting processes of a pure, transcendental, intersubjective consciousness.

At this point Husserl makes an uneasy compromise with a quite different notion of intersubjectivity. In locating the transcendental ego in the body Husserl provides the beginnings of a defensible notion of a genuinely intersubjective consciousness. But in *Cartesian Meditations* he develops the argument in relation to what might more properly be termed an 'interactive' ego. In the 'Fifth Meditation', by far the longest and most complex, Husserl attempts to combine the notions of intersubjectivity and interactive subjectivity. Following the general development of his thought, one way of doing this is to claim intersubjectivity is the 'pure' collective consciousness upon which the empirical interactive ego is founded; thus, 'within myself, within the limits of my transcendentally reduced pure conscious life, I *experience* the world (including others) – and, according to its experiential sense, *not* (so to speak) my *private* synthetic formation but as other than mine alone [*mir fremde*], as an *intersubjective* world, actually there for everyone, accessible in respect of its Objects to everyone' (1967, 91). Of course there is already an ambiguity over the term 'experience' here, a term properly referring to the empirical rather than the transcendentally reduced ego, and the parenthetical equivocation (which is, after all, no parenthesis in the phenomenological sense but just what is not to be 'bracketed') is immediately brought into the open: 'and yet each has his experiences, his appearances and appearance unities, his world-phenomenon; whereas the experienced world exists in itself, over against all experiencing subjects and their world-phenomena' (1967, 91).

The issue, however, becomes more complex and raises serious difficulties. It is here less a problem of articulating a relation between the pure transcendental intersubjectivity and the empirical interactive ego than an issue of gaining insight into the apparent opposition, within *both* spheres, of the sense in which the world is shared with others, and the equally compelling sense in which this world is exclusively a world-for-me. Husserl tries to bridge this gap with an elaborate 'transcendental theory of "empathy"' (1967, 92). He makes the important observation that, in spite of the intentional structure of consciousness, it is a remarkable fact that, as pure ego, I can nevertheless contrast myself with another self and not just with objects in the world. The character of this other self is just that it remains immediately inaccessible to me. This 'presupposes that *not all my own modes of consciousness are modes of my self-consciousness*' (1967, 105). For Husserl the problem of the 'other' is just how it can be that 'the ego has, and can always go on forming, in himself such intentionalities of a different kind, intentionalities with an existence-sense whereby *he wholly transcends his own being'* (1967, 105). How, in other words, can we constitute within the synthesis of consciousness anything 'other?' This difficulty raises in an acute form the problem posed by the enigmatic character of reality; the sense in which the self-constituted world is nonetheless experienced as something given to us.

We immediately recognize the other as another *person* and, thus, a centre of self-conscious activity and self-presence, yet we cannot gain access to the immediate experience of *their* world. This means that we must, mutually, constitute the world as an intersubjective and exterior reality. However, Husserl makes the issue unnecessarily complicated and obscure by trying to relate intersubjectivity to the ego conceived as an experiencing monad, yet the whole tendency of his argument has been away from such naturalistic fallacies. The monad is not an adequate description of the empirical ego, which is always an interactive subject (rather than pure collective intersubjectivity), and is just the kind of theoretical construct Husserl himself was so fond of exposing and rooting out. There is no need, in Husserl's own understanding at this point, to found the interactive subject, or intersubjectivity more generally and primordially, on empathy. In fact, in terms of our immediate experience, Husserl is clear that empathy is not an inductive process (this would send us all the way back to psychologism), but is itself a constitutional unity of any consciousness. The other is another person in a primal sense that does not require further clarification. We do not deduce the existence of another: 'What I actually see is not a sign and a mere analogue, a depiction in any natural sense of the word; on the contrary, it is someone else' (1967, 124).

Jan Patočka nicely conveys the subtle complexity of Husserl's view: 'Other living beings are not accessible to us in their original experiencing, in their stream of living … The others are posited to us through their appearance, as a phenomenon only and not in their primordial being … At the same time and in spite of that we have constantly the impression that others are not before us only as the front side of an object, a wall behind which something is taking place … The other as a life is present to us after all' (1998, 63).

The constraint of time

Husserl's *Phenomenology of Internal Time Consciousness* is a complex text, the major part of which was composed as a lecture course in 1905 and is among the first products of his new phenomenological method. His focus, thus, is on the pure essence of time as the general condition of any consciousness whatever. This is not conceived, of course, as a categorical *a priori* in the manner of Kant; indeed, it is not and cannot be conceived at all. There is, however, an apprehension of the *immanent time* of duration that remains quite independent of time measured by clocks, or constituted in social conventions: 'the moments of experience that specifically found temporal apprehension as the apprehension of time … are phenomenologically given'. But, just as sensation does not reveal the thing-in-itself, 'One cannot discover the least thing about objective time through phenomenological analysis' (1990, 6). And while the essential qualities of succession and duration, like other intentional forms, cannot be traced to, or explained by, empirical experiences, they can be grasped, nonetheless, in their pure eidetic form. Thus, 'The duration of sensation and the sensation of duration are two very different things ... The succession of sensations and the sensation of succession are not the same' (1990, 12).

Time consciousness is curiously binding upon all experience: 'Even in phantasy every individual is extended in time in some way, having its now, its before, and its after; but the now, before, and after are merely imagined' (1990, 43). We cannot escape the absolute condition of temporality; in memory and imagination, as in perception, a single temporal givenness is the condition of consciousness. All appearance is 'one thing at a time' and 'one thing after another'. Husserl is taken aback by this evident but overlooked characteristic of experience: 'As shocking (when not initially even absurd) as it may seem to say that the flow of consciousness constitutes its own unity, it is nevertheless the case that it does' (1990, 84). Contents of all kinds, sensations, appearances, objects, acts, 'reproductive modifications' all come to consciousness with a particular temporal marker, a sign of 'now', that points back and probes into the future towards vague horizons of retention and protention. In a supplementary text he emphasizes that phenomenology must deal with the givenness of experienced time alone (again equivocation over the notion of experience) and that now *with* its past and future are given immediately. 'What is "given" to perception is necessarily something temporally *extended*, not something with the character of a mere point in time' (1990, 173). Time consciousness, as phenomenologically reduced, is extended, filled with temporal adumbrations; 'That all reality lies in the indivisible now-point, that in phenomenology everything ought to be reduced to this point – these are sheer *fictions* and lead to absurdities' (1990, 174).

Husserl discusses the perception of tone and melody (a topic much discussed in psychology since Helmholtz) as a critical example. All immediate impressions are modified as a 'retentional consciousness'. But this is not a simple linear series of dissolving now points. Each retentional modification simultaneously modifies prior retentional modifications, the characteristic 'running-off phenomena' of temporal consciousness. Memory, thus, is a continually transforming experience of the past, continually remade as an aspect of the constitution of present consciousness.

The pure transcendental ego is given temporally. That is to say, the intersubjectivity that founds the experience of the world and ourselves as *given* realities is a transforming temporal construction; it is historical as well as temporal.

History

The forms in which consciousness founds experience, that is to say, are *historical* forms of intersubjectivity and appear as the development of human culture. Every act of consciousness is a synthesis: 'Yet precisely this synthesis, as a synthesis having this form, has its "history", evinced in the synthesis itself. It is owing to an essentially necessary genesis that I, the ego, can experience a physical thing and do so even at first glance' (1967, 79).

The relentless pursuit of insight into the given character of consciousness involved Husserl in a series of decisive modifications of his starting point and its assumptions. Consciousness is first narrowed through a rigorous exclusion of all hypothetical and unfounded theoretical concepts, and then clarified by the suspension of all positing activity. This all takes place within the historically limiting assumptions of modern individualism. The Cartesian starting point – the starting point for the purposes of exposition – means that consciousness is to be grasped in transparent *self*-understanding; and the 'self' appears irresistibly to be the living subjectivity of an individual person. This is symmetrical with the fundamental methodological principle that all givenness is given *individually*. However, the phenomenological reduction pointed inescapably to the transcendental reduction and the ever expanding investigation into spheres of intersubjectivity. Self-understanding, thus, involves its relation not only with other, already formed, selves but with an entire shared world; the intersubjective character of reality comes to light as the real foundation of every individual and individually taken acts of consciousness. It is, above all, the intersubjectivity that is concealed in and by the natural attitude.

This opens the way for a fresh historical perspective on the insights won by Husserl in his penetrating philosophical reflection. *Both* the natural attitude, which is its point of departure, *and* the complex spheres of inter-subjective reality, which are revealed by phenomenological reflection, can be grasped historically as two sides, so to speak, of the development of modern society and modern culture. Husserl himself develops a historical view of his critique of the natural attitude, and the ways in which his own phenomenological explorations can fruitfully be contextualized, historically and culturally, will be taken up in subsequent chapters.

After *Cartesian Meditations* Husserl became increasingly interested in and concerned over the most general historical significance of his work. From the early attacks on psychologism to the mature and magisterial dethrone-ment of the natural attitude as an adequate starting point for philosophical reflection, his work had shown increasing sensitivity to the relationship between the emergence and development of modern scientific thought, on the one hand, and the possibilities of critical reflection, on the other. The historical issue was given greater urgency, for Husserl, after his reading of Martin Heidegger's *Being and Time*. His one-time student, collaborator, and designated successor Heidegger not only came to represent for him a pro-found misunderstanding of the method of phenomenology and an obscuring of its most vital insights, but exemplified a 'faddish' 'philosophy of freedom' that amounted to nothing other than a betrayal of the entire project of modernity and its fundamental commitment to reason.

Influenced by the writings of Georg Misch and the stimulating thought of his new assistant, Eugen Fink, Husserl once again recast his phenomenological starting point (Elveton 2000). Rather than work through the Cartesian problem finally to discover its ground in intersubjectivity, he began with the 'higher-order' constitution of reality as modern spirit. His earlier, occasional, historically contextualized remarks – as in the *Logos* article – became a new point of departure for a genuinely historical-critical understanding of the natural attitude and the withering of the spirit of reason that Husserl believed it represented. His 'reflection upon the origin of our critical scientific and philosophical situation' (1970a, xxiv) was not a new application of his phenomenology, but a new point of departure for yet another full-scale working through of his philosophical method. The two came together in an enquiry into 'the origin of the modern spirit', which was manifest above all in the development of the natural sciences: 'the authority behind the natural attitude of everyday life with which it is ultimately continuous'.

Husserl's phenomenology moves relentlessly from its starting point in modern logic and psychology, and the *topos* of individual consciousness, to broader issues of intersubjectivity and history (Brainard 2002). His final work recognizes, in the context of the actual political and cultural crisis in which he was living, the task that lay ahead, and reconfirms, in spite of the often tragic failure fully to realize them, his deep commitment to the continually unfolding values of modernity:

> The type of investigation that we must carry out … is not that of a historical investigation in the usual sense. Our task is to make comprehensible the *teleology* in the historical becoming of philosophy, especially modern philosophy, and at the same time to achieve clarity about ourselves, who are the bearers of this teleology, who take part in carrying it out through our personal intentions … we are attempting ultimately to discern the historical task which we can acknowledge as the only one which is personally our own … Only in this way can we, who not only have a spiritual heritage but have become what we are thoroughly and exclusively in a historical-spiritual manner, have a task which is truly our own … the task stands before us not merely as factually required but as a task *assigned* to us. (1970a, 70–1)

3

Variation: Method and Theme in the Development of Phenomenology

Being is the proper and sole theme of philosophy.

Heidegger, *The Basic Problems of Phenomenology*

Dasein is fascinated with its world.

Heidegger, *Being and Time*

The pure I, the subject of the transcendental consciousness in which the world is constituted, is itself *outside the subject: self* without reflection – uniqueness identifying itself as incessant awakening.

Levinas, *Outside the Subject*

All that exists consists of interpretation.

Nietzsche, *Will to Power*

In addition to the originality and evident importance of Husserl's published writings, his impressive personality and committed teaching attracted a growing number of exceptionally talented students. Through them Husserl's phenomenology made a powerful impact not only on academic philosophy but, more generally and to a growing extent, on the intellectual life of modern society as a whole. In spite of the difficulty and austerity of its founder's published work, phenomenology was quickly recognized as offering a fresh point of departure for almost every type of critical inquiry into the character of modern life and its forms of self-understanding. The unusual combination of intellectual rigour, radical argument, and undogmatic openness to experience made phenomenology relevant to investigations of the most varied sort, many of which were quite remote from Husserl's own immediate interests. And, in spite of Husserl's articulation of the historical commitment of his philosophy, phenomenology became associated with quite divergent and even contrary ideological and political commitments. It was invoked to justify a radically secular world view and, equally, new religious and theological positions; it supported reactionary, progressive, and revolutionary political programmes; it inspired innovations and established traditions in the arts as well as a variety of new and old aesthetic perspectives; and, not least, it fuelled discrepant valuations of modern technology (Spiegelberg 1969).

Within philosophical discourse more strictly defined, Husserl's work was received in a hardly less varied manner. The growing number of philosophers who identified their own work as phenomenological rarely, in fact, followed Husserl consistently and many explicitly rejected aspects of his method, or contested its results. The diffusion of Husserl's thought, beyond as well as within the academy, was accompanied by the proliferation of contending interpretations of the original and rival versions of its essential insights. But it was in relation to Husserl's original work that every new position was defined and defended so that, in a process very similar to the development of modern thought after Descartes, and later Kant, the most acute exploration of *experience* took the form of debates over the meaning and significance of philosophical texts.

From the outset, beyond Husserl's immediate circle of advanced students and co-workers, quite different versions of phenomenology appeared. Early enthusiasts tended either to stress the 'objective' and given character of phenomena, portraying Husserl's approach as a new and legitimate form of empiricism, or to focus on 'subjective', self-constituting activity, regarding phenomenology as a valid development of idealism (Elveton 2000). Reductive and eclectic strategies, indeed, have remained influential (Ey 1978; Hundert 1989; Petitot et al. 1999). However, rather than follow chronologically the emergence and complex interrelation of divergent interpretations of phenomenology, which is of considerable historical interest, the more particular connection between phenomenology and sociology is better approached retrospectively in terms of a simplified schema of 'orthodox' and 'heterodox' positions.

Many earlier 'heterodox' views are now, with the progressive revelation of Husserl's voluminous notebooks, plausibly seen as elaborating aspects of Husserl's programme that remained undeveloped in his published work rather than as distinct or alternative versions of phenomenology. Thus, for example, the phenomenological approaches that took their point of departure in the experience of religion (Scheler, Otto), or art (Dufrenne), or politics (Ortega), or the body (Merleau-Ponty) – in the belief that Husserl's method excluded, rather than simply neglected, such significant 'given' realities – have to a large extent been overtaken by the emergence of Husserl's own account of these matters. Similarly, those works offering distinctive phenomenological approaches founded on feeling (Strasser), or willing (Ricoeur), rather than perception, must now be read in relation to Husserl's wider-ranging investigations of 'regional ontologies' that have more recently appeared.

Existence

Husserl's phenomenology was not a systematic *theory* of phenomena. It was rigorous but incomplete; indeed, if it was genuinely to follow 'phenomena themselves' it could hardly be otherwise. But the sprawling character of

Husserl's unpublished work, flowing out as it did from the closed Cartesian *cogito* to the complex intersubjective constitution of the life-world with its infinitely rich historical content, threatened not only to overwhelm its author but to dissolve phenomenology itself into diffuse and incoherent research. Husserl's unequalled strength as an original thinker lay in his radical insight, his fearless development of new positions, and his patient unfurling of all the implications of novel perspectives. But, in spite of his own precision and rigour, he increasingly felt the need to establish a systematic framework for its presentation and further detailed development. It was primarily to fulfil this task that he worked directly with a number of advanced students and assistants, most significantly with Martin Heidegger in whom he quickly recognized his future legitimate successor. However, in the late twenties, in the aftermath of Heidegger's major work *Being and Time*, Husserl came to see in his assistant's work not only a rejection of his own phenomenological method, but a distortion of his entire philosophical project and its central task of articulating anew the historic project of modernity (Hussert 1997a).

Heidegger claimed a central place for his own philosophy within the phenomenological revolution. Yet, far from providing an appropriate framework for the exposition of Husserl's work, it challenged his teacher's most cherished positions. Certainly it begins, as does Husserl, with a decisive rejection of modern metaphysical dualism. However, breaking free from what he regarded as the self-enclosed world of phenomena, Heidegger insists on enquiring into the being, and not just the appearing, of things; and into the Being of beings, rather than the constitution of experience.

For Husserl the phenomenological reduction laid aside the natural attitude directed towards preconstituted objects but, importantly, these objects were neither annihilated nor ignored. They came into focus in a new way once the reduction was effected. The result was a progressive uncovering of aspects of reality and its formation that normally remained concealed in the obviousness of the everyday world. Heidegger advanced his own version of the phenomenological reduction and outlined its methodical character in lectures prior to the publication of his major work:

> *For Husserl*, phenomenological reduction ... is the method of leading phenomenological vision from the natural attitude of the human being whose life is involved in the world of things and persons back to the transcendental life of consciousness and its noetic-noematic experiences, in which objects are constituted as correlates of consciousness. *For us*, phenomenological reduction means leading phenomenological vision back from the apprehension of a being, whatever may be the character of that apprehension, to the understanding of the being of this being. (Heidegger 1982, 21)

Although recent scholarship has sought out continuities between the work of Husserl and that of Heidegger (Crowell 2001), the latter's insistence that 'being is the proper and sole theme of philosophy' (1982, 11) makes clear the fundamentally different direction of their thought. This is a method which is distinct from any version of scientific 'detachment', but 'requires at the same time that we should bring ourselves forward positively toward being itself' (1982, 21).

For Heidegger, the ordinary world cannot be 'bracketed'. What he termed *Dasein* is the human mode of being that is always a being-in-the-world; our *interest* in the world is not a voluntary orientation towards being but is, rather, *given* with being itself. Human *existence* is necessarily and always implicated in its own world; it always comes enshrouded in worldness. Heidegger's existential version of phenomenology goes back to, and rests heavily on, the writings of the nineteenth-century Danish religious thinker, Søren Kierkegaard. In an extensive, complex, and elusive series of works Kierkegaard confronted the Hegelian 'reduction' of reality to a 'presuppositionless' metaphysics with actually living individuals continually engaged with their own existence (Ferguson 1994; Westphal 1996). Heidegger develops Kierkegaard's existential understanding of modernity. Whereas for modern philosophers and scientists the objective knowledge of nature is a privileged region of modern consciousness, Heidegger follows Kierkegaard in grasping that for every living being 'subjectivity is truth'. The appropriate modality of self-understanding is subjective; that is to say it involves an active self-grasping in, and *living through*, the conventions of everyday life, and should not be confused either with the acquisition of knowledge or with its phenomenological reduction. Science and philosophy, in misconstruing humanity as a particular kind of 'object', placed everything vital in modern life beyond any possibility of understanding from 'within'. Humanity, however, cannot be detached from itself, does not appear to itself as an object and, therefore, does not pose an issue of 'knowledge' at all. The issue raised by humanity is not how to *explain* itself to itself but how authentically to *be* human. Humanity is subject, not object, and must be grasped subjectively in its own peculiar modality. From the outset, thus, Heidegger views humanity in terms of the historical character of existence as a continuously self-transforming subjectivity. Philosophy and science are misguided to the extent that they attempt to begin at the beginning. *Dasein* always finds itself in its own world as active *being-in-the-world*. Human being, *Dasein*, is characterized as *care* and *throwness*; that is it is always given in the inescapable direction of our interest as a project of worldness.

Heidegger, thus, views Husserl's phenomenology as insufficiently radical in its rejection of the positivist and empiricist prejudices of the modern 'natural attitude'. Husserl retains, as a fundamental and unclarified assumption of his entire philosophy, the notion of 'objectification' as the 'natural' movement of human subjectivity in all its forms. Husserl's questioning, that is to say, is still guided by an uncritical acceptance of modernity's drift into objectivism. Heidegger, however, invoking a reading of Kierkegaard in the context of European romanticism rather than Reformation theology, takes this entire tendency as an indication of the *inauthentic* character of modern culture as a whole. Modern subjectivity conceals itself in the illusions of objectivity; and this is no mere misconception, but a consequence of *Dasein*'s historical distortion. Husserl's method, in spite of its principled rejection of empiricism and psychologism, is inextricably bound up with the historically limited and, in a larger view, inauthentic reality of modern life. Husserl's phenomenology, in fact, becomes an example of *Dasein*'s modern misunderstanding of itself. That 'Because the Dasein is historical in its own existence, possibilities of access and modes of interpretation of beings are themselves diverse, varying in different historical circumstances' (Heidegger 1982, 22).

Heidegger's approach is, curiously, at once both more and less cautious than his one-time mentor's (Keller, 1999). On the one hand he denies the real possibility of phenomenological reduction. Detachment is conceivable only as the adoption of a specific *theoretical* interest in the world, an interest in philosophizing. On the other hand, Heidegger equates Being (*Dasein)* with the modern theme of human autonomy as *freedom*, and *both* with the pure streaming of time. He pertinently asks: 'Can such a thing as a pure intuiting be found in the finite knowing of beings? What is sought is an immediate, although experience-free, allowing of an individual to be encountered ... the pure representing which takes things in stride must give itself something capable of being represented. Pure intuition, therefore, must in a certain sense be "creative"' (1990, 31). By dissolving reality into the ultimately free Being of humanity, unencumbered of any characterization other than temporality, the problem of self-understanding and self-representing re-emerges. Only in an act of pure intuition can we grasp *Dasein* or, rather, only in a free act of intuition does *Dasein* condescend to the finite being of actual human experience: 'Pure intuition is required as the essential element of ontological knowledge in which the experience of being is grounded' (1990, 34). However, the now point of streaming *Dasein* is not 'reduced' to empty temporality: 'What is represented in pure intuition is no being (no object [*Gegenstand*]), i.e. no appearing being, but at the same time it is plainly not nothing' (1990, 31). The pure intuition of time is the primal unity of the field of consciousness and its horizons; it is within it, and only within it, that the 'belonging together' of one thing with another can appear. 'What is encountered itself, however, has already been comprehensively grasped in advance through the horizon of time which is set forth in pure intuition' (1990, 54).

The Being of human being is the Being of time. And for Heidegger *Dasein*'s 'reckoning with time' is 'a way of reckoning which precedes any use of measuring equipment' and owes its origin to 'a way in which primordial time has been levelled off' (1962, 456–7). The immediately intelligible and recognizable temporality of all experience is not to be confused with the '*ecstatical* character of the Present' (1962, 461), which is its primordial source. As distinct from the absolute ontological freedom of the now, all ontic experience is a present which has already 'been understood and *interpreted* in its full structural content of datability, spannedness, publicness, and worldhood' (1962, 469). The ordinary measurement of time 'covers up' the now and conceals it. *Dasein* loses itself in the world.

Subjectivity is identical with time primordially rather than with the phenomenal structure of duration, succession, and the relentless birth and death of the now point. Husserl had also arrived at this view, but he was careful to limit his phenomenological method at this point. Time, ultimately, was given in a unique way; as pure exteriority, as an inescapable condition of our existence. The *same* stream of time appeared and reappeared through every modulation of experience and, thus, remained absolutely beyond the ego; whether understood empirically or through the transcendental reduction. For Husserl, this meant that pure subjectivity was, ultimately, something absolutely beyond experience, something *outside* consciousness. This was the limit, not just of phenomenology, but also of any experience including any reflection upon experience. And this, ultimately, founded the necessity that the world was experienced as something outside us, something in-itself given.

In Heidegger's version, however, phenomenology leads all the way back to primal being in relation to which all social-historical constitution of experience remains essentially mysterious. All givenness dissolves into the pure fluidity of time. Heidegger's problem, thus, is to give some account of the emergence of empirical reality, of all finiteness, from the streaming now point. The solution must simultaneously give the finite with the infinite:

> Ontological knowledge 'forms' transcendence, and this forming is nothing other than the holding-open of the horizon within which the Being of the being becomes discernible in a preliminary way ... If ontological knowledge unveils the horizon, then its truth lies precisely in (the act of) letting the being be encountered within the horizon ... Hence, it must at least remain open as to whether this 'creative' knowledge, which is always only ontological and never ontic, bursts the finitude of transcendence asunder, or whether it does not just plant the finite 'subject' in its authentic finitude. (1962, 87)

Being always anticipates its ontic forms, makes itself known in advance and, as productive imagination, is not dependent on what has already been revealed. Imagination first brings into view 'something like constant presence' (1962, 93).

In Heidegger the 'everydayness' of *Dasein* is something equivocal because, at the same time, *Dasein* is and has the possibility of revealing itself as other than everyday. *Dasein* 'manifests' itself as authentic phenomena, indeed the appearance of the everyday is quite distinct and actually disguises or veils *Dasein* in its primal sense. It is difficult, however, to resist the thought that Heidegger has taken 'everydayness' in a literal way, that his rejection of the world of ontic blandness leads directly to a spiritual retreat and nostalgia to a 'worldness' in which the ontic and the ontological are seamlessly identical. Interestingly Husserl, by setting aside ontic everydayness, succeeds in *preserving* its objectivity and its astonishing givenness; while Heidegger, who cannot suspend concern of being for its world and therefore the guiding interest of any thought, actually loses all objectivity and givenness. This paradox is resolved in recognizing that Husserl brackets appearance only to bring back, and to preserve, the actual content of experience; while Heidegger, with the entire world of thingly objects at his disposal, to engender a critical philosophical reflection, plunges them, and himself, into pure flowing subjectivity.

Heidegger's difficulty (as Pascal's and Kierkegaard's) is to find in the fallen state of ontic being a clue to the authentic Being that, nonetheless, lies hidden within it. The 'who' of *Dasein* is the 'self', but not the ego of direct empirical experience that identifies itself in its experiences:

> When saying 'I', Dasein surely has in view the entity which, in every case, it is itself. The everyday interpretation of the Self, however, has a tendency to understand itself in terms of the 'world' with which it is concerned. When Dasein has itself in view ontically, it *fails to see* itself in relation to the kind of Being of that entity which it is itself. And this holds especially for the basic state of Dasein, Being-in-the-World. (1962, 368)

He finds in the least well-defined aspects of contemporary experiences the starting point for his interrogation of Being, at every stage, so to speak, outwitting the clinging ordinariness of the everyday. To allow Being properly to manifest itself we must distrust everything clear and precise and fall back, rather, on the vagueness of 'moods'. The starting point of questioning is not curiosity, doubt, wonder or even suspension of interest, but a vague 'moodiness', which is the fundamental 'attunement' of the present.

Yet it is difficult not to read much of *Being and Time* as a striking and valuable *psychology* of contemporary existence. In particular Heidegger's precise and richly textured accounts of the more diffuse and 'empty' feelings that characterized modern life, such as anxiety, boredom, guilt and so on, attracted a great deal of attention and, justifiably, continue to do so. It was often difficult, however, to discern a methodical route that yielded these compelling insights. And in relation to his most general conclusions, the reader was frequently presented with provocative assertions rather than insights. In claiming, for example, that 'Care, as a primordial totality, lies "before" [*vor*] every factical "attitude" and "situation" of *Dasein*, and it does so essentially *a priori*' or that 'Willing and wishing are rooted with ontological necessity in Dasein as care' (1962, 238) it is unclear how such assertions are to be supported independently of his own idiosyncratic use of words. Where Husserl's method is painstakingly slow and cumulative, Heidegger, as it were, aims *through* every reality to a 'primal manifestation' of Being, which is, in principle, unconnected with any ontic reality. One is reminded of Pascal, and in a larger framework of ontology, St Anselm; faith furnishes him with a vision of primordial reality (here 'care' rather than happiness and unhappiness) and this becomes a clue for the reinterpretation of all other experiences in its light. The *formal* requirement of care is simply the unity of Being-in-the-world; but in designating this as 'care' Heidegger is evidently filling it with a special content that – in his highly charged philosophical language – fills it out with an entire world; indeed, with worldhood as such. 'Being-in-the-world is a structure which is primordially and constantly *whole*' (Heidegger 1962, 225). But is this just the hidden rational assumption in Heidegger's otherwise radical freeing of phenomenology from the conditions of modernity? It is not so simple to eradicate metaphysical assumptions and replace them with the substantive freedom of *Dasein*, as the absolute 'other' that is also a 'self'.

The distinction between Husserl and Heidegger can be made in terms of substantive and historical, as well as of methodological, issues central to phenomenology. Husserl might be viewed, in retrospect, as proposing a phenomenology framed by a commitment to being as *distinct* from time. All being, that is all possible experience, comes, so to speak, with a temporal 'marker'; all possible experience is singular and comes *in* time. Essential insight, apodictic truth, and ontological knowledge are eternal, in the sense that their temporal markers (their possible psychological associations and context) are not relevant to *those* aspects of reality which, as particular thoughts, insights and forms of experience, are also given exclusively *through* singular events, objects, feelings, and so on. Both the world given in the natural attitude, and the *philosophical reflection* that brings to light the reduced data of pure eidetic forms, are accessible only as temporal objects. Yet time 'itself' and *any* form of experienced reality remain, in a strict sense, incommensurable. Time is something wholly outside experience. The 'now moment' is not an experiencable 'quantum' of a pure temporal flow, as it were, built into the world of things; it is, rather, the fundamentally mysterious and impenetrable *fact* of the relentless *appearing* of phenomena. Time is wholly 'other' than the phenomenal. Heidegger insists, on the contrary, in viewing time itself as indistinguishable from *Dasein*. The pure stream of time is nothing other than the absolute freedom of *Dasein*. As a result all actual experience is 'fallen'. The entire phenomenal world is rendered alien, a realm of estranged, equivocal being. Yet, as time and authentic being cannot be distinguished, even the impoverished existence to which we are presently condemned bears imperishably within it the promise of humanity. Heidegger's philosophy increasingly diverged from the founding assumption of modernity. Human autonomy, in his view, and not just reason, was fatally compromised, on the one hand, by repeated failures fully to seize the freedom that founded all human action, and on the other hand, and more fundamentally, because *Dasein* could not ultimately disclose itself through any process of objectification. It was in the non-objective states of anxiety, boredom, happiness, and so on that *Dasein* made its presence felt; while all objective being, by its fall into the absolutely determined temporal flow, alienated its freedom and became responsible for the restless negativity of modern life. Heidegger's later work makes clear the powerful strain of anti-modernism that had animated his work from the beginning. In contrast to Husserl and rather than viewing science as a valid, if uncritical, form of rational knowledge, Heidegger considers it an expression of modern self-misunderstanding and hubris. Science emerges 'only when truth has been transferred into the certainty of representation' and the worldness of reality is grasped as a *picture* of the world (Heidegger 1977, 127). The ensuing critique of technological reason has much in common with modernist disquiet over modernity, such as that articulated by Max Weber, but Heidegger associates it with a historically unfounded and misleading nostalgia for the premodern *Gemeinde*.

This contrast helps to clarify the extent to which Husserl's philosophy is opposed to the idealist tradition as well as to modern empiricism and psychologism. Heidegger's phenomenology lapses back into idealism. Paradoxically his radical existentialism reveals a distinct lack of security in the 'self-evidence' of his own existence; the ego-*cogito* does not carry any special weight of self-evidence. As a result his inspirational reading of Kierkegaard sees 'through' his mentor to the romanticism of Schelling and Fichte; positions Kierkegaard had, in fact, rejected.

After the appearance of *Being and Time* Heidegger's influence was immense and spread well beyond the already extensive network of gifted and highly original students who had been attracted by his teaching. After World War II, and particularly in France, his work became an important focus for the diverse strands of thought that merged in the general cultural movement of existentialism (Rockmore 1995). While phenomenology remained an important background and source of inspiration for this movement generally, progressively it tended to distance itself not only from Husserl's programme but also from Heidegger's own ontology.

Sartre, for example, reading Heidegger in relation to a particular version of Hegel's philosophy, championed a radical, libertarian, doctrine that laid claim to the heritage of phenomenology in spite of its equal remoteness from Husserl's rigour and Heidegger's rhetoric. Sartre forces together empirical self-reflection and the transcendental demand for absolute freedom. The empirical ego is intoxicated with infinite possibility and an unlimited freedom of self-realization, as if both were made actual in mundane experience. Sartre makes absolute what Kierkegaard had termed the aesthetic choice, in which the self is dissolved in contingent events and dignifies arbitrariness as authentic selfhood (Sartre 1969; 1999; Zaner 1970; 1971).

Jacques Derrida, who saw in phenomenology the beginning of a radical rejection of the western metaphysical prejudice in favour of presence over representation, took up Heidegger's existentialism in quite a different way. Derrida's early work on Husserl elaborated Heidegger's implicit criticism of his teacher. Focusing on the theory of signs outlined in *Logical Investigations*, Derrida rejects Husserl's phenomenological reduction as a new version of idealism that involves a duplication of reality. Husserl's effort to overcome the paralysing dualism of subject and object fails because that very distinction is reproduced in the difference between the phenomenologically reduced ego (phenomenological psychology) and the transcendental ego (pure ego). To escape the traps of solipsism Husserl's language breaks free of the monism of consciousness and subverts his methodological commitment to intentionality. A categorical distinction between 'fulfilled' and 'unfulfilled' expectations makes clear Husserl's continuing metaphysical prejudice in favour of the 'real' presence of the object of perception independent of the consciousness of the perceiving subject (Derrida 1973). Priority is given to the passive perception of objects over the active synthesis of 'quasi' perceptions of imagination, memory, illusion, and so on.

Derrida views Heidegger's dissolution of subjectivity into unfounded streaming of temporality as a progressive step towards overcoming the lingering dualism of Husserl's thought. But cleansing the western 'onto-theology' of presence requires a yet more determined and radical programme of 'deconstruction'. There is no 'founding' to the process of representation; nothing stands as a bare presence that begins signification. All signifying is the linking of representations, which should be grasped as arbitrary marks, as pure *différance*, rather than as signs of absent 'real' objects (Derrida 1976).

Derrida has moved a long way from both Husserl's (early) phenomenology and Heidegger's romantic anti-modernist existentialism. His celebratory, postmodern, non-metaphysical anti-philosophy has become significant for investigations of every aspect of contemporary culture. Ironically, in claiming no real difference 'underlies' the meaningfulness 'given' as everyday life, as art, as religion, as science, and so on, his own deconstruction of contemporary experience is clearly 'founded' in the early work of Husserl.

Alterity

The protean character of Husserl's phenomenology is nowhere more evident than in the contrast between those of his followers who have read his works as a bold extension of the 'subjectivism' of modern thought and those, alternatively, who welcome his writings as a challenging restatement of the irreducible 'objectivism' of modern experience.

Among the earliest protagonists of a distinctively phenomenological philosophy, therefore, were thinkers who situated themselves within a specifically religious tradition. A significant *religious* phenomenology (Scheler, Otto, Marcel), as well as a *phenomenology* of religion (Van der Leeuw, Eliade), thus developed. Where Husserl sketched out the essential contours of his phenomenology through a consideration and reconsideration of the emergence of science within the western tradition (Funke 1987), alternative versions that took their point of departure in religious world views rapidly emerged. In spite of the strong commitment of Husserl to the general project of modernity and, more directly, the continuing antipathy of all phenomenological positions to any form of abstraction or to any account of reality made in terms of hypothetical concepts, it is not at all surprising that the new philosophy should have explored religious phenomena and religious aspects of experience. These interests were compatible with Husserl's own development towards investigations into the cultural-historical realm of spirit, and proved to be one of the most fertile areas of phenomenological research.

The resilience of the world to any subjective act of negation – its sheer *thereness* – survives the most radical process of reduction. Indeed, the progressive suspension of all positing of reality as actual reveals ever new aspects of the world which, in their ceaseless appearing and disappearing, present themselves as simply *given*. And every effort further to analyse the given, to find in it a wealth of intersubjective cultural history, does nothing to overcome the powerful sense of exteriority which is, in fact, the only modality through which essential data *can* appear. Essential insight into *either* the object of the natural attitude, *or* the empirically experiencing subject, reveals reality standing within consciousness as *something*; that is, as something that is *neither* object nor subject, something *other* than object or subject. It is possible then to interpret this something as a *difference from* consciousness, as a pure presence registered by and in consciousness but always as something other than itself, as an appearing/disappearing present; or to view it as a *difference in* consciousness, a phasic transformation from ego to non-ego modes of apprehension.

It is, above all, due to the extraordinarily original work of Emmanuel Levinas that a phenomenological account of the other has become central to the clarification of contemporary experience. Levinas's first publications were translations and commentaries on Husserl; in fact his French translation of *Cartesian Meditations*, like Ricoeur's translation of the first book of *Ideas Pertaining to a Pure Phenomenology*, had had a greater impact than their German originals and stimulated wide-ranging innovations within, or related to, the phenomenological movement (Levinas 1995; 1998a). His prize-winning *The Theory of Intuition in Husserl's Phenomenology*, first published in 1930, already stressed humanistic rather than formal epistemological aspects of Husserl's work. By focusing on the notion of intuition, rather than the historical or thematic structure of subjectivity, he sought to develop the essential phenomenological insight into the peculiar *exteriority* of consciousness. Insight always involves an *encounter* with something initially mysterious or puzzling but, equally, always projects ahead of itself a potential resolution and means of assimilating this difference. Insight begins in anticipation: 'Husserl had an intuition of his philosophy before he made it a philosophy of intuition' (Levinas 1995, liv).

Levinas grasps insight in such a way as to preserve and emphasize its limitations. Not everything is, or can be, penetrated by insight. The phenomenological reduction, ultimately, 'is an act of violence that man does to himself ... in order to find himself again as pure thought' (1995, 36). The radical sense in which Levinas intended these remarks only became evident at a much later date, with the publication of *Totality and Infinity* (1969). Here, in direct opposition to Heidegger's avoidance, and Derrida's outright rejection, of the metaphysics of presence, Levinas insists that *all* subjectivity, all sense of selfhood, comes to itself in an encounter with otherness. Genuine metaphysics is not the western prejudice in favour of the *logos* but an unavoidable longing for reality, and is not to be mistaken for theoretical knowledge or formal reasoning in which everything is dissolved in abstraction and then systematically articulated; rather, 'metaphysical desire tends toward *something else entirely*, toward the *absolutely other*' (1969, 33). Levinas insists upon the 'absolute exteriority of the metaphysical' and the 'radical heterogeneity of the other' (1969, 35–6).

It is just the refractory character of reality that, for Levinas, arouses and sustains our interest; it is always something outside us; it resists us. In contrast to Heidegger 'who subordinates the relation with the Other as ontology', the significance of Husserl's phenomenology is just that, albeit it in an unclear and inarticulate way, it acknowledged the otherness of our world. And this criticism of Heidegger applies *a fortiori* to Derrida: 'Representation consists in the possibility of accounting for the object as though it were constituted by a thought' (1969, 128).

The other is not a differentiated fragment, or projection, of what is first internal to consciousness, nor can it be assimilated to consciousness in any way; it is and remains 'outside the subject'. Levinas, in other words, is not simply and in an uncritical way acquiescing to the 'natural attitude' and making it absolute. His claim, rather, is that otherness becomes manifest as a result of carrying through the phenomenological reduction in a radical fashion. What emerges with the reduction of the actively constituted object-world of everyday life is neither the transcendental ego, nor the pure transition of temporality, but the mysterious, brute fact of exteriority.

In a remarkable way Levinas elaborates a phenomenology of *enjoyment* as part of his investigation of the experience of the world that emerges in the inescapable encounter with otherness. While the other remains, by definition, outside any possible experience, experience in the face of otherness, in recognition of the impenetrable exteriority of reality, is characterized as 'enjoyment'. In the sharpest possible contrast to Heidegger's delineation of the experience of modernity as anxious, empty, and despairing, Levinas seeks to reinstate a frankly utopian vision of homeliness in the face of an impenetrable reality: 'Enjoyment – an ultimate relation with the substantial plenitude of being, with it materially – embraces all relations with things' (1969, 133). The modern prejudice is not empiricism of the metaphysics of presence but, rather, the hubris in which all reality is assimilated to the absolute freedom of subjectivity. But, mounting his own criticism of the dominant tendency of modernity, Levinas insists that 'The love of life does not resemble the care for Being, reducible to the comprehension of Being, or ontology. The love of life does not love Being, but loves the happiness of being' (1969, 145).

Happiness, as all truth, requires that we encounter the other as other. Levinas is not referring to remote and inaccessible causes of phenomena. The other is, first of all, another person. Closeness and intimacy do not overcome the abyss of otherness; this is just the error of all modern forms of romanticism. Closeness in human terms, rather than assimilate the other to the self as in the Hegelian dialectic of self-recognition, is a relation of mutual strangeness: 'The Other remains infinitely transcendent, infinitely foreign; his face in which his epiphany is produced and which appeals to me breaks with the world that can be common to us' (1969, 194); a view admirably expressed also by Derrida (1997) and by Blanchot (1997). And quite contrary to the uncritical assumption that the face 'expresses' the 'character' and interior world of the other, a view that rose to prominence in late-eighteenth- and early-nineteenth-century fascination with physiognomy (Richards 2002), he develops a rich phenomenological account of its utterly alien aspect, which 'resists possession, resists my powers' (Levinas 1969, 197).

Levinas's work might well be viewed as the annexation of modern phenomenology to the world view of Ancient Judaism, as distinct from Heidegger's attempt, via Nietzsche, to place it within the context of pre-Socratic Greek philosophy. Certainly there are clear affinities between Levinas's work and the influential writings of Martin Buber (1937) and, strikingly, of Franz Rosenzweig (1985). A phenomenology of otherness, however, is by no means restricted to those historical and cultural antecedents and has also been developed in a significant way in the context of modern western theology. From the early work of Max Scheler under the immediate influence of Husserl's writings, through the more ambiguous writings of Gabriel Marcel, to the more recent and impressive development of the theme by Jean-Luc Marion, the 'givenness' of *our own* reality has been an essential mystery. In this view phenomenology is a version of negative theology and, far from expressing a modern secular spirit, points decisively to the relevance of an older theology for which ultimate reality was certain but enigmatically closed to human knowledge (Zaehner 1957; McGinn 1992).

This raises in a different context the obscure connection between phenomenology and scholasticism, to which Brentano had alluded in his notion of the intentionality of consciousness. What, more generally, connects them is the astonishment that *any* world at all should exist. This is just the orientation to reality that phenomenology reintroduces into western culture; an orientation apparently 'superseded' by the emergence in the early modern period of curiosity, doubt, and despair.

Astonishment links the hypermodern with the premodern, and both with the theological mystery (for a world view in which reality is given as God) that anything should appear at all. In the medieval world this was discussed as the problem of creation. Why should God create anything when God, by definition, is self-sufficient? This question has a certain priority over any further investigation into reality. Any creation assumed the forms of empirical objects, is subject to the natural restrictions of time and space and so on; yet God, we know, is not thus restricted. This is a kind of inversion of the phenomenological reduction. By suspending our belief in the actuality of creation we can, once again, be astonished that anything at all exists. This becomes a fundamental motif for a different kind of modern philosophy in Hegel and more acutely in Schelling (Žižek 1996, 2000), before it finds its way once again into the centre of all questioning; questioning which, in its radical character, is quite involuntary and itself part of the essential 'givenness' of the reality it questions.

Interpretation

Husserl established his position within modern philosophical thought through a radical reworking of its fundamental themes and, in particular, by

74

clarifying its absolute autonomy from psychology. It was only gradually that a historical-cultural perspective emerged in his writing as an essential dimension of all constituting processes. Existential phenomenology, defining itself against what was taken to be Husserl's narrow epistemological interest, identified itself with subjectivity liberated from all historical constraint, while the phenomenology of otherness grasped the phenomenal in relation to an ultimately incomprehensible and ahistorical givenness. A third distinctive version of phenomenological philosophy also developed, focused directly on the historical character of phenomena as constituted through social-cultural processes of *interpretation*.

Hermeneutics developed independently of, and prior to, Husserl's phenomenology. And rather as Heidegger took up themes from Kierkegaard and Hegel in elaborating what he claimed was a phenomenological philosophy, others turned towards Husserl's older contemporary, Wilhelm Dilthey, and the distinctive development of modern thought in which his work is centrally located. Dilthey's original point of view, which in important respects anticipates Husserl's later development, serves as an important point of reference for an alternative construction of modernity.

Modern hermeneutics has its roots in the critical biblical scholarship inspired both by Reformation theology, including Martin Luther's epochal translation of the Bible into vernacular German, and Enlightenment attacks on religious ideologies. Biblical material stood in urgent need of clarification in the light of reason and historical scholarship (Szondi 1995; Mueller-Vollmer 1997; Jeanrond 1991). What rapidly emerged from a sustained consideration of the difficulties of translation and contextualization was the realization that *no* text could, in fact, 'speak for itself'. Whatever the intention of the author, or authors, and whatever the circumstances of the text's original production and distribution, the 'meaning' that any particular reader might grasp as lying within it was, ultimately, an interpretation placed upon it and not an objective independent and verifiable fact. The meaningfulness of the text always appeared for the reader to be something given in and with the text, something to which reading contributed nothing significant. But for different readers at different times and places, and for the same reader, indeed, on different occasions, the meaning revealed in the act of reading was altered and surprisingly unstable. The text, originally an interpretation of some event or sequence of events, or particular kinds of experience, and so on, was itself subject to innumerable reinterpretations. Every text, like the reality to which it was thought to refer, remained undetermined in relation to its immanent meaning.

This view is readily generalizable to all texts and, as in modernity all reality can be viewed as composed of representations, everything that appears externally to be given as a world and in the world is best understood textually. All human activity is a process of active interpretation of the world in which it finds itself and which forms its arena. Hermeneutics is just the methodological implication of modernity as human self-activity; as the declaration of autonomy in which modernity is inaugurated.

The hermeneutics perspective, then, seems at odds with radical, subjective or objective, versions of phenomenology. For it, there are no phenomena other than those given with a point of view, no reality other than an interpreted reality; nothing is simply 'given'. The urgent issue is critically to understand how the process of interpretation enters into the constitution of reality as an apparently 'given' object. This, of course, is a restatement of Husserl's programme rather than an alternative to it. What is given is not one particular interpreted reality rather than another, but a reality that always appears as a world with certain kinds of formal characteristics. What is given, outside and prior to any interpretation, is just the process of interpretation itself as the continuing activity of reality construction.

The particular significance of Dilthey within the hermeneutic tradition lies in the impressive manner in which he brings into prominence the role of collective and historical processes in the development of all modern self-understanding and self-interpretation. Where psychologists were elaborating a descriptive phenomenology of individual experience within the natural attitude (and Husserl regarded this as a vital and legitimate task), the hermeneutic tradition provided a rich source of critical investigations into the emergence, in a variety of intersubjective and historically specific contexts, of a series of distinctive natural attitudes.

Certainly at the time Husserl formulated his phenomenology, Dilthey's work provided an incomparably broad historical and cultural context for its reception. Indeed, Dilthey's historical studies of the emergence of scientific naturalism were significantly in advance of Husserl's initial phenomenological investigations conceived, as they were, within a narrower framework of modern epistemology. What Husserl at first saw as a general and universal clarification of experience was viewed by Dilthey, from the beginning, as itself an aspect of the particular historical constitution of modernity. The whole notion of experience and its possibility, indeed, was given in a unique way with modern society, so that phenomenology is nothing other than modern self-understanding and, consequently, stands in need of historical contextualization. The larger context itself is an essential aspect of the modern experience of life: 'We have entered an age of historical consciousness. We feel surrounded by an entire past' (Dilthey 1985, 35).

Dilthey and the later Husserl come together in terms of a historical grasp of philosophy and a philosophical grasp of history. In a letter of 1927 Husserl acknowledges Dilthey's own phenomenological insight but claims the latter had been mistaken in his initial reaction to phenomenology: 'Concerning eidetic phenomenology it was a serious mistake for Dilthey to think that with my study of essences I will never reach actual life and that I want to exclude historical and factual inquiry' (Makkreel and Scanlon 1987). But late in his life, Dilthey acknowledged 'how much I owe to the *Logical Investigations* of Husserl, which are epoch-making' (Dilthey 2002, 34). And as early as 1907, in an essay on 'The Essence of Philosophy', Dilthey looks forward to themes later taken up in Husserl's *Crisis*:

What remains after the immense efforts of the metaphysical spirit, is the historical consciousness which is recapitulated in philosophy. Thus philosophy experiences the unfathomable depth of the world through the efforts of spirit. The last word of spirit, having passed through all world-views, is not the relativity of each of them, but is the sovereignty of spirit over against each of them, and at the same time the positive awareness about the way the one reality of the world exists for us in the various attitudes of spirit. (Makkreel and Scanlon 1987, 16)

Dilthey pursues this history of spirit as it is inflected in the world views of western society. But throughout there is a clear grasp that the 'lived experience' of a 'life-world' is the singular actuality from which world views arise: 'Lived experience can never be reduced to thoughts or ideas. However, it can be related to the totality of human existence through reflection … and thus it can be understood in its essence, that is, its meaning' (1985, 59). The primacy of a 'subsoil of life' involves not one singular mode of experience and connection but, rather, three fundamentally distinct types of meaningful content: 'object apprehension, evaluation, and the positing of purposes emerge as types of attitude with countless nuances that merge into each other' (Dilthey 2002, 153–4). Cognition, evaluation, and volition can be viewed as the given 'ontological regions' of the 'subsoil of life'. In this context the emergence of the human sciences is the consequence of a reflection on the specific mode of interconnectedness of activities: 'The human sciences form an epistemic nexus that strives to attain objectively engaged and objectively valid conceptual cognition of the interconnectedness of lived experience in the human historical-social world' (2002, 23). The modern life-world, in fact, is rich in differentiated inner forms and relations: 'In its tranquil flow, life constantly produces all sorts of realities' (2002, 27).

Dilthey also shares Husserl's fundamental insight that 'The manifold of what is given as content is boundless' (2002, 43). All ontological distinctions merge and flow together in the unity of psychic life such that 'Representations, judgments, feelings, desires, acts of will are always interwoven in the psychic nexus; this is the empirical given of psychic life' (2002, 145). And, anticipating Sartre as well as Husserl, he claims that within this nexus every content is given as 'being there for me' (2002, 47).

Every understanding of this world itself springs from developments within it; that is, such an understanding is also part of that world. And an adequate grasp of this complex world requires more than a purely conceptual elaboration of its cognitive content; attention must also be paid to 'the determination of value, the setting of purposes, and the establishment of rules' (2002, 66). It is not obvious that we can grasp feeling or will, for example, in terms of a conceptual structure that springs exclusively from cognitive aspects of the life-world.

Dilthey's suggestive work has remained an important point of reference for a historical phenomenology. Hans-Georg Gadamer, for example, highlights Dilthey's rather than Husserl's exploration of the life-world and particularly the emergence of modern aesthetic valuation within it. Gadamer begins with a historical-social understanding of the life-world as the immediate reality of experience: 'It is clear that the life-world is always at the same time a communal world and involves the existence of other people as well' (1975, 219). And, as such it is 'an essentially historical concept, which does not refer to a universe of being, to an "existent world" ... [it is] the will in which we live as historical creatures' (1975, 218).

Dilthey's work is also a prominent source for the thought of Paul Ricoeur, whose wide-ranging writing is among the richest developments of the hermeneutic tradition. Ricoeur connects Dilthey to the long-range history of western textuality and narrative. His is a phenomenological history on a grand scale. And, though he explicitly rejects Husserl's eidetic method, he embraces the 'infinite task' of uncovering the horizon of consciousness of ourselves as historical beings and sets in motion a ceaseless movement forward and back across the entire range of the western history of the subject as an interpretive activity.

Ricoeur's wide-ranging and broad-minded assimilation of western culture is guided, nonetheless, by a residual commitment to Husserl's insight. Rather than dissolve the given into a pure history of interpretation he draws it out from that history and emphasizes the narrative of the human encounter with what remains *uninterpreted* in humanity. Ricoeur stresses the relationship between a hermeneutics of meaning and the process of interpretation. Humanity, in his view, cannot become transparent to itself; there is always something opaque in consciousness. His work can be viewed, thus, as a social-historical expansion of a Husserlian insight overlooked in the descriptive elaboration of the life-world: 'the being of the world "transcends" consciousness ... and that it necessarily remains transcendent, in no wise alters the fact that it is conscious life alone, wherein everything transcendent becomes constituted, as something inseparable from consciousness, and which specifically as world-consciousness, bears within itself inseparably the sense: world – and indeed: "this actually existing" world' (Husserl 1967, 62).

Ricoeur first locates the incommensurable difference between immanent meaning and transcendental mystery in the intimate confrontation between nature and freedom in the human body and, particularly, in the phenomenon of voluntary movement (Ricoeur 1966). Then, in an original way, he focuses on the phenomenon of human *fault* as the central theme of developing western hermeneutic practice. From defilement, through sin, to evil, the incomprehensible fallibility of humanity generates a complex history of self-interpretation (Ricoeur 1967a; 1986; 1992). The incomprehensible, as well as the transparently meaningful, has a cultural history and hermeneutics includes both in a developing and dynamic interrelation. Where hermeneutics began in a critical examination of the sacred text, it has been transformed with the development of modernity into an immanent social practice through which humanity takes account of its own impenetrability. And this account consists largely in generating interpretations of the mystery of human being in such a way as to make it appear meaningful (Ricoeur 1990).

Ricoeur, thus, continues the legacy of Husserl against both the existentialism and the structuralism that pervaded French thought after World War II, as in a different way does the interesting work of Vladimir Jankélévitch (2001; 2003). Ricoeur (1969) emphasizes the multiplicity and conflicting character of interpretations. There is no uninterpreted social reality; but nor is there a single coherent 'story' that adequately interprets that reality. Society is the arena of hermeneutic contestation.

Description

The differentiation of the phenomenological movement into distinctive and at times opposed positions has not prevented the emergence of common themes and an accumulation of striking non-doctrinaire and eclectic studies that have been influential outside the sphere of phenomenological philosophy. The primary significance of such phenomenological studies has been to introduce, to a broad range of more specialized fields, approaches that reject the object–subject dichotomy still prevalent throughout the human sciences. Such descriptive approaches, in psychology especially, were explicitly 'non-transcendental' explorations within the natural attitude and aimed first of all to provide a systematic criticism of the dominant positivistic framework. Aron Gurwitsch, for example, in a fine presentation of phenomenology for an American academic audience, and particularly American psychologists, draws attention to descriptive similarities between Husserl's work and the psychology of William James. This serves as a telling criticism both of behaviourism and, more unexpectedly, of its leading alternative, Gestalt psychology.

For James all sensible impressions 'fuse into a single object' and what requires explanation is dissociation, individuation and differentiation – which James accounts for in terms of 'selective interest': 'Interest alone gives accent and emphasis, light and shade, background and foreground', interest which operates within the mind to organize the 'primordial chaos of sensation' (James 1981, 288). However, classical empiricism, James, the Gestalt school and Piaget all account for the organization of field of consciousness from the originally indifferent flow of pure content: 'Rather we venture to assert the existence of a universal, formal pattern of organization, realized in every field of consciousness regardless of content' (Gurwitsch 1964, 55). And he does not claim this gives rise only to 'idealized' objects, but holds that it is constitutive of the actually perceived object.

Phenomenology rejects the 'atomistic' approach to consciousness, but also versions of Gestalt which view 'structures' as ready-made forms. There is, rather, an 'infinitely open perceptual process' (1964, 223). In their perceptual organization, 'parts' 'do not merely co-exist but, rather, imply, envelop, symbolize, and qualify each other. These parts stand in a thoroughgoing interdependence and interdetermination of one another. Such an organizational form is also realized in our embodied existence' (1964, 301). And, thus, the 'unity and identity of the perceived thing are correlative of the unity and identity of the body' (1964, 303).

In common with many such studies, Gurwitsch makes prominent a thematic interest in the human body as the unitary *terminus a quo* and *terminus ad quem* for all forms of differentiated experience. Of course the phenomenal character of the body was stressed by a number of major phenomenological thinkers, notably by Husserl himself, and including Gabriel Marcel, Emmanuel Levinas and, more recently, Michel Henry (1975; 2002).

The most influential descriptive phenomenology of the body, however, is to be found in the writings of Maurice Merleau-Ponty whose important book, *The Phenomenology of Perception* (original French edition 1945), was among the first fully to exploit Husserl's, at the time unpublished, manuscript of the second book of *Ideas*.

Prior to that work Merleau-Ponty had already mounted a powerful attack on the dominant behaviouristic psychology from the perspective of a non-transcendental descriptive phenomenology (Merleau-Ponty 1963). The fundamental phenomenological insight is to undo or reverse the naturalistic illusion of exteriority, not through symmetrical idealist illusion that dissolves the world into spirit, but through a phenomenological account of natural consciousness. Here 'The world is the ensemble of objective relations borne by consciousness' (1963, 3), but the manner of the 'borne by' is precisely the issue of phenomenology; its equivocal character requires clarification.

Merleau-Ponty views the givenness of the world and the being of the body in the world in a non-transcendental way; it is to be grasped not as an aspect of pure consciousness, but as the reality in which consciousness is essentially implicated. The world is not 'outside' the subject as a puzzling exteriority; rather it is in worldness that the mystery of interiority, as well as exteriority, appears. The reductive programme of modern psychology distorts the character of experience, invading the body, so to speak, with exteriority. Thus, for example, 'The living physiology of the nervous system can only be understood by starting from phenomenal givens' (1963, 88). That is to say, 'the object of biology cannot be grasped without the unities of signification which a consciousness finds and sees in it' (1963, 161).

But consciousness cannot be other than the very worldness that appears to confront it. Merleau-Ponty views the transcendental character of objects as arising in and with the world and not either *first* in consciousness or in the mechanical combination of imperceptible things-in-themselves. The world, and designated objects within it, are given immediately in a perspective: 'I grasp *in* a perspectival appearance, which I know is only one of its possible aspects, the thing itself which transcends it' (1963, 187).

In *Phenomenology of Perception* Merleau-Ponty develops the positive side of the argument by emphasizing the primal character of the natural attitude as a corporeal reality. The natural attitude of exteriority is, in fact, just the peculiarly modern form in which worldness appears for us and, thus, betrays a deeper necessity in the implication of consciousness in the world itself. Phenomenology here reinterprets the natural attitude as a specific kind of implication or absorption in the world, rather than an error of some kind. Its aim is that of 're-achieving a direct and primitive contact with the world' (1962, vii). By revealing the 'illusory' character of the subject–object structure of reality and refocusing attention on worldness, both the immanence of subject–object in *modern* worldness, and seeing *through* this consciousness of reality to its immediate unity, come into view. Thus, 'the world is not what I think, but what I live through' (1962, xvi). And this is not grasped in a reflective process but, rather, comes to consciousness as an activity: 'there is no inner man, man is in the world, and only in the world does he know himself' (1962, xi).

Merleau-Ponty, as in a strikingly similar but independent and previously overlooked study by Samuel Todes (2001), is at pains to express Husserl's thought free of any residual epistemological interest. Consciousness as living unity of worldness means that attentiveness is a differentiation of a pre-existing reality rather than an independent process of perceiving: 'Consciousness is no less intimately linked with objects of which it is unheeding than with those which interest it' (Merleau-Ponty 1962, 28). 'Attachment' to the world is not an external relation, motivated by a particular interest or wish, but a continuously achieved unity of experience.

In emphasizing the centrality of Husserl's insight into embodiment as the central phenomenological structure of reality, Merleau-Ponty is able to situate in a broader framework a number of pioneering studies that, without breaking free of orthodox methodological prejudices, had nonetheless effectively undermined standard functional models in psychology. In particularly the classic work of Henry Head on aphasia, Gelb and Goldstein's laboratory researches, and the original, eclectic studies of body images by Schilder (1964) and Lhermite (1960) were brought into close relation with Husserl's work: 'my whole body for me is not an assemblage of organs juxtaposed in space. I am in undivided possession of it and I know where each of my limbs is through a *body image* in which all are included' (Merleau-Ponty 1962, 98). And from another perspective this means that reality is fully *incarnated*; all experience is bodily experience. The primal body has no meaning for me as a pure object, 'The body by itself, the body at rest is merely an obscure mass' (1962, 322); nor does it have any significance for me as a pure subject, 'I am no more aware of being the true subject of my sensations than of my birth or my death' (1962, 215). This is an influential view echoed by Marcel, 'The primary object with which I identify myself, but which still eludes me, is my own body' (Marcel 1949a, 163); Ricoeur, 'My body is neither constituted in an objective sense, nor constitutive as a transcendental subject – it eludes this pair of opposites. It is the existing I' (1966, 16); Patočka, 'we elude facticity' (1998, 24); and many others. Indeed, a phenomenological statement of this sort has become a standard preface to many studies in the humanities and social sciences and, as generally with prefaces, has little to do with the work that follows. Phenomenology, that is to say, has reached a much wider audience through the writings of Merleau-Ponty, Sartre, and Ricoeur but its insights have been added to the list of available perspectives without transforming, as its philosophical pioneers intended, the entire domain of self-understanding. The problem of knowledge is rooted in the body's self-effacement: 'The obscurity of the external world is a function of my own obscurity to myself' (Ricoeur 1966, 13). In contemporary research, however, phenomenology all too easily slides into subjectivism and the uncritical and undemanding transparency of 'cultural studies'.

The three major phenomenological positions that quickly emerged in direct contact with Husserl's activity have remained lively and continue to develop. Derrida, for example, has self-consciously advanced Heidegger's existential phenomenology as a comprehensive and now enormously influential critique of metaphysics. Jean-Luc Marion (1998; 2002) has developed, in a most impressive fashion, a theologically oriented phenomenology that extends Levinas's unflinching encounter with the otherness of experience (Janicaud et al. 2000). And in a variety of ways phenomenological reflection includes a historical hermeneutics of contemporary experience (Steinbock 1995; Ihde 1993; Sallis 1995; Mensch 2001). There is little point in seeking to synthesize these discrepant and incompatible views of the phenomenological project; there is no possibility of arriving, by addition or interrelation, at a satisfactory account of reality 'as a whole'. And rather than place them in conflict or treat them as equivalent alternative interpretations of the same 'underlying' reality, it is more revealing to regard each as a wholly adequate account of a specific 'ontological region' of experience. This suggestion will be taken up in Part II of the present discussion but, prior to a fuller development of such an approach, it is helpful to examine the way in which phenomenology has impinged upon social thought in general and sociology in particular.

4

Dialogue: Phenomenology in Social Theory

> The structure of the social world can be disclosed as a structure of intelligible intentional meanings.
>
> Schutz, *The Phenomenology of the Social World*

> The concrete sciences of cultural phenomena ... are related to that mundane sphere which transcendental phenomenology has bracketed.
>
> Schutz, *Collected Papers*, vol. 1

> Transcendental philosophy must remain in tension with any sociology of collective consciousness and any philosophy of history.
>
> Ricoeur, *Husserl*

The first generation of phenomenologists were not directly interested in sociological issues. Not surprisingly philosophical problems, and especially epistemological questions, dominated the initial reception of Husserl's work. Sociology was conceptualized as falling into the region of 'applied' philosophy and, therefore, was considered of marginal relevance to phenomenological issues proper. And from the perspective of sociology, phenomenology was of interest, if at all, as symptomatic of a contemporary loss of reality (Psathas 1973; Löwith 1998). Mutual disregard, however, was gradually displaced by a methodological concern. Phenomenology, it was suggested, might be regarded as a new methodological foundation for sociology and currently phenomenology is still known to sociologists primarily as one among a number of methodological critiques of positivism in the social sciences. In a larger sense, however, as phenomenology itself demonstrated in a decisive way, methodological issues never stand alone and are always related to practical matters of substance that are significant not only for an adequate understanding of experience but also for the formation of that experience 'in reality'. Explorations of what at first seemed to be inconsequential borderline areas progressively brought into focus issues that touched all the fundamental questions of *both* disciplines *and* the experience upon which they reflected and in which they were rooted.

The systematic interrelation between phenomenology and sociology emerged in a shared interest in clarifying the nature of intersubjectivity. Phenomenological insights pointed directly to the centrality of intersubjectivity, that is, both the natural attitude and the phenomenologically reduced transcendental ego were intersubjective in character. And in as much as sociology investigated intersubjective realities directly, each discipline was implicated in the other. Sociology could not be independent of phenomenology, nor could phenomenology proceed without regard to the knowledge of intersubjective realities revealed by sociology.

Sympathy

The first sociologically oriented accounts of phenomenology, inspired primarily by philosophical interest in Husserl's writings, thus, stressed the central importance of intersubjectivity. In its reception by Max Scheler, and later by Ortega y Gasset, important reflections on what was seen, by Husserl himself, as at best incomplete and provisional areas of phenomenological insight, were seized upon as the key to the development of a new understanding of modern society.

Scheler was the first to see the resolution of central problems of both philosophy and sociology in terms of a further clarification of the meaning of intersubjectivity. In particular he argued against Husserl's initial formulation, that no process of deduction or projection could be involved in the formation of the peculiarly shared character of experience. Husserl had, indeed, claimed in *Cartesian Meditations* that only the physical reality of the other was immediately given in experience. We were aware of others as bodies, as bodies like our own. And in as much as our own consciousness was inextricably linked to our own body, in an essential way, we were bound to assume that these other bodies housed *alter egos*, that is, they were physical carriers of other centres of conscious experience. Scheler argued that, in fact, what was immediately given in direct interrelation with others were other *persons* in the full sense as human beings and not just ghostly human bodies. There was no need to appeal to a hypothetical psychic function of *empathy* to account for the intersubjective character of social life. While Husserl is certainly correct in recognizing that 'a man's *bodily* consciousness, like the individual essence of his *personality*, is *his and his alone*' (Scheler 1954, 33), social interaction is founded on a genuinely collective and shared spirit; on *sympathy* or 'fellow-feeling'. Projective and hypothetical empathic understanding, as Dilthey and Weber demonstrated, provided a means of grasping the meaning of that spirit in situations outside the range of our direct experience. In immediate interrelation with others, however, we did not project our own consciousness into the position of the other body and, as it were, imaginatively adopt that new location in attributing to the other the full panoply of experiential forms.

It is not clear, however, that Scheler's criticism is justified. Certainly, Husserl himself felt that the problem of intersubjectivity was fundamental to the development of his phenomenology and was not himself satisfied with his early formulations of the issue and its proposed solution. Yet, what this early formulation does succeed in throwing into sharp relief is the absolute givenness of the relation between body, consciousness, and our sense of individuality. The other is given directly as a meaningful unity of human experience and expression but, uniquely, is given as *other* than ourselves. The immediacy of lived experience is given only as *self*-experience and is always centred on our own 'interior' life. Every aspect of our normal experience is singular, yet the phenomenological clarification of any aspect of that experience, including the spiritual quality of sympathy, ends in the inescapable postulate of their intersubjective character. This amounts to repeating, in a different way, the central insight of phenomenology: that reality is given to us as experience, and all experience is the experience of something; something there. Sympathy remains as mysterious and hypothetical as empathy. *That* the other appears to us as a human being is not at issue; its possibility, however, remains obscure.

Scheler's criticism of Husserl, however, was linked to an interesting and original development of a phenomenology of feeling and valuing. The intersubjective reality that founds society is not to be grasped, first of all or essentially, according to Scheler, in the context of classical epistemological problems as valid *knowledge* of the same world; the puzzle of intersubjectivity is not a problem of knowledge at all. Intersubjectivity, rather, makes itself *felt*, moves in us, and through us as *feeling* and *value*. The central phenomenological problem, that is to say, is better approached by way of 'regional ontologies' other than that which had so far dominated modern thought. We can see at once that the whole tendency of Scheler's thought will then consist in avoiding the difficulty raised by Husserl, rather than resolving it. If knowledge is not the problem, if reality is first of all felt, and adumbrated in values, rather than apprehended as sense data, then he can fall back on an appeal to some rather vague sense of collective consciousness. 'All primordial comportment toward the world,' Scheler says, 'involves values, emotions, and feelings which we do not "perceive". Our primordial orientation to the world is in terms of values and feelings' (1973, 198), which 'precedes all representational acts according to an essential law of origin' (1973, 201). Value is reached, in his view, by the phenomenological reduction of 'goods' through which they appear but in relation to which they remain ultimately independent (1973, 17). But Husserl's epistemological difficulties also emerge in this region. Feeling and value are just as individuated in terms of experience as perception or knowledge. It is just the unclarified nature of feeling that conceals this or, rather, allows him to obscure the real issue; the issue between the transcendental ego and the interactive reality generated from particular empirical egos.

Husserl's own reflections on such matters, at the time unpublished, were consistent and radical. The progressive movement of his own thought towards 'passive' syntheses of feeling and vague and cloudy states of consciousness is not to be seen as an effort somehow to break out of the monad in which the ego was imprisoned. Rather, feeling, just as the sharpest cognition, was intersubjective in the full and puzzling sense; it was available to us only as an experience, and as experience it remained uniquely our own. And where feeling seemed to refer ever inwards rather than outwards it gave on to a reality that was, equally, beyond us; something transcending the immediate experience of the living subject. The depth of the soul, in other words, was just as much 'outside' the subject as the noumenal 'object'. Consciousness was an intermediate realm, a cushion between the object and the subject, rather than a unification of outer and inner.

Consciousness bore within it, indeed in its every fleeting transition, the marks of an intersubjective reality. The issue was not, given the fully individuated character of conscious experience, how we know, or how we reach, the 'other' that it acknowledges and implies. The issue is, rather, given the intersubjective character of reality, how experience is born and contained *within* the confines of an always singular ego. And it is this problem that Husserl had introduced in a radical way through his discussion of the essential relation of consciousness to the body.

Phenomenology and the Sociological Classics

An equivocal relation between sociology and philosophy is evident throughout the classical sociological literature. On the one hand it is clear that the work of Marx, Durkheim, Weber, and Simmel emerges in the closest relation to the development of modern philosophical reflection and particularly to the original thought of Hegel, Kant, and Nietzsche (Ollman 1976; Schluchter 1996; Lukes 1973; Meštrović 1992). At the same time the distinctive character of sociology was established through a critical reinterpretation of that tradition. But that both phenomenology and sociology defined themselves in opposition to the main traditions of modern philosophy did not immediately draw them together. For the emerging discipline of sociology, phenomenology was readily viewed as the apotheosis of just those illusions and misconceptions with which sociology had to contend. The exclusive focus on consciousness, individualism, and confinement to an inner world of experience, all ran counter to the sociological grasp of reality in terms of social-historical relations, institutional structures, and the collective characteristics of modern society. Indeed, it seemed that phenomenology would deny to 'society', as a hypothetical abstraction, any reality whatever. That such views misjudge the real import of phenomenological thought emerged only with the benefit of hindsight and the publication of Husserl's notebooks. Initially, it is certainly understandable that sociologists should look to the classics as a secure position outside and opposed to phenomenology and, indeed, it was not difficult to find support for such a contention.

Marx, thus, famously declared 'it is not the consciousness of men that determines their being, but their being determines their consciousness' and went on to outline a historical understanding of society as a continually developing 'ensemble of relations'. Durkheim, equally forthright, insisted we regard 'social facts as things' and seems to recommend a brand of positivism inimical to the very idea of phenomenology. Max Weber's sociology is articulated in terms of a complex comparative institutional history that constitutes its reality in terms of 'ideal types', derived from but not identical with actual experience. And Simmel's rich account of social reality gains its coherence in terms of abstract, formal criteria rather than in the experience of phenomena themselves.

Phenomenology, thus, could easily be overlooked by sociology, and, if encountered, quickly dismissed as 'idealism' of an exaggerated sort; it was an example of speculation that had lost all contact with the very reality it sought to grasp and into which it claimed to have gained insight. It is worth considering, nonetheless, and in a preliminary way that 'adumbrates' a fuller discussion in a later chapter, potentially fruitful points of contact between phenomenology and the classics; relations that have remained undeveloped but which in retrospect might now be seen quite differently and in a more positive light. What strikingly links Husserl's phenomenological insight and classical sociological perspectives generally is a critical understanding of the immediate consciousness of social reality as an *inessential* and ultimately unfounded representation. That is, for both, what is most commonly taken to be 'real' is, in fact, a 'tissue of ideas' that veils reality.

Marx has frequently been read philosophically and significant interpretations of his writings appeared as part of a reassessment of Hegel (Kojève 1969; Hyppolite 1969). Like Kierkegaard, Marx explicitly rejected Hegel's work, regarding it as an *inverted* image of the real relations that conditioned social life (Löwith 1964). This was not to say that Hegel's writings should not be taken seriously; quite to the contrary, his philosophical analysis could itself be inverted, resulting in a valid account of the real character of modern society. Given the intimate relation between Marx and Hegel, and Hegel's announcement of his own philosophy as a phenomenology, a *prima facie* case could be made for looking more positively for a meaningful connection between Marx and the further development of phenomenology. Indeed, in different ways, Michel Henry (1983) and Duc Thao Trân (1986) have presented highly sophisticated phenomenological readings of Marx. What is decisive in Marx's work, here, is his radical rejection of the natural standpoint and his reduction of the scientific understanding of society that is continuous with this attitude; that is, with political economy. The rational individualism and utilitarianism of political economy are themselves aspects of the veiling of the real character of modern society. The practical activity through which society comes into being and renews itself simultaneously produces an ideological representation of itself. An ideology, that is to say, is neither an error nor a deliberate deception but, rather, a counter-image of reality that arises from the same processes that generate that reality itself. It is the commodity, and not a misplaced idea, that is the source of ideology. The commodity is produced 'as if' it existed as a pure thing independent of human activity and the social relations that are obscured by this objectification (Marx 1976a, 163–77).

Marx seeks to restore this reality to the realm of self-conscious activity, to praxis: 'Man's self-production is always, and of necessity, a social enterprise.

Men *together* produce a human environment, with the totality of its sociocultural and psychological formations' (1976b, 69). Externalization and objectification are, thus, *given* as an anthropological necessity: 'Human being is impossible in a closed sphere of quiescent interiority. Human being must ongoingly externalise itself in activity' (1976b, 70). In a strikingly similar manner Husserl 'sees through' the objectivities of the natural attitude to its transcendental (historical and intersubjective) constitution; for both writers, in fact, consciousness is a *practical activity* that ceaselessly produces objects in such a way as to obscure the very process of their construction. Consciousness, like the commodity, always reproduces itself as something alien; something 'there' over against the creative powers of the subject.

Husserl can also be considered positively in relation to Durkheim's sociology. This, equally, depends upon a view of Durkheim's work that is quite distinct from either positivist or functionalist research agendas that subsequently developed in his name. So, just as there is required an '*epoché* of Marxism to understand Marx' (Henry 1983, 14), so influential interpretations of Durkheim have to be discounted in order to focus on those aspects of his work that are phenomenologically significant.

What must be stressed here is Durkheim's unfashionable insistence upon the reality of what he terms the *conscience collective*. A certain embarrassment among his most ardent followers, especially in Great Britain and America, arises at this point. The sense in which there may be a genuinely 'collective subject' for the sociologist has been rejected as 'metaphysical' and understood in Durkheim's work as nothing more than a manner of speaking. But Durkheim has no metaphorical intention here; society is nothing other than a collective subject, and society lives through its members as *collective representations* and not representations *of* the collectivity. The genuinely collective character of experience is brought out particularly in his account of 'mechanical solidarity' that finds its most precise articulation in terms of the ritual life of the most 'primitive' societies. At the same time, however, even in the most complex and highly differentiated society, which can be grasped in terms of specific interrelations of the division of labour and within which 'moral particularism' of distinct social groupings predominates over any sense of the totality of social life, that totality is still felt in the ordinary experience of individuals.

For Durkheim, the collective subject is not only prior to any individuated experience or differentiated social relation, it is a prerequisite for the appearance of such experiences and relations. The collective subject is eminently historical; it is not just a logical *a priori* construct that allows the sociologist rationally to reconstruct society as a possible experience, it is the real foundation of practical social life. Durkheim, that is to say, offers a realistic sociology as a response to Kant's categorical analysis of the consciousness as the 'mind'. It is society in which the categories are inscribed; and as such are not fixed *a priori* but enter fully into the historical process.

Individuals feel collective subjectivity as a moral obligation; precisely as the 'exteriority and constraint' of social facts. The thing-like character of social facts is a consequence of the translation of collective subjectivity into the meaningful content of individual representations. This content is encountered as a moral force; the interior 'ought' of conscience and the overwhelming sense of conviction in 'true' beliefs. Yet, at bottom, this content is arbitrary and wholly conventional. It is not just made possible by the historical character of solidarity; its realization could always be otherwise than it is. And the radical conventionalism of everyday life is difficult to detect because it has its source in the overwhelming 'objectivity' of the collective subject that stands over against any individual experience. The 'natural attitude' that Husserl came up against as an obstacle to 'essential viewing', that is to say, is just the 'collective representation' through which society comes into existence.

Possible links between the work of Georg Simmel and phenomenology have also remained unexplored within mainstream sociology, but Simmel's conception of formal sociology might, paradoxically, be viewed as an *eidetic* viewing of society. Simmel 'brackets' the specific psychic content and interests, which always belong to individuals, that arise in a variety of social contexts in order to bring into view the formal structural features of, for example, 'twoness' as distinct from 'threeness' in social relations, the characteristics of superordination or subordination, the peculiarities of the secret, fashion, or, above all, money relations. Significantly, like Husserl, Simmel likens his method to geometry: 'Geometrical abstraction investigates the spatial forms of bodies, although empirically, these forms are given merely as the forms of some material content. Similarly, if society is conceived as interaction among individuals, the description of the forms of this interaction is the task of the science of society in its strictest and most *essential* sense' (1950, 21–2, emphasis added). Simmel's approach to modern society has frequently been criticized, in fact, just because it runs counter to the 'natural attitude' toward and within which social life both stimulates and is sustained by the inner motives and interests of individuals. Here society exists as something transcendental; opening up a realm of 'pure sociology' to a method of 'essential viewing'.

And in a more concrete way Simmel's description of the experience of modern urban life bears a striking resemblance to Husserl's phenomenological account of perception; walking through city streets can well be described in terms of an ever moving horizon, the adumbration of objects, a shifting focus of attention, the penumbra of half-noticed objects, a continual interplay of modalities, and so on (Simmel 1997, 174–87; Frisby 2001, 100–59). For Husserl, there is always, a 'radical incompleteness' in every perception of the object' (1997b, 44). Simmel, equally, recognizes the 'radical incompleteness' of our grasp of the world into which we are plunged:

> the typical problematic condition of modern humanity, the feeling of being surrounded by an immense number of cultural elements, which are not

meaningless, but not profoundly meaningful to the individual either; elements which have a certain crushing quality as a mass, because an individual cannot inwardly assimilate every individual thing, but cannot simply reject it either, since it belongs potentially, as it were, to the sphere of his or her cultural development. (1997, 73)

In relation to the work of Max Weber, however, a more intimate relation to phenomenology emerged from the outset. In developing a comprehensive historical and comparative sociology of *spirit*, Weber's work has close affinities with the thought of, on the one hand, Dilthey and, on the other, Husserl. Weber, significantly, grasps spirit as a process of objectifying value; a process that in the modern world takes the form of producing material things rather than ideas or beliefs. He concludes a famous essay by drawing attention to the pure materiality of modern culture: 'Since asceticism undertook to remodel the world and to work out its ideals in the world, material goods have gained an increasing and finally an inexorable power over the lives of men as at no previous period in history.' And though Weber arrived at this conclusion by a very different path to that followed by Marx, he nonetheless echoes the opening sentence of *Capital* in which modern society is described as an 'immense collection of commodities'. Weber's insisted that the 'inexorable power' of things in modern society, whatever its origin, was now 'bound to the technical and economic conditions of machine production which today determine the lives of all the individuals who are born into this mechanism ... with irresistible force' (1930, 181).

Phenomenology and classical sociology, it might even be argued, not only display interesting points of contact but converge significantly, without yet meeting, not only in the thematic investigation of modernity as a particular kind of experience, but also and critically in grasping the enigmatic character of that experience as the central historical problem of intersubjectivity.

The puzzling inside–outside character of consciousness leads Husserl relentlessly towards the historical perspective of his later writings; that is, towards the classical sociological account of modernity. Correlatively, the classical sociological perspective, in which society is grasped as a historical, intersubjective reality, is driven up against the strange outside–inside character of modern experience. These streams of modern thought, that is to say, point towards a common *problem*, rather than a joint solution. Both classical sociology and phenomenology directly confront issues of human autonomy and self-understanding immanent with the development of modern society since the Renaissance.

The actual emergence of phenomenological perspectives within sociology, however, took place in unfavourable circumstances and developed in quite a different direction. It was associated directly with the flight of many German intellectuals from the Nazi regime after 1933 and, in particular, with the work of Alfred Schutz at the New School for Social Research in New York.

Phenomenology and American Sociology

In the context of post-war American social thought Anton Gurwitsch summarizes a phenomenological perspective derived from the later work of Husserl, which is in principle friendly to both sociology and psychology. He describes the 'field of consciousness' as an actual social experience – rather than an essential insight into the natural attitude. Here the reduced data of consciousness emerge as an accurate description of the *empirical* character of modern life and the 'life-world' is transposed into an empirical ethnography of modern everyday life: 'The life-world is defined as comprising all items and objects which present themselves in pre-scientific experience, and as they present themselves prior to their scientific interpretation in the specific modern sense' (Gurwitsch 1964, 48). For this world, 'the foundation of sense has become obscured, obfuscated, and forgotten. Since the beginning of the modern development, the life-world has been concealed under a "tissue of ideas" [*Ideenkleed*] which has been cast upon it like a disguise.' The result in modernity is that 'the only truly real world has been relegated to the inferior status of a merely subjective being' (1964, 48). The aim of phenomenology, for Gurwitsch, is to restore the life-world to reality; to strip it of scientific pretension.

The restoration of reality to the life-world makes it eminently historical: 'Historical reflections strip any cultural world of the matter of course character which it has for those who simply live in it. In the light of such reflection, our cultural world appears as one among a great many others' (1964, 56). The historical perspective already introduced by Husserl is taken up by Gurwitsch in a promising way to confront emerging issues of relativism: 'Whatever differences might obtain between the several cultural worlds and, correspondingly, between the several particular forms of conscious life in which the cultural worlds originate and of which they are the correlates, the general reference of any such world to the corresponding consciousness, which underlies all relativities, is not relative itself' (1964, 55).

Alfred Schutz and the domestication of phenomenology

It was, however, in an ahistorical, functionalist form that phenomenology made its way into American sociology. A seemingly fertile point of contact between sociology and phenomenology was established with Alfred Schutz's arrival in America. Initially Schutz, like Scheler, focused on the issue of intersubjectivity as the unresolved difficulty in Husserl's phenomenology. Prior to the publication of Husserl's *Crisis*, Schutz was already developing a distinctive sociological approach to the problem. From the outset he conceived intersubjectivity as a socially constituted phenomenon; that is, as a constructed and actively regenerated reality. Only as a socially constructed reality, indeed, could anything appear to us as something 'given'; something exterior to the immediate flow of self-feeling and self-presence.

Schutz's primary interest, that is to say, was firmly rooted in the natural attitude; with the reality that appeared to us as something simply 'there'. Transcendental phenomenology, he claimed, was misdirected and superfluous. It was not that the *philosophical* problem of consciousness, rooted in the Cartesian *cogito*, was to be solved sociologically; rather, that problem simply did not arise within a sociological framework. Society and social action were both the precondition for, and the consequence of, the ever renewed positing of the natural attitude itself. What struck Schutz as characteristic of social reality was just that, even where we recognized its thoroughly conventional character, we could not easily suspend belief in its reality; it remained overwhelming and irresistible precisely in its quality of givenness. Schutz, indeed, inverts Husserl's method:

> Phenomenology has taught us the concept of phenomenological *epoché*, the suspension of our belief in the reality of the world as a device to overcome the natural attitude by radicalising the Cartesian method of philosophical doubt. The suggestion may be ventured that man within the natural attitude also uses a specific *epoché*, of course quite another one than the phenomenologists. He does not suspend belief in the outer world and its objects, but on the contrary, he suspends doubt in its existence. What he puts in brackets is the doubt that the world and its objects might be otherwise than it appears to him. We propose to call this *epoché* the *epoché of the natural attitude*. (1962, vol. 1, 229)

The key issue, for Schutz, was not to investigate what remained after the natural attitude was dismantled but, rather, to understand just how this persistent and compelling belief was constituted and generated, directly and unreflectively, through social action. Schutz was concerned, thus, to articulate links between the immediate and vital interest we had in various projects of action, and the persisting structure of society as a given intersubjective reality.

Schutz turned at once to the writings of Max Weber, and more particularly to his methodological considerations, for clarification of this issue. In fact, Schutz saw Husserl and Weber as intimately related, and a synthesis of the two as the most promising way forward for a sociology in which existing philosophical problems would be subsumed. What attracted Schutz to Weber was the latter's insistence that sociology be grasped as a science of social action, where action is behaviour that is 'subjectively meaningful'. Husserl, in the most general way possible, had described reality in terms of consciousness; that is, as the givenness of *meaningful* content. Schutz argues that Weber and Husserl come together in the proposition that 'The structure of the social world can be disclosed as a structure of intelligible intentional meanings' (1967, 7). Meaning is inscribed in reality as an essential condition of its possibility. And as human behaviour is 'already meaningful when it takes place, and is already intelligible at the level of daily life' (1967, 10), the aim of Schutz's work 'is to interpret the actions of individuals in the social world and the ways in which individuals give meaning to social phenomena' (1967, 6).

Meaning, however, does not lie *in* experience itself. Rather, 'those experiences are meaningful which are grasped reflectively' (1967, 69), which is not to say abstractly in the light of specific concepts but, rather, as the product of an attentive attitude that delimits a specific segment of the ongoing stream of practical activities: 'when I immerse myself in my stream of consciousness, in my duration, I do not find any clearly differentiated experiences at all', but 'The very awareness of the stream of duration presupposes a turning-back against the stream, a special kind of attitude toward that stream, a "reflection" as we call it' (1967, 47).

Schutz seizes upon the notion of meaningful action and argues that Weber has not fully developed the insight upon which it rests, and claims (unjustifiably) that he fails properly to distinguish between the subjective meanings of action for actors engaged in the flow of events and the meaning an observer ascribes to it. More pertinently, Schutz points out that, although differentiating natural causality from meaningful understanding, Weber fails clearly to distinguish between 'because' and 'in order to' motives as key modalities of meaningfulness.

Schutz here assimilates Weber's methodological principle to what he conceives to be Husserl's fundamental problem of intersubjectivity. The 'solution' to the problem of intersubjectivity (within the natural attitude at least) consists simply in viewing that reality as the 'stock of knowledge' and 'frames of relevance' that sustain, and are sustained through, social interaction. The 'transcendental ego' in fact becomes an awkward and unnecessarily obtuse formulation of something that is, in fact, much simpler: the available store of ready-made meanings through which actors can explicate their own and others' ongoing action.

This leads Schutz to an elaboration of the meaningfulness of social action in terms of the 'common-sense' experience constituted as an 'everyday world'. This represents an original point of view in Schutz's work and should be distinguished from Husserl's focus on the 'life-world', which appears only as a result of the rigorous transcendental reduction of every form of common sense. The coherence and meaningfulness of the world in general are a consequence of 'sedimentation' of past and present reflections, including scientific, metaphysical, and religious discourse, in the mundane reality of everyday life: 'the so-called concrete facts of common-sense perception are not so concrete as it seems. They already involve abstractions of a highly complicated nature' (Schutz 1962, vol. 1, 3). It is just the structure of common-sense 'typifications' that Schutz makes the content of his sociology. It is through the ceaseless constituting and reconstituting of such typifications that a 'common world' emerges (1962, vol. 1, 144) that is made up of a 'stock of knowledge' of the world as 'a system of constructs and its typicality' (1962, vol. 1, 7).

The subjective world, thus, 'is from the outset an intersubjective world of culture' (1962, vol. 1, 10). And an adequate understanding of this world does not require the exhausting method of transcendental reduction, but yields immediately to direct investigation once the fundamental insight has been securely grasped. Just as, for phenomenological philosophy, consciousness is understood in terms of its own intentionality, the world that is an 'everyday reality' is historical and cannot be grasped as 'founded' on something other than itself. 'There is no primordial experience upon which all subsequent knowledge could possibly be founded' (1967, 75), and invoked as the putative origin of our present system of typifications and frames of relevance. That system, the characteristic reality of modern society, is ordered, according to Schutz, first of all in terms of a 'biographically determined situation', which is the primary frame of reference or 'relevance structure' of experience. Schutz's focus on the biographical situation of determined life-plans and subplans as the framework within which a choice of more specific *projects* emerges gives his work a distinctively existential flavour but, whereas European existential thinkers stressed the inner freedom of the subject in the choice of life-project, Schutz turns his attention to the pre-existing social contexts of meaning through which such choices emerge. Intersubjectivity also means that the world is experienced as extending beyond the sphere of immediate contact; it 'contains' its own past and future as well as remote places. It includes, in other words, realities that we cannot and some imaginary ones that we could not ourselves experience at first hand, and appear to us exclusively in the form of *typifications*; characterizations of distant objects, people, events, places and so on. *Both immediate life-projects and typifications must be understood as constituting social processes.*

Schutz argues that modern society is characterized by the multiplicity and variety of social realities that have become available to us. In one of his best-known essays, and with explicit reference to a famous chapter of William James's *Principles of Psychology*, Schutz stresses the distinctive character of modern life as a movement among a multiplicity of different realities (1962, vol. 1). All realities can be described in terms of their theme and horizon; but all are founded in the socially constituted paramount reality of everyday life, which is the concrete result of innumerable historical sedimentations. Each reality is, additionally, marked by a specific level of 'tension' appropriate to it; the alertness, say, required by a specific practical task as compared to a relaxed state of rest. In the complex interrelation of different realities and levels, the immanent coherence of experience (which Schutz seems still to require as a 'philosophical' premise) becomes threatened: 'Although experienced as a unity, what I am doing is not one single activity; it is rather a set of heterogeneous activities, each of them taking place in its own appropriate medium' (1962, vol. 1, 10).

Schutz singles out the world of work as a privileged location of everyday reality, the centre of vital interests and the focus of conscious and deliberative social action; 'The world of working in daily life is the archetype of our experience of reality. All the other provinces of meaning may be considered as its modifications' (1962, vol. 1, 233). The world of work is characterized by the highest level of attentive tension:

> By the term '*wide-awakeness*' we want to denote a plane of consciousness of highest tension originating in an attitude of full attention to life and its requirements. Only the performing and especially the working self is fully interested in

life and, hence, especially the working self is fully interested in life and, hence, wide-awake. It lives within its acts and its attention is exclusively directed to carrying its projects into effect, to executing its plan. (1962, vol. 1, 213)

In contrast to such conscious, directed, and unified activity, 'In passive attention I experience, for instance, the surf of indiscernible small perceptions' (1962, vol. 1, 213). It is only in the 'vivid present' of the wide-awake, acting, working subject that experiences are formed into a unity:

Living in the vivid present in its ongoing working acts, directed toward the objects and objectivities to be brought about, the working self experiences itself as the originator of the ongoing actions and, thus, as an undivided total self. It experiences its bodily movements from within; it lives in the correlated essentially actual experiences which are inaccessible to recollection and reflection; its world is a world of open anticipations. The working self, and only the working self, experiences all this *modo presenti* and, experiencing itself as the author of this ongoing working, it realizes itself as a unity. (1962, vol. 1, 216)

In reflection and in the actual practice of everyday life 'this unity goes to pieces'. The multiplicity of realities are interrelated in a more complicated fashion than William James had suggested in his juxtaposition of 'sub-universes'. There are, rather, delimited 'provinces of meaning' each characterized by a specific 'cognitive style' and 'accent of reality' and particular 'tension of consciousness', such that a shift from one to another is experienced as a 'shock': 'The world of dreams, of imageries and phantasms, especially the world of art, the world of religious experience, the world of scientific contemplation, the play world of the child, and the world of the insane – are finite provinces of meaning' (1962, vol. 1, 230–2).

Schutz attempts to classify the multiplicity of realities based on the various levels of attention and tension of consciousness. Interestingly, in addition to the hierarchy of attentiveness that culminates in the concentration of deliberative work, Schutz notes that not all states of relaxed consciousness are the same. Thus, first and at the lowest level of attentive consciousness, we find various worlds of 'phantasms; day-dreams in play, jokes, fancy; initial withdrawal from everyday waking reality and its demands and pragmatic tasks, less resistance in exteriority, floating beyond the range of immediate reach in time and space' (1962, vol. 1). These states are intermittent and normally everyday reality impinges upon us in such a way as to force us once again back to *its* reality; phantasy images are transformed, reasserting the world of actualities, and we resume some ordinary activity. Secondly, a world of dreams may emerge upon a complete withdrawal of vital interest in practical tasks: 'The sleeping self has no pragmatic interest whatsoever in transforming its largely confused perceptions into a state of partial clarity and distinctness' (1962, vol. 1, 240). Unlike phantasy 'the dreamer has no freedom of discretion, no arbitrariness in mastering the chances … the inescapableness of the happening in the world of dream and the powerlessness of the dreamer to influence it' (1962, vol. 1, 241). And, thirdly, a world of scientific theory is linked to the special position of the 'disinterested observer', which is free from the 'fundamental anxiety' that is the tension of everyday life and no longer involves observing and thinking in context of personal biography, practical aims, and so on.

Schutz's development was away from both Husserl and Weber and towards American sociology and it is a distinctively American style of phenomenological analysis that Schutz developed (Cox 1978). In particular he saw his own work in close relation to symbolic interactionism and its philosophical background in pragmatism (1962, vol. 1; Joas 1985; Aboulafia 1991). One of the difficulties of Schutz's work, indeed, is his somewhat eclectic embrace of distinct and quite different points of view as if they were mutually confirming insights. Though at odds with the growing dominance of Talcott Parsons's theory of social action, his stress on the constituting character of action, the arbitrary and conventional nature of meaning, and, most of all, the intersubjective unity of society conceived as relevant knowledge for the operations of everyday life, also characterize American functionalism.

What primarily separates Schutz from Husserl is that the former, increasingly at home with post-war American optimism, takes horizon and theme to be a matter of self-definition, and the 'definition of the situation' to be a matter of motivational relevance and interest for the individual and group; the sense of the situation being 'given' is attenuated and, thus, the *phenomenological* problem of constitution – precisely that self-constitution is simultaneously the constitution of exteriority and vice versa – is similarly avoided rather than resolved. Schutz's sociology, that is to say, becomes characteristically voluntaristic. Thus, in spite of his rejection of Parsons, Schutz implies a conception of the social order as a meaningful consensus of just the sort Parsons advanced (Grathoff 1978). A shared 'stock of knowledge' and shared typifications play the same role in Schutz's work that shared norms and values do for Parsons. And, similarly, the origin of such knowledge and how it is shared do not arise as issues. Schutz's merging of phenomenology and American sociology marks an important departure from the development of phenomenological thought in Europe, and points towards the transformation of phenomenology into a *theory* of society.

From Phenomenology to a Sociology of Knowledge

Schutz's transformation of Husserl's critical, genetic phenomenology into a version of pragmatism is taken up and integrated with mainstream American functionalism in different ways by Harold Garfinkel's programme of ethnomethodology, and by Peter Berger and Thomas Luckmann in their well-known *The Social Construction of Reality*.

Garfinkel proposed a research programme as follows: 'Ethnomethodological studies analyze everyday activities as members' methods for making the same activities visibly-rational-and-reportable-for-all-practical-purposes, i.e., "accountable," as organizations of commonplace everyday activities' (1967, vi). The specific focus of ethnomethodological studies is precisely that they take everyday practical activities as self-constituting processes of social life. The routine 'explanations' and descriptions of these activities, by those actually involved in producing them, are regarded as both the subject matter *and* a valid account of local social routines. Ethnomethodology takes seriously the phenomenological distrust of theoretical concepts. Equally understanding and meaning come under suspicion as arbitrarily constructed concepts brought to bear on situations by observers. Social structure consists, rather, in everyday practical routines; practices that embrace, in their contextual and embedded character, the accounts people give themselves and each other of just those practices: 'In short, recognizable sense, or fact, or methodic character, or impersonality, or objectivity of accounts are not independent of the socially organized occasion of their use' (1967, 3). These accounts render 'rational' and comprehensible the complex moral order that implicitly organizes activities. The sociologists should not go beyond these accounts or impose upon them some other objective or theoretical explanation: 'I use the term "Ethnomethodology" to refer to the investigation of the rational properties of indexical expressions and other practical actions as contingent ongoing accomplishments of organized artful practices of everyday life' (1967, 11).

Common-sense understanding of everyday activities is constitutive as well as explanatory of these practices:

> Common sense knowledge of the facts of social life for the members of the society is institutionalized knowledge of the real world. Not only does common sense knowledge portray a real society for members, but in the manner of a self fulfilling prophecy the features of the real society are produced by persons' motivated complexes with these background expectancies. (1967, 53)

Ethnomethodology tended to restrict the scope of phenomenology to the explication of implicit rules and competence of practical reasoning; and, furthermore, to a linguistic approach to such explication. Ironically, having developed out of a rejection of linguistic philosophy as excessively formalistic, phenomenology here ends in technical, albeit contextualized, linguistic studies (Cicourel 1974).

Schutz and Garfinkel explicitly highlight the 'natural attitude' as itself the institutional, interactive structure of society; and seek to explicate in different contexts and with differing levels of generality how this structure emerges and operates, how it is renewed and persists. It is as if phenomenology had sought to appropriate the 'results' of Husserl's investigation while dispensing with his method, assumptions, and goals. Uneasy with the pursuit of a transcendental reflection, these developments sought, nonetheless, to transfer Husserl's transcendental insights – that referred, it must be remembered, to essential or 'pure' phenomena reached deliberately through a process of turning away from the 'taken-for-granted' character of reality – to the empirical and contingent content of experience.

Where ethnomethodology focused on the micro-processes of social life, Thomas Luckmann, with Peter Berger, utilized phenomenology to explicate social structure in terms of macro-processes of 'objectification' and 'socialization'. Here the phenomenological heritage is turned back into a problem of knowledge, and the development of a phenomenologically inspired sociology of knowledge is viewed as the central problem for a theory of society.

For Berger and Luckmann, 'reality is socially constructed and ... the sociology of knowledge must analyse the process in which this occurs' (1966, 3). And for them, reality is restricted formally to a specific aspect of the 'definition of the situation', 'a quality appertaining to phenomena that we recognize as being independent of our own volition', and knowledge is identified as 'certainty that phenomena are real and that they possess specific characteristics' (1966, 13). Here the natural attitude is taken as a starting point for a critical and comprehensive sociology of knowledge. But even for the natural attitude reality is defined more generously; it includes much that is dependent upon our will and mood, and treats much knowledge as uncertain. More importantly for the natural attitude the issue of knowledge does not arise. Reality is experienced and lived through; it is intimately bound up with our volition and spontaneous activity and, therefore, does not constitute an object of knowledge at all. For Berger and Luckmann, however, all phenomena are subsumed under a sociology of knowledge, which enquires into 'the processes by which *any* body of "knowledge" comes to be socially established *as* reality' (1966, 15).

They take the 'taken-for-granted' world, like Schutz, to be the 'paramount reality' of society:

> Compared to the reality of everyday life, other realities appear as finite processes of meaning, enclaves within the paramount reality marked by circumscribed meanings and modes of experience. The paramount reality envelops them on all sides, as it were, and consciousness always returns to the paramount reality as from an excursion. (1966, 39)

The key sociological and phenomenological issue is focused on the integration of sub-universes of reality into a unified and coherent totality. This is solved by an appeal to symbolic levels of integration at ever higher levels. That is, a Parsonian scaffolding is invoked to guarantee order at the highest level. But this seems to contradict the starting point, which is rooted in everyday reality as the level at which integration actually takes place.

Here unreality comes to the rescue of reality as its legitimating myth. Language is the fundamental mechanism of legitimating the social world as an objective reality. Social order requires differentiated knowledge of the world, and this different universe of knowledge can be held together by a shared and common reality; at the concrete and everyday level, language, 'such knowledge constitutes the motivating dynamics of institutionalised conduct' (1966, 83), but at a symbolic level, and more importantly, it exists in ever higher spheres of symbolic integration – myth, religion etc. Thus the 'definition of the situation' is viewed structurally and historically rather than individually and voluntaristically. But the requirements of systematic wholeness and completeness are as firmly held as in Parsons: 'Legitimation "explains" the institutional order by ascribing cognitive validity to its objectivated meanings' (1966, 11) and does so through reference 'upwards' to symbolically integrated spheres of knowledge.

Neither Garfinkel's nor Berger and Luckmann's versions of Schutz, nor Schutz's work itself, made a lasting impression on American sociology. They were not so much criticized as ignored; the central interest shifted from Parsons's theory of order to perspectives that came from European sociology, history, and cultural studies that, ironically, had themselves been influenced, and in quite different ways, by developments in phenomenological thinking. In America the more lasting influence of phenomenology was in psychiatry, where a typically existential variant derived as much from Bergson as Husserl made a fitful, underground, impact on orthodox positions (May et al. 1958; Lawrence and O'Connor 1967; Minkowski 1970). Functionalism was eclipsed, at least as a unifying theoretical framework for sociology, and as phenomenology had entered sociology as co-present with functionalism, the shift in attention left it stranded. Phenomenology survived sociology in an attenuated form as a methodological critique of the persisting dominant research tradition of positivism.

Part II

Implications

A horizon is not a rigid frontier, but something that moves with and invites one to advance further.

Gadamer, *Truth and Method*

5

Experience: Historical Sociology of the Natural Attitude

> How are we to overcome the difficulty, which all the human sciences face, of deriving universally valid principles from inner experiences, which are personally limited, composite, and yet incapable of analysis?
>
> Dilthey, *Poetry and Experience*

> Lived experience can never be reduced to thoughts or ideas. However, it can be related to the totality of human existence through reflection ... and thus it can be understood in its essence, that is, its meaning.
>
> Dilthey, *Poetry and Experience*

The 'natural attitude' that was the critical animus for all phenomenological studies of consciousness found a sociological equivalent in the somewhat belated thematization of 'everyday life' as a critical research focus. Simmel, in a pioneering essay on 'Sociology of the Senses' that anticipated many subsequent developments, advanced a new focus for sociological study: 'the real life of society, provided by experience, could certainly not be constructed from those large, objectivized structures that constitute the traditional objects of social science' (1997, 110). This call for a new approach, in spite of its explicit recognition of the centrality of experience for an adequate sociology of modern life, was developed in ways and in contexts that seemed remote from any phenomenological interest. It has become associated in particular with more recent historiographical perspectives, including the global social history of Fernand Braudel (1985) and the *Annales* school, as well as neo-Marxist and positivist orientations, in which the development of modern society is viewed 'from below' (Lüdtke 1995; de Certeau 1984; 1988; Lefebvre 1971; 1992; 2001). These studies were also, and to an increasing extent, influenced by philosophical positions inimical to phenomenology, particularly structuralist and poststructuralist reassessments of the role of consciousness as 'discourse' (Foucault 1970; 1972). There emerged at the same time a notable resurgence of interest in aesthetics as an alternative to any economic-rationalistic theory of value, but that approach, equally, rejected phenomenological perspectives as unduly 'subjective' (Bourdieu 1978).

In more specific contexts, however, distinctive historical and sociological studies of such phenomenological topics as time, space, the body, feeling, sensing and so on have become well established. And, in spite of rejecting or ignoring phenomenological writings, these studies have frequently proved their value in offering accounts of modern experience that parallel phenomenological insights. New thematic concerns and new perspectives have, thus, at an implicit level already gone some way towards establishing a genuine phenomenological sociology. The aim of the following chapters is, through reading phenomenological texts sociologically, and sociological texts phenomenologically, to make explicit this latent synthesis and indicate its value as an account of modernity.

Embodiment

The phenomenological investigation of consciousness rejoined the mind to the body by revealing ever more general, constitutive processes that gave rise to objectifications of all sorts. These processes were focused, on the one hand, in embodied individual experience and, on the other, in historical-cultural crystallizations of spirit. Phenomenology developed from a recognition of the living body as the primary phenomenon to a historical-social understanding of intersubjectivity rooted in bodily experience. Classical sociology, on the other hand, beginning with large-scale historical studies of objectified spirit, moved towards the discovery or, rather, rediscovery of embodiment as the secret of modern society. Embodiment, thus, presents itself as an obvious point of contact and transition between phenomenology and sociology, and the essential starting point for the development of any phenomenological sociology.

In retrospect, of course, it is possible to read into the works of Weber and Marx, in particular, a fundamental preoccupation with issues of embodiment. The classical literature provides, in fact, a number of sophisticated insights into the historical peculiarity of modern forms and processes of embodiment; that is, into the manner in which modern social relations are realized in specific bodily forms and practices. In fact the classical literature throws up a number of suggestive characterizations of modernity as a process of *disembodiment*.

Weber, for example, famously discusses the manner in which modernity is inscribed in the body as a specific form of asceticism. This allows him to link the bodily experience of modernity with remote periods of western history and, at the same time, to provide an incisive characterization of the particular experience of the modern age. Weber makes clear the specifically modern character of asceticism that, for the first time, links self-denial to the organization of work. Modern asceticism, shorn of religious presuppositions, takes on the character of a widespread secular *discipline* unconnected with esoteric religious practices (Wimbush 1995). Rather than turning its back on the world and seeking in heroic acts of spiritual athleticism wholly to master the world by overcoming every natural appetite, asceticism now takes on the character of rigorous self-control and the systematic denial of *spontaneous* enjoyment.

Equally, though in quite a different way, Marx makes the process of embodiment central to his understanding of modernity by focusing attention on the process of *labour* as both the social power for producing commodities and the source of their exchange value. This view introduced a radically historical understanding of embodiment. Labour was the central activity through which human beings created themselves as human beings; as social creatures. This meant that human activity in general, including the purposive interaction between human beings and their natural environment, was brought under historical forms and could only adequately be grasped in historical terms. Human beings do not live immediately in union with nature, rather, they must actively create a supporting environment for themselves, not only one in which they can survive in an animal sense, but one in which they can live as human beings (Marx 1976b, 322–41). In the historical process thus established, human beings experience needs and wants that arise independently of nature. Yet these 'needs' are felt in the same body that has an organic and natural form. Embodiment, that is to say, is a process of inscribing in the natural corporeal form specific historical demands and possibilities that arise within a particular 'mode of life'.

But in modern capitalist society everything that human beings produce has become detached from the process of creation, from labour in any free and original sense. Labour, rather, has become corrupted as work, and is itself a product or commodity that can be bought and sold. The historic medium of human self-creation is thus turned against human beings themselves and is made to serve the apparently ineluctable laws of the commodity as an ideal object. Value seems to inhere in objects and bears no relation to the human process of production. In a general sense, then, Marx provides an analysis of modernity as *dis*embodiment rather than embodiment. Modern society is peculiarly abstract and appears to be dominated by abstract laws; and in a more particular sense the process of humanization, in which the body is cultivated and matures as a living vehicle of civilization, is wasted and destroyed. The body of the worker becomes impoverished and worthless; assimilated, on the one hand, to the empty abstraction of the commodity form and, on the other, to the terrifying power of productive machinery.

Marx and Weber open new ways to an understanding of the social character of embodiment and disembodiment, to a radical insight shared with phenomenology: that your body is never quite 'your own'.

While such classical works invite continued reflection and reassessment as sources for a general historical sociology of embodiment, their insights remain embedded in the most complex general theories of society and thus defy simple extraction. It is, thus, to more recent writers (albeit ones deeply influenced by the classics) that we should turn as the proximate sources of the current interest in embodiment as a central theme for historical sociology; notably to the writings of Norbert Elias and Michel Foucault.

Incorporation

Both Elias and Foucault situate their key works in the context of early modern western society. For Elias this is identified with absolutism, the pre-eminence of court society, and the subsequent erosion of its authority and power by an aspiring bourgeois class. The aristocracy of the *ancien régime*, that is to say, is viewed as the progenitor of the modern age rather than the apotheosis of feudalism. The modern bourgeois class adopted the *manners* that characterized the court society it replaced. Manners required, and were exemplified by, new forms of comportment and bodily self-control. Elias illustrates *The Civilizing Process* (1994) with a host of specific examples, many drawn from early etiquette books, and in particular Erasmus of Rotterdam's *Education of the Christian Prince* (1997).

The new body consciousness, which was to develop into the general requirements of both respectability and hygiene, focused primarily on continuous self-monitoring and the exercise of bodily self-control in every possible respect. Appropriate dress, appearance, polite modes of eating and drinking, acceptable means of dealing with coughing, sneezing, urination and defecation, the proper restraint in gesture and forms of interaction, and the provision and protection of personal space all featured in the new corporeal pedagogy. The bodily training Erasmus's text enjoins not only on the prince but far more generally on all educated people, Elias claims, represents and is instrumental in realizing an unprecedented degree of individuation, privatization, and pacification in social life. The institutionalization of *manners* is nothing less than a 'civilizing process' and both the means by which, and the medium through which, the modern 'self' is constructed as a specific kind of bodily awareness; a new kind of embodiment (Muchembled 1988; Renaut 1997; Judovitz 2001).

Erasmus's text, thus, has a far wider significance than medieval works on knighthood, such as that of Ramon Llull (Herlihy 1971), which are addressed to a specific group whose appearance and behaviour are circumscribed by obligatory sumptuary laws (Bumke 2000; Le Goff 1982). A notable transition can be found in Balthasar Castiglione's *Life of the Courtier* (1976), which, written for an aristocratic elite required to demonstrate their good breeding, subsequently became a model of gentlemanly conduct that was widely adopted (Burke 1995; Marin 1988; Becker 1988).

Whatever objections might be raised to the details of Elias's views (Van Krieken 1998), they served in an exemplary fashion to focus social thought on a new theme, and have succeeded in making the process of embodiment a fundamental concern of any general sociology. Presenting his views in the context of a discussion of the relevance of phenomenology to modern social thought, however, may still appear ill-judged. Elias presented his sociology forthrightly as an alternative to and rejection of philosophy and vigorously denied any connection of his own thought with previous or contemporary philosophical discourse. Yet his views make little sense *outside* a general phenomenological framework. In spite of his own views of the matter his work can usefully be seen as among the first serious essays in historical phenomenology, albeit it one that offers important correctives to all the significant variants of its purely philosophical development.

In this respect the other *locus classicus* of contemporary interest in embodiment, Michel Foucault's (1977) *Discipline and Punish*, which was written a generation and more after *The Civilizing Process* but coincided in its English publication with the translation of Elias's work, happily embraces philosophy. Foucault also situates his work in the early modern period, which he terms the classical age. Foucault presents the 'civilizing process' in a striking and dramatic fashion. He also takes the crisis of the old regime and a pervasive sense of disorder and insecurity as the significant starting point for the emergence of modern society and its culture. In many ways this seems to mark a return to an older historiography; charting the emergence of absolutist regimes through the systematic use of force and violence, the establishment of new organizational weapons, the military revolution, the imposition of taxation systems, and so on, with their ideological elaboration in the doctrine of divine right or the secular, and cynical, acknowledgement of the necessity of brute force. What is new in Foucault's account is the emphasis he places on the human body as the primary *locus* of this process. The body is the focal point for the emergence of new institutional structures of the absolutist state and, subsequently, the vehicle for its transformation into modern, rationalized, bureaucratic regimes.

Foucault begins with an exception – a veritable *tour de force* (one is tempted to call it a *tour de ferocité*), the ritualized execution by torture and dismemberment of an attempted royal assassin. Like the opening of *les mots et les choses* (a famous discussion of Velázquez's painting *Las Meniñas*) it has somewhat overshadowed the subsequent text devoted to characterizing the emergence and establishment of new disciplinary regimes, epistemic as well as juridical, educational, and medical, which have as their object the new kind of embodiment that, in fact, renders the introductory *mise-en-scène* a discarded exception.

Foucault, in fact and perversely, deals only in exceptions. The greater part of *Discipline and Punish* is taken up with the *failure* of absolutism and the early modern state, and the surprisingly rapid transformation of punitive regimes that seek inwardly to transform the transgressor rather than wreak corporeal vengeance on the delinquent. But this strategy was only possible and only made sense because the 'normal' person did not transgress and did not require to be controlled any longer from 'above' or 'outside'. Foucault is concerned with the fate of those in early modern society who could not or would not exercise self-control. The implicit assumption throughout is just that most people, most of the time, could and did. And while he stresses the importance of schooling and military training as human *dressage* that has as its aim the inculcation of correct comportment, it is clear that such forceful educational techniques are one aspect only of a more pervasive shift in the culture of modern society; one increasingly ordered according to the rational demands of the market, capitalist production, and the bureaucratic state. A society, that is to say, within which reason, by a complex historical process, is *embodied* in the lives of modern individuals and serves adequately to guide their action into predictable and orderly channels.

As in the case of Elias, exception can be taken at many points to Foucault's narrative of power and secrecy, which is far more wide-ranging and provocative than can be indicated here (Florike and Mason 1997), but it has served, as from a quite different political and cultural direction has that of Elias, to establish a new research agenda and a fresh perspective for historical-sociological studies.

What has been assimilated to contemporary sociological and historical studies includes a new appreciation of the significance and power of embodiment as a significant focus for the institutionalization of modernity. The modern consciousness of the body, which is simply embodied self-consciousness, should not be regarded as a concept, or symbol, or metaphor; it is not primarily a 'natural symbol' of modern society (Douglas 1970). The embodiment of modernity is here just the *experience* the body gains of itself through its activity in the world. It is, and is not just a product of, an 'ensemble of social relations'. The incorporation of modernity transforms the body into, on the one hand, a living tool of the individuated subject and, on the other, the self-regulating instrument of the modern state (Heller et al. 1986; Izenberg 1992; Rose 1990). In an important way Elias and Foucault both appropriate phenomenological insights and meaningfully locate these insights in the emergence of modern society. Phenomenology, in other words, is not just about consciousness, it is about embodied self-consciousness, which is the embodiment of modernity; and sociology is not just about society, it is about the way in which we can experience the world, including ourselves.

Talk of 'the body' or even 'embodiment' tends almost irresistibly towards the construction or reconstruction of an architectonics of modernity. The body, after all, is something palpable and altogether 'real'. One feels it is the 'most real' kind of reality there is. The Aristotelian table of categories, redrawn by Kant, finds its living archetype in the body; the active structure which, in turn, orders the world. Thus, in a somewhat different perspective, a historical sociology of embodiment replaces the intellectual history of western civilization; but with something that turns out to be strikingly similar. It serves as a significant critique, however, of an overly idealist interpretation of history by offering a narrative of the real foundation of that history *and* a final and irrefutable foundation for the *logos* (Lakoff and Johnson 1980; Judovitz 2001).

Spatiality

Kant, reflecting on both the scientific and the philosophical conceptions of reality that had risen to prominence in his own time, treated space as an *a priori condition* of experience. Both phenomenology and sociology, however, focus on the *experience* of space rather than its theoretical conceptualization and, consequently, view the indifference of pure extension as a *post*-experiential intellectual construction. Rather than forming an empty continuum *within which* bodies appear and interact, space itself is constituted in the same social processes in which the body comes to self-awareness (Lefebvre 1991). We cannot appeal to any presumed formal unity of space, therefore, to guarantee the continuity of the experiencing subject. Indeed, modern society is marked by a characteristic proliferation of different kinds of spatial experience with characteristic accompanying objects, relations, moods, and so on. Modernity, which in one perspective is nothing other than the radical 'geometrization' of space and the thorough working through of the implications of the breakthrough 'from the closed world to the infinite universe', in other respects differentiates spatial experience in new ways that break into and render discontinuous the ideal spatial unity it theoretically requires (Koyré 1957; Casey 1997). Space in premodern society was organized in terms of a cosmological body image in which simple distinctions – right/left, up/down, front/back, inside/outside – were the substantial symbols of a divine order. Modern space, in contrast, is linear, continuous and ordered according to relative nearness and farness.

In the modern world space both shrinks to nothing (as in instantaneous telecommunications) and expands to infinity (Kern 1983). In both cases, and in the multiplicity of spatial forms characteristic of modern life, space is also and always *embodied*. Whether as location, place, site, inside, outside, public, private, transitional, closed, open, bounded, bordered, or as particular kinds of objects, events, performances, and so on, 'space-in-itself' is as illusory to experience as the thing-in-itself (Perec 1997). This rich qualitative variation is, in part at least, a consequence of the modern freedom of movement; it is because we are not *fixed* in a definite position within a cosmological and social order, and move more or less freely through our world, that we experience a multiplicity of different places, and different kinds of space, which hitherto had been the exclusive locality of a specific community. Movement is not just linear displacement; it is experienced as purposive and in its orientation towards an end becomes both a journey and the external realization of an inward movement of the self. The phenomenological account of perception is, first of all, a description of the characteristically modern experience of movement; oriented in terms of a self-directed embodied observer in relation to a horizon of continually appearing objects.

The experience of space is organized in terms of a particular body image. The individuation and closure of the modern body image are associated with two specific aspects of spatial experience: separation and objecthood. The separation of the embodied self as the active centre of sensibility from the exterior world, and the breaking of all immediate links between the two, mean that external objects can only be grasped as representations within the self. Every representation introduces a certain kind of *distance* between itself and the putative 'thing' for which it stands. There is, in principle, no limit to the distance to which objects may be withdrawn. And distance, in itself, does not signify unfamiliarity. Giordano Bruno was astonished that we could see all the way to the stars; and stars were among the most familiar and constant of exterior objects. At the same time, as we moved through the modern world, we encountered innumerable strange and curious objects close at hand. Distance is linked to the *scale* of body images. New observational techniques disclosed hitherto unknown objects and bodies that lay beyond the range of ordinary perception and, therefore, were experienced as remote; replenishing in spectacular fashion the diminishing stock of irresistibly astonishing phenomena (Stafford 1994).

The embodied self is a centre of sensible qualities such that representations of distant objects are always experienced as 'things' outside and other than the body itself. Space always lies outside and beyond the pure 'hereness' of embodied self-feeling. Exteriority is grasped as a particular distribution of objects, of regions of space filled with 'bodies' that are, in certain essential respects, like our own bodies. Thus, while the representations of all exteriority cannot resemble their exciting causes, which remain essentially beyond our reach, the abyss between embodied self-presence and external object is overcome in the experience of these representations as other *bodies*. The body image as an individuated, bound, and filled unity enshrouds the object with the spatial experience of the body itself. Body and object are modern twins; arising together they nonetheless confront each other as strangers. The object is modelled on the body image (Lakoff and Johnson 1980; Schilder 1964; Strauss 1963; 1966).

The object, which always retains its bodily thinghood, is located in relation to our own body as more or less distant. Modernity continually extends this distance and thus enlarges the sphere of objects, all of which are ultimately familiar as bodily kin. We sense objects, that is to say, in terms of our immediate *non*-represented bodily self-experience. In that sense we remain under the sway of anthropomorphic thought; what distinguishes our conception of things as modern is the historic transformation of the body image that informs the *metaphorical* experience of space.

The externalized object, its inner nature forever reticent, can be related to us only through intermediary representations. This is not because the senses are deceptive or lack penetration but because we do not know anything definite about our own insides and can ascribe to the object only a vague sense of substance as a 'heavy mass' (Schilder 1964).

The modern normative body image is a closed unity, a monad and, thus, the ideal object is an external, uniquely located, impenetrable body. The modern experience of space, however, is highly differentiated and corresponds to a wide range of body images and objectivities, varying in terms of their mutual openness and permeability. Only the briefest indication of the range of body–object relations and their characteristic spatial forms can be given here (Appadurai 1986).

The things that in modern society became personal property enter into relation with people externally through the act of exchange; in buying and selling. Property is just what we have a legal right to sell; that is to alienate from ourselves. Property is owned but not possessed. The object that is so much like us (or like we imagine we ought to be) in its complacent indwelling composure taunts us with its careless independence. This contrasts with the object that may be possessed (the gift) or cannot be other than possessed (the totem) (Gregory 1982; Mauss 1970; Durkheim 1995). The characteristic modern passion for ownership, for accumulating objects, is an important aspect of spatial experience. It is our *inability* truly to possess the object that fuels the desire to own it and, at the same time, is the source of our disappointment at discovering that we *only* own it (Balzac 1968).

Not all things are pure objects in this sense. A variety of thing-like objectivations characterize the range of embodied spatial experience available within modern society. Toys, for example, are exterior, open rather than closed objects that invite participation in creating and sustaining an imaginary world. The physical structure of toys is quite independent of their functionality or use; whatever their appearance they can 'be' anything at all. The meaning of the object is defined by the momentary exigencies of play, and is free to alter. Toys enjoy an absolute spatial freedom, undergoing continuous metamorphosis, including multiple repetition of previous incarnations. Toys, that is to say, generate their own imaginary space and resonate with the player's spatially liberated and sensuously mobile body image (Tiffany 2000). Many of the most widely used products of advanced technology are popular just because they are embodied as toy-like objects; a 'new toy' is fun. Mobile communicators and other hand-held gizmos are irresistible and, unlike the alien objectivity of merely useful or conspicuously valuable commodities, they invite manipulation, and lead the hand to rediscover its primal function of exploring space.

We play *with* toys, but we just play musical instruments. The instrument is an object that *dictates* its use to us. In relation to instruments our freedom is severely curtailed yet they lure us into new kinds of spatial experience. The instrument has to be learned and mastered before it repays the virtuoso with the sense of 'soaring' beyond the restricted range of the mundane world. The conquest of space, here, results from the complete assimilation of the instrument to the body and vice versa. The player 'becomes' the instrument in the way in which an actor might be said to become a particular role; equally the instrument 'belongs' to the player in quite a different sense to that of ownership. Instruments of other sorts, scientific and medical devices in particular, require a different kind of skill. Here the mastery of technique is in the interest of a skill that is put to use in a deliberative and concentrated manner. The use of instruments in this way calls forth a particularly focused body image, in which space shrinks to that required for the task in hand. In a medical procedure, for example, the relevant site is isolated and treated as an independent location detached from the 'patient'. These objects remain intermediaries between the concentrated endeavour of the skilled user and the effective completion of a task. In related ways, equipment, tools (Harman 2002), furniture (Auslander 1996), machinery (Giedion 1948), and so on, may be distinguished, each related to specific transformations in the normative modern body image and its spatial experience.

Exteriority and movement characterize all modern public space – the world in which the embodied self appears as an anonymous object, equivalent in its closed unity to any other object. Modernity, however, is also characterized by the careful construction and protection of personal space. In modern society all three have developed along with the appearance of the spatialized object as pure exteriority. Thus, in addition to the empty surrounding of things, space in a modern sense is also experienced as a series of discontinuous transformations. Bachelard describes the 'intimate' space of the home, in an idealized way to be sure, but in what remains a suggestive fashion. The modern western home developed towards a highly differentiated interior structure which not only protected the privacy of the family as a whole, but also encouraged and even formalized the provision of individuated private space (Bachelard 1969; Ariès and Duby 1991).

Temporality

The historical transformation in which modernity had its origins left nothing untouched. A new temporal order and new experiences of time were central aspects of the embodiment of modernity (Rossum 1996; Pomian 1984). But, while the abstraction of infinite, empty, and continuous space contrasts with the qualitative differentiation of spatial embodiment, so the incorporation of temporality was primarily in the direction of standardization and uniformity. Husserl's phenomenology pays particular attention to this difference. For him, time remains elusive and resists full embodiment. Modernity might be characterized, in fact, as a confrontation with time's ineluctable exteriority; a movement that aims at nothing less than the complete incorporation of time into the experience of the world; a movement that, ultimately, fails.

Modernity, first of all, meant a break in continuity with the past. The founding of human autonomy required an act of freedom; a movement out of the atemporal structure of the premodern cosmos and into a continually developing, temporally constituted human world. Time, that is to say, is newly seized as the immanence of human freedom and human self-determination. The radical character of modernity is characterized as a *beginning*, and the beginning of modernity is, above all, the emergence of a new temporal horizon; the incorporation of time into the human world as its immanent flow. It is not the case, of course, that time played no part in constituting experience prior to modernity but, in a paradoxical fashion, the fundamental constituting temporality of the premodern appeared as the *eternal*. The permanence of the divine alone possessed being and existed simply without temporal qualification or modification of any sort. Self-sufficient being lay outside the transient and valueless realm of immediate experience, which existed in subordinate, dependent and changeable states. For corrupt and decaying humanity the eternal beckoned and, in spiritual contemplation and material death, oriented the earthly realm towards ends that lay beyond experience. And for this world mundane events were grasped analogically in relation to eternal truths revealed in biblical narratives. Past and future were fixed in divine acts of condescension; creation, incarnation, apocalypse (Gurevich 1985; Kleinschmidt 2000, 15–32). From a human perspective these miraculous interventions inaugurated and appeared as events 'in time', one following and symbolically replicating the other. But irruptions of the eternal, if recognized as such, overwhelm reality and transform every limited experience into tokens of the absolute. Experience is cleansed of temporal significance; neither for individual not for collective life can any fundamental significance be attached to succession or duration. The 'art of memory', like the biblical pattern of 'history', conformed temporal events to a spatial logic (Carruthers 1990; Yates 1964).

In contrast to all views for which mundane existence appears to be the transient bearer of symbols of timeless being, modernity constitutes itself as a radically historical reality. Time is infinitized, nothing that is can be outside its flowing unity. All events are connected sequentially; related both causally and meaningfully in terms of the unbroken continuity and directionality of time. Both history and memory define the past as an essential aspect of the present and its distinctive identity.

The incorporation of time into modern society was effected primarily by measurement and standardization (Crosby 1997; Landes 1983). These processes have nothing to do with the technology of timekeeping; the mechanical clock, and later the watch, were the means of extending and generalizing a process that already had a long history. Like the development of money, however, improved means here eventually had significant consequences of their own. In premodern monasteries, for example, a variety of timing devices were introduced and used to indicate the 'hours' to be devoted to different forms of worship, or study, or work in accordance with the rule of the order (Mumford 1963). These divisions of the day were also to some extent standardized, so that monasteries dispersed throughout Europe observed the same time, ignoring marked local variation. Such cases, however, remained unusual and the real spur to standardization only came with the new freedom of movement that characterized the end of feudalism and the emergence of the modern age. Time could be localized and marked in terms of community activities only so long as such communities remained more or less closed and isolated one from another. The increasing 'dynamic density' (Durkheim) of modernity required and promoted the adoption of a standard time covering ever larger areas. The real importance of new technologies of timekeeping lay less in accuracy and reliability than in the relative ease in which a standard time could be moved from one place to another. A clock could travel by carriage and arrive at its destination still showing the 'correct' time; movement could be contained within a single 'time zone'. It was only with the development of much faster travel over long distances, by railway, that insurmountable difficulties in standardizing to a single time became apparent and it became necessary also to establish and regulate the boundaries of time zones and their transitions.

The development of watches rather than large-scale clocks is significant here; it allowed individuals to carry the time around with them and guarantee they were in harmony with the local, possibly unfamiliar, locality. The personalized timepiece was extremely popular and its spread was out of all proportion to its practical utility. That time became at once abstract, standardized, mechanized, and personal as distinct from concrete, local, ritualized and communal is part of a total transformation of a way of life rather than the consequences of any specific technical innovation (Landes 1983; Le Goff 1982). This creates a sense not only of the human control of time, but also of its ownership.

The personalization of time is of much greater significance in modern society, however, as the 'interior time' of recollection. Modern experience is formed as self-experience and the self is essentially a temporal relation. Time was internalized as a continuous biographical narrative. This was directly related, not only to the general individuating tendencies at work in modern society, but more particularly to the continuous surveillance and monitoring of private as well as public aspects of life (Donzelot 1979). Rather than defining a life cycle by periodic, communally observed *rites de passage*, each individual ideally formed a continuous arrow of time that left a unique official trace. Transitions from childhood to adulthood to old age became blurred, movements into and out of work increasingly depended on market conditions unrelated to age, episodic changes in family and household circumstances went uncelebrated and unnoticed. Personal memory was gradually conformed to, and confined within, a continuous, internal monologue. From Rousseau's *Confessions* to Proust's and Freud's reconstruction of personal narrative, time became increasingly significant as the medium of selfhood.

Modernity can be characterized in terms of transformations in the experience of space and time, and their typical modes of embodiment. Modern body images, in their bewildering and overlooked variety, reveal the mutual implication of spatiality and temporality. Novalis neatly expresses the normative relation here: 'Time is *inner space* – space is *outer time*' (1997, 136). But new body images and related forms of spatiality and temporality arose and interacted in complex ways; in the modern world, the processes of objects, events, actions, ideas, and so on were constituted as meaningful unities. This world can further be characterized, both phenomenologically and sociologically, in terms of 'regional ontologies' that distinguish essential *differences* in the constituting processes of embodiment that characterized modernity. These regions may be indicated in a preliminary way as *sensing*, *willing*, and *feeling*.

Sensing

In sensing the formal unity of the body is continually dissolved into qualitatively distinct aspects of consciousness: seeing, hearing, touching, and so on. If modernity required, and was made possible through, new body images and new forms of embodiment, equally it brought the senses into prominence in a new way, threatening even as it did so the architectonic unity apparently established by these same processes. The world apprehended visually was not identical to the world revealed in sound, nor was it easy to relate to the world that was touched or tasted. The senses were differentially incarnated; the body that looked was distinct from the body that listened, or stretched out a hand to touch and hold (Strauss 1963; Katz 1935; 1989). This either put into question the unity of the body and its world or left unclarified its coherence as a manifold. In the modern period the senses became the privileged, indeed, exclusive sources of knowledge of the world. And although the disciplinary regimes of modernity invoked an ascetic ideal as the foundation of order, reason and legitimate pleasure, the senses were also celebrated and valued to an unprecedented degree and in new ways. In relation to these issues a convincing phenomenological sociology of sensing has yet to be fully developed, but recent scholarship in a variety of disciplines has opened fresh perspectives towards such a development (Classen 1993; Howes 2004; Jütte 2005).

The early modern period has been characterized as the baroque; marked, above all, by devotion to the senses and by an extraordinary development of sensuousness of every kind (Maravall 1986; Božouē 2000). It is the baroque spectacle that Foucault alludes to in the opening pages of *Discipline and Punish*, hinting at an entire world of sensuous excess that bourgeois society will repress. The banquet, the festival, the performance, opera, as well as characteristic architecture and the heightened and dramatized bodily forms in painting characterize the sensuous world, as it was reborn from the neglect of a medieval culture that sought reality in symbols (Camporesi 1988; 1994; Harbison 2000; Bouwsma 2000; Buci-Glucksmann 1994).

In the sensuous awakening of modernity, a process that locates the origins of modernity firmly in the Renaissance and views the later emergence of bourgeois society as something of a late development, or even a deviation from its more fundamental form, a new ordering of the modes of awareness and a fresh articulation of their interrelations are adumbrated. Vision, it has been claimed, becomes the pre-eminent sense and the cultivation of seeing the most significant distinguishing feature of modern humanity (Foster 1988; Levin 1993; 1997; Shapiro 2003). Of course vision had been highly valued in the Judaeo-Christian tradition; the divine *light* came into existence prior to humanity and every act of seeing dwelt in its luminous essence. The blind were excluded from immediate participation in the primary manifestation of the divine mystery and their misfortune, thus, tinged with sin roused fear more than sympathy (Barasch 2001). It is just in this respect, however, that a fundamental difference between the premodern tradition of vision as revelation and the modern articulation of seeing becomes evident. For the religious cosmology of the premodern west seeing is the first (and not necessarily the most vital) medium in which the person draws near to something other than the envisaged object. It is an *intimate* sense, in which and through which the divine spirit is conveyed to its human host. Vision at once puts humanity 'in touch' with its creator and a strong mystical tradition in western religious thought longed earnestly for the moment in which God would be glimpsed 'face-to-face' (McGinn 1992; Leclerq 1978). But within modern society the priority of seeing is a function of its role as a *distance* sense. Vision becomes consecrated to a wholly secular task of 'picturing' the world as an external scene.

Some, of course, regret the loss of intimacy that seems irrevocably to be the consequence of this transformation. And a sense of loss and separation, palpable in every contemporary access of nostalgia and melancholy, as a result colours the experience of even the most committed of modernists. It is not only the priority of the visual sense over any other, but the dominance of immediate seeing over revelatory vision that robs the world of its enchantment. Such views are easily exaggerated and invoke a somewhat fanciful narrative of a past, shared world in which the living presence of another speaker makes hearing and listening the primary senses for conveying and experiencing fellowship (Derrida 1976; 1981).

This view has also been associated with somewhat exaggerated claims, in a quite different ideological perspective, for the significance of printing and book production in the emergence of modern culture; specifically that the *circulation* of the written word encouraged the rapid spread of humanism and played an important part in a general intellectual transformation that remains notable for the rise of modern science (Eisenstein 1983). In the premodern scholastic community the manuscript text was usually read aloud to a group of listeners, and its transformation into the printed and individually available book allowed learning to free itself from the dominance of ecclesiastical authority, and encouraged scholarly communication among physically and socially remote individuals, forming an early 'virtual' community that initially required little institutional support. The transmission of culture became primarily a matter of visual reading rather than communal listening.

Such views are exaggerated. The immediacy of the spoken word may be a harsh and inescapable word of command that dehumanizes and humiliates, rather than the familiar voice in which a cherished and intimate relation is borne. Equally, the detachment of the text from the community does not always signal the liberation of the reader and thinker from traditional (or novel) constraints; most importantly, perhaps, the growing authority of the author who could now exercise an uncanny power over the isolated and unprotected reader. Not surprisingly the early modern period was productive of superstition, magic, heresy, and nonsense as well as seeing the birth (or rebirth) of the rational sciences, the invention of the novel, and Europe's greatest age of drama (Martin 1994; Chartier 1994).

More importantly these views fail to note the transformation in hearing that *along with* the emergence of new ways of seeing distinguish the modern social world. It is only recently that a more general social history and anthropology of hearing have been taken seriously (Attali 1985; Kahn 2001; Erlmann 2004). Now the history of music and the 'soundscape' of the environment form important themes for the historical phenomenology of modernity. Alain Corbin, in particular, has begun the task of describing the characteristic sound of early modern society. And just as new pictorial conventions in the Renaissance stimulated, amongst artists and non-artists alike, a search for valid forms of visual representation, rules and conventions for perspective drawing, and adequate techniques of illusionism, so musicians, including Galileo Galilei's father, Vicenzo, and many non-musicians became concerned with formulating a satisfactory physical and mathematical account of musicality (Cohen 1984; Crombie 1990).

Vision and hearing are often described as the distance senses; privileged in the modern period as the means of gaining knowledge of the external world. In the development of modernity, however, the division between outside and inside is constituted both by the architectonics of the body and by a division of the senses. The senses of smell and more particularly taste are taken to be indicative of a purely personal region and these senses become increasingly confined to a region of incommunicable interiority. The doctrine of primary and secondary qualities, which played such an important part in the development of the physical sciences after Galileo, systematized and refined what was a general cultural transformation in the sphere of sensing. Vision and hearing were construed as remote sensing devices that revealed the character of a common, shared exteriority; taste and smell, on the other hand, depended for their identifying qualities as much on the moral character and inner cultivation of the individual as on the nature of the object. Aesthetic looking and listening depended on the general cultivation of the individual's senses and, thus, became primarily a matter of 'taste' rather than a mere registering of what was 'there'. This very ambiguity, of course, became a focus for the development of philosophical aesthetics, particularly after Kant's determined efforts to establish common criteria for judgments of taste (Kant 2000).

The transformation in the sense of smell is one of the most revealing aspects of the history of modernity. Corbin has elegantly described the transition from the collective understanding of smell as organized around the foul and fragrant, to a modern odourless environment. There is a considerable effort to eradicate odour of all sorts, the 'toning down' of smells in the modern period (Corbin 1996; Classen et al. 1994).

Interestingly, at the same time, a developing passion for stronger tastes, both sweet and spicy, becomes evident and is not accounted for simply on the basis of new sources of availability (Schivelbusch 1993; Flandrin and Montanari 1999). Medieval food would seem, to modern palates, mostly bland and unappetizing; medieval smells would be suffocatingly pungent. The difference here is related to more general orientations; smell and taste are individuated senses but where taste, as it were, points outward and can be a mark of distinction, aroma is the secret inwardness of the person, lodged deep in the body. The 'odour of sanctity' and the 'smell of corruption' refer still to an unknowable interiority. Pleasant smelling scent *masks* the odour of decay, and if intense serves only to emphasize its unfortunate necessity. Good taste, however, can be publicized (Kass 1999).

In being interiorized and personalized, smell and taste have come to play a special role in the structure of recollection. Taste and smell often function to trigger and mark such memories, particularly those spontaneous recollections celebrated by Proust, in which the past seems to well up and live again within us, saturating our consciousness with the repetition of some forgotten event.

The history of touching and feeling in the emergence and development of modernity is the least studied of sensory transformations (Montagu 1986; Harvey 2003; Classen 2005; Derrida 2005), yet its importance for a culture in which the surface of the body serves as a double boundary, simultaneously distinguishing each individual from any other and differentiating the outer world of objects from the inner life of the subject, is evident. The zone of touch is our only point of contact with both the inside and the outside, self and world. In marking the boundary between inside and outside, self and other, the skin, enveloping the body, plays a vital role in uniting the architectonic and the sensitive aspects of embodiment (Anzieu 1989). Touch marks out our place in the world and hollows out a mysterious abyss within us; it defines the peculiar region, seized by Pascal, in which we actually live; a finite haven between two qualitatively distinct infinities. This is a region and not a line; an indefinite and variable zone.

'Sensitivity' is, first of all, the awareness of contact. Sensitivity is distributed over the entire surface of the body and animates its image as a living unity (Schilder 1964). The sensitive zone registers the resistance of the world without, and the recurrence of appetite and needs from within; it is also in the flesh that feelings of all sorts arise; the shock of grief, the twinge of recrimination, the ache of desire. We feel disgust as a special aesthetic and moral revulsion at *touching* anything impure, and awe at coming into contact with the sacred (Scheler 1987; Miller 1997; Kolnai 2004). What most excites disgust is the body's own waste products and discharges (the intriguing exception of tears remains puzzling); a reaction that is so firmly institutionalized in the culture that most people have difficulty conceiving that it is not a universal and natural condition. Yet we need only consider the evident joy with which an infant will, accidentally allowed the opportunity, play with its own faeces to realize that here too we are dealing with a history of conventions. Equally challenging is the extent to which the erotic overcomes disgust, and might even be defined as the overcoming of a general fear of touching.

Historically the sense of touch also underwent a fundamental transformation and became part of the modern sensorium. The kiss and other forms of embrace became eroticized (Perella 1969). Violence became 'civilized' in the duel and organized through weapons that kept the protagonists apart. The transmission of power or healing directly through the hand was attenuated (Kantorowitz 1957; Marin 1988). Yet even slight accidental contact can cause offence and, where bodily contact is unavoidable as in busy subways and lifts, is highly ritualized. The potency of touch, ideally withdrawn from public life, continually threatens to break into and disrupt its orderly flow.

Willing

The mysterious synthesis in which bodily phenomena arise does not come about as the result of some sort of conceptual or reflective process; it arises immediately in the activity of willing; that is, in activity. The living body as the architectonic model of the world and the locus of differentiated sensations is spontaneously united in willing. And willing manifests itself, first of all, in voluntary physical movement. It is just in the dynamism of the body that we find the *liveliness* of life; the prototypical vitality of all willing.

Voluntary movement is immediately given as an embodied possibility. Willing consists, first of all, in the effortless *freedom* of bodily activity: 'Genuinely voluntary motion is one which passes unnoticed because it expresses *the docility of a yielding body*' (Ricoeur 1966, 309). In a related sense we also speak of our 'willingness' to act for someone, to yield to their decision, and refer generally to a 'willing' as distinct from a 'wilful' child. The first instance of willing can be considered in relation to the phenomenon of play. Play is the pure form of voluntary movement; it is movement without purpose or end and is characterized precisely as *effortless* activity (Fink 1966; Gadamer 1975; Spariosu 1989, 1997). At the same time we commonly associate willing with resolution, determination, and effort; with a summoning and seizing of inner energy to overcome the *resistance* of the body. Paradoxically we exercise the will to act against our inclination and in spite of our own 'unwillingness'. In this sense willing has to be grasped in relation particularly to the exhausting activity of work (Rabinbach 1990).

Just as phenomenology revealed the natural attitude in relation to the externality of the world and its objectivity was the end result of a complex intersubjective process involving specific, philosophically arbitrary and historically contingent assumptions, so the natural attitude in relation to willing has reconstituted its original givenness in an almost opposite sense. In modern society constraint not freedom, resistance rather than movement, seem ineradicably to characterize its every appearance. Historical-sociological studies provide some hints towards a clarification of this situation.

The identification of willing with voluntary movement has an important political significance for the emergence of modern society. In medieval society freedom of movement was reserved for elite individuals who, in a very direct way, were uniquely distinguished by the free exercise of the will

(Bloch 1962). The overwhelming majority of people lived in communities that strictly limited their movement and to which they belonged and upon which they were dependent. Law within the territorial jurisdiction of a feudal lord was defined by his personal rule, his will. And establishing a relation of vassalage through the ritualized oath of loyalty was to surrender the will, to become 'the man of another man' (Le Goff 1982). The general phenomenon of willing, that is to say, was configured as a will to obedience; humility, institutionalized in the monastic life, was the most praised virtue (Leclerq 1978; Lawrence 1998).

But elite culture itself sided ultimately with freedom. The rise of humanism not only revived secular learning, it made radical claims for human freedom; boldly expressed in the first instance in the demand for *dignity*, which consisted in the ability and freedom of *self-movement*; that is, in *willing* (Kristeller 1972). The passive will to obedience – obedience to God, to nature and to their human representatives – was transformed into an active freedom of movement. The long and confusing processes in which feudalism ended liberated people from the land and expelled them from communities, creating large numbers of rootless migrants throughout Europe. The first priority of emergent modern states, monarchical, imperial, or princely, was to bring this population under the direct control of centralized authorities. The humanist and baroque passion for bodily discipline, stressed in different ways by Elias and Foucault according to their particular focus (Reformation or Counter-Reformation, northern or southern, rising bourgeoisie or declining aristocracy), reveals a profound understanding of nascent modernity in the phenomenological novelty of willing. If freedom is to be brought under control and harnessed to the demands of the state and the interests of a ruling class, voluntary movement, in which willing first takes on its characteristic modern appearance, must be integrated with a new corporeal order. This is as vital as the market or the state to the full development of modernity. If people are free to move they must be taught to move correctly; comportment is the first requirement of the new age and the initial step in a process that will ultimately transform the freedom of willing into a 'rational' and, hence, expected pattern of 'decisions' and 'choices'.

The internalization of controlling mechanisms finds its point of self-generating stability in the agency of 'conscience'. As Max Weber makes clear, the fundamental importance of the Reformation for the development of modern society lies in the specifically moral, rather than religious, sense it gave to willing and the manner in which the constituting of this 'ontological region' became allied to the process of modern rationalization in every sphere of life. *Willing* becomes the *self-limiting* of freedom as distinct from the freedom of movement. This decisive phenomenological transition is the central *motif* in the development of the most characteristic features of modern society and modern culture. Willing, thus, becomes identified with a self-imposed determination either to act or not to act in a particular way. And, certainly, Kant may be viewed in this context as the culmination of the baroque insinuation of self-control into the spirit of modern humanism. Enlightenment, in Kant's famous essay, means *civilized* reason and the reason of civilization. It is as practical reason, the recognition of, and willed surrender to, binding values on the part of an embodied conscience, as well as in the economic calculation of pure reason, that modern society is established as *self-regulating* (Schmidt 1996; Unger 1975).

The unifying notion of willing, for the central period of modernity, thus, becomes one modelled on physical effort rather than freedom of movement. Willing involves, first of all, a decision or choice and then an action executing that choice. The second part is generally viewed as the source of the effort involved in exercising the will. Fatigue, and the inertial resistance of the body, must in some way be overcome to realize an inner decision. The freedom of the will consists just in the unqualified interiority of this decision. There is in principle no limit to *what* the will might, as it were, alight upon as its goal or object and, more importantly, no exterior agency that can determine this choice. And it is this ineradicable inner freedom that requires the internalization of a specifically moral content for practical reason; the guarantee that an appropriate goal or object will be selected. Modern society becomes self-regulating, that is to say, through the successful institutionalizing of a specific, regulative principle of willing.

Where early modern society depended on the active and willing cooperation of large numbers of people it was vital that they willed to act 'correctly'. But once regulative norms were embodied in the self-moving, willing subject, that subject became theoretically free. It was just the apparently radical character of willing that inebriated the Romantic movement and, at the same time, its purely theoretical freedom that rendered harmless its subversive ideology (Bloch 2000; Löwy and Sayre 2002; Lacoue-Labarthe, Nancy 1988).

If willing was interiorized as absolute freedom it could not ever be 'exhausting'; its playful quality was restored and could never be experienced as other than spontaneous. Whence, then, the feeling of effort that during the modern period has been viewed as the inevitable accompaniment and most faithful companion to every act of willing? An obvious answer might be that our everyday activity, after all, does not issue spontaneously from free acts of willing but, rather, is coerced and requires a strenuous effort of self-suppression. Modern life, after all, is not all play. The significance of the modern construction of willing is evident in the extent to which such an obvious view was countered. William James, for example, interestingly argued that every feeling of effort lay in the struggle among contending *possible* actions; carrying out an action is effortless once all alternative lines of action have been suppressed. Effort, that is to say, stems from an excess of freedom (James 1981, 83–126).

It is in the consistency and freedom of willing, therefore, that selfhood emerges as a specific form of embodiment. Willing is best grasped, thus, not in relation to action as its cause or its motive but in terms of other forms of volition; wanting, wishing, longing, desiring, and so on. Willing does not 'do' anything, it simply wills; the issue is not how it effects a result in the 'real' world but how it forms itself into a temporal unity as the self, character, or personality.

Feeling

It would be an exaggeration to say that sociology until quite recently had almost entirely ignored the realm of feeling but, certainly, it is only recently that sociological writing on feeling has become prominent (Giddens 1992; Bauman 2003; 2005; Williams 2001; Franks and McCarthy 1989). And this recent interest coincides with its reappearance, also in mainstream philosophy and, to a lesser extent, psychology (Hirschman 1977; Solomon 1983; Frijda 1986; Elster 1999; Ben-Ze'ev 2000; Sorabji 2000; Nussbaum 2001).

The difficulty in naming and distinguishing feelings, evident both in their scholarly neglect and in the lack of consensus on how adequately to describe their most elementary forms and characteristics, should not mislead us into considering them either insignificant or dependent on other, more elementary, states of being. Wilhelm Dilthey rightly insists on the 'omnipresence of feeling in psychic life' (2002, 68) and clearly distinguishes its ontological region and mode of 'interconnectedness' from either the causal explanation of nature or the meaningful understanding of history.

In modernity feelings were thematized, first of all, as *passions* and in this context Spinoza may be regarded as epochal, as Descartes was to sensing, or Leibniz to willing. However, whereas Descartes's philosophy of doubt immediately initiated a continuously developing reflection on modern experience as a process of representation, Spinoza's grasp of the real presence of feeling has been only intermittently the occasion of sustained discussion (Unger 1984; Luhmann 1986). The tendency within modern society has been, rather, to either a naturalization or a rationalization of feeling as *emotions*.

Feeling has been considered, that is to say, primarily from the perspective of 'reason' and defined relationally and by contrast as irrational (Hirschman 1977). By bringing the passions, even negatively, within the sphere of intellect this very irrationality was contained and organized, if not actually spirited away. The passions were codified, collected, ordered, and subjected to a proper scientific investigation and, more significantly, they could be 'explained' within the framework of naturalism. This procedure was already developed with impressive Aristotelian gusto by Robert Burton at the end of the seventeenth century in his *Anatomy of Melancholy*. Here the passions constituted the interior 'force' (on the model of *impetus* in late medieval physics) 'driving' action. And for Hume, similarly, the passions propel action, not only energizing but also directing activity towards certain kinds of goals. To some extent this is still the case for Freud, though he adds to this, alongside it so to speak, an interpretive understanding of passions considered as *motives*; as ultimate sources of meaning. Furthermore, a general confusion between willing and feeling has obscured both systematic and historical issues. In both cases the passions serve as ultimate explanatory concepts devoid of any experiential content; they are expelled, as it were, from the human world proper and made tokens of a purely natural, organic process. On the other hand, as emotion, feelings are robbed of their primordial givenness. What we generally mean by emotion is something more specific and secondary in character; a complex and contingent structure of psychic life rather than a continuously present quality of experience. The realm of feeling has remained the most obscure of phenomenological regions, but this is not to say it should be treated as somehow less 'real' than sensing or willing. The obscurity and confusion attendant on the modern discourse on feeling, rather than indicating intellectual difficulties alone, or their status as secondary 'higher-order' social and mental constructs, betray a general unease with the phenomenal reality of feeling itself (Redd 2001).

Feelings appear *along with* sensed and willed objectivities, but are quite distinct from them. They suffuse the world of spatio-temporal objects and beings with a specific 'colour' or 'tone'. Happiness, melancholy, boredom, excitement, pleasure, and so on are feelings that bathe the world (however it is constituted) and 'blend with a more global bodily sense' (Strasser 1977, 47). Feeling is always a general characteristic of the world of experience. If we are bored *everything* is dull and lifeless, if we are joyful *everything* is fresh and lively: 'The collected contemporaneous state of affairs remains always embedded in the total whole of feeling' (Krueger, quoted in Strasser 1977, 89). The realm of feeling, however, is not a property or an attribute or a predicate of 'world' as an object. The same world, the same objects, the same circumstances, may be felt in turn as sad, joyful, anxious, hopeful, and so on.

We talk of feeling as a tone or colour; it has no predetermined form, no architectural structure. Novalis talked of *moods*, of 'indeterminate sensations' whose 'modulations' were felt as happiness and unhappiness (1997, 107). Nor has it an inherent temporal direction or location; love or grief comes and passes, and returns as the same feeling. There is no causality here and no definite object in view: 'The scream of the anguished, the blush of the embarrassed, the pallor of the terrified, the restlessness of the joyful do not point to something yet to be attained, something which is not emotion; they are themselves emotion. They break forth from the deepest interior of man and stream into the natural and social environment – in a completely planless and unintentional manner' (Strasser 1977, 82).

But where feelings colour the world in general, what might be referred to more precisely as emotions often display intentionality in a conventional sense. Emotions are feelings in relation to a specific object. When we are angry it is 'about something' and usually directed at someone. When we are in love, we love someone in particular. But the 'scope' of emotion can vary a great deal. Modern romantic love, for example, defines our relation to another person in every circumstance and in relation to every particular characteristic of the person; we love not merely some particularly lovable characteristics of the person, but the person as an individual. And love may be thought of as a feeling in relation to a person rather than in relation to the world in general. Guilt may, equally, have a broad range of reference as, for example, sharing in a collective sense of responsibility for a war and its atrocities, but may also be particularized in extremely narrow and often surprising ways. We are irresistibly drawn to the conclusion, which is the founding assumption of the 'natural attitude' in relation to feeling, that emotions are the objective causes of feelings. We are happy because we are in love; we are depressed because of thwarted ambitions or disappointed hopes.

To list and classify emotions is rather like naming colours; it is a question not of organizing a pre-existing field, so much as of coming to distinguish and recognize ever finer gradations and differences. The best psychologists of feeling, that is to say the best novelists, are the most sensitive to such fine distinctions. Proust, for example, fills an entire volume with the seemingly endless variations and fine shadings of jealousy; or Albert Cohen, in his remarkable *Belle de Seigneur*, writes voluminously and no less precisely on the inner development of boredom.

Prior to their differentiation as specific and socially meaningful psychic contents, therefore, it is important to grasp the more general phenomenological standpoint implied in any such approach. Of course, just as we can focus not on sensing as such but only on particular acts of sensing, so feeling, however vague, indeterminate, or difficult to characterize, appears for us always as a particular feeling act and not as 'feeling as such'. We can, nonetheless, in an appropriate historical context, gain some insight into the more general phenomenal characteristics of feeling and its transformation through the emergence and development of modernity.

In the modern period, feeling, like sensing and willing, remains utterly impenetrable in its original givenness; as Ricoeur nicely remarks, 'beyond all representation affectivity remains unreachable and really incomprehensible. In a general way, affectivity is the non-transparent aspect of the Cogito' (1966, 86). Feelings simply arise and subside as waves of happiness, boredom, affection, anger, and so on. Feeling continually colours every act of sensing and willing with its peculiar quality. Feeling is ever present; it is given *with* sensing and willing and may also be a specific focus of attention. Just as one cannot will a specific sense impression, one cannot will a feeling. Feeling is involuntary. Although it seems to come to us from *within*, it remains radically outside our control. In feeling we always feel the presence of something alien, something other than ourselves. Feeling takes hold of us; it moves us. As distinct from willing, which takes possession of what it lacks, feelings possess us; they flow through us, and carry us along. Feeling sweeps through the body in quite a different way, therefore, to desire, which is essentially related to willing. In an older, and striking, vocabulary, feeling is first of all passion in the sense of *suffering*; the passion of Christ is his absolute passivity and receptiveness to his earthly fate.

Of course we can, and do, instigate specific feelings by various means thought to be capable of provoking them. Sombre music, solemn ritual, whispered voices, and saddened looks at a funeral *may* be accompanied by a feeling of grief; but if we do feel grief on such an occasion it always comes to us of its own accord and not at our instruction. Similarly intense anger, love, jealousy and so on have the character of 'welling up' spontaneously and breaking into the closed world of the self and shattering its coherence. Feelings may be suppressed or 'managed' in some way, but they cannot be summoned at will.

In the early modern period feeling was mobile, open, and public. Daily life, it seems, was marked by strong and rapidly oscillating emotions. Violence was commonplace (Huizinga 1955), people were quick to anger, driven by fear and hatred, and often appeared indifferent to the suffering of others (Naphy and Roberts 1997). These are aspects also of the greatest literature and drama of the period; one need only think of Marvell, Shakespeare, Cervantes and Rabelais. The whole emotional tone of life was more intense and unpredictable and the most noticeable, but least discussed, aspect of the development of modernity has been a general 'cooling' of the passions. Feeling and emotion always appear in relation to a world and the historical transformation of the world is accompanied by the emergence of new feelings and the passing away of old ones. Compunction, acedia, and fury slip beneath the horizon of feeling; romantic love flares into life, melancholy appears and in its turn gives way to depression. A critical psychology of feeling emerged as an important aspect of the philosophical programme of phenomenology from the outset (Husserl 1977; Dilthey 1977) and developed in significant ways during the interwar period (Reymert 1967; Kockelmans 1987). These promising developments were subsequently eclipsed by the rise of behaviorism and the more reductive forms of cognitive science. A phenomenologically inspired cultural history of feeling is now overdue (Reddy 2001).

Phenomenology and sociology come together in a critical historical account of experience as a complex and changing manifold. They both seek to clarify the character of modern society through new ways of grasping and understanding its experience as a process of embodiment. Embodiment is prior, but gives rise to, the logical and practical dualities that have structured the natural attitude of modernity. To grasp modernity as a historical phenomenon means to recover the sense in which the natural attitude is inscribed in the body, and the sense in which the process of embodiment itself constitutes that attitude.

6

Equivocations: Modern Trinitarian Conundrums

> Anyone who has a lively intuition of these three (memory, understanding, and love) ... has thereby found the image of that supreme trinity.
>
> Augustine, *The Trinity*

> Humanity's indispensable demand for pure and absolute knowledge (and what is inseparably one with that, its demand for pure and absolute valuing and willing).
>
> Husserl, 'Philosophy as a Rigorous Science'

> Man projected his three 'inner facts', that in which he believed more firmly than in anything else, will, spirit, ego, outside himself.
>
> Nietzsche, *Twilight of the Idols*

The embodiment of modernity did not result in a unified experience of the world or of the self. In modern society a variety of irreducibly distinct ontological regions with their characteristic phenomena emerged and were institutionalized. Furthermore, although modernity above all bestowed value on what was new, not everything in modern society was novel. In fact a vast collection of premodern forms either remained or were deliberately reintroduced as 'traditions' of one sort or another. Nonetheless, the complexity of the phenomenological map of modern experience may be reduced without serious distortion by focusing, in the first instance, on major developments within an exclusively modern framework, and by following the immanent 'logic' of the qualitatively distinct ontological zones of experience outlined in the previous chapter. This procedure might be seen as a simplified and free adaptation of Dilthey's pioneering studies.

Phenomenological investigations suggest that sensing, willing, and feeling are constituted as primary and given data of modern experience. Sociological studies insist (rightly) in viewing these regional ontologies in a broader historical context in relation to which their significance becomes contingent. Laying aside issues of method for the moment, some further insights may be gained by internal investigations of each of these regions. That is, rather than use historical sociology to relativize or even deconstruct phenomenological accounts of primordial experience, historical-sociological studies can be exploited to fill out these phenomenal forms with a rich and distinctive content. Sensing, willing, and feeling become points of entry for a phenomenological sociology of modern experience; each opens on to a specific and complete *world* that can be grasped internally in terms of its own specific characteristics.

Implicit phenomenological sociology, that is, grasps modern experience in terms of three quite different orders of phenomena. Each order is characterized by a specific *quality* of experience that is given in a distinctive way. We can gain insight into sensing only *as* sensing, willing *as* willing, and feeling *as* feeling; all theoretical system-building that seeks to grasp one in terms of the other and all in terms of some more 'fundamental' *concept* obscures the reality in which our vital interests are rooted. Properly grasped, these distinctions become points of departure for the exploration of the distinctive *worlds* of modernity. An indeterminate series of trinities emerge as parallel constituting unities of these worlds, which may be characterized in terms of, for example:

- regulative principle (reason/striving/pleasure)
- ideal form (thing/self/other)
- substantial unity (body/soul/spirit)
- meaningful coherence (explanation/understanding/interpretation)
- meaningless incoherence (contradiction/paradox/mystery)
- perfections (truth/authenticity/faith)
- social sphere (circulation/production/consumption)
- goods (commodity/gift/given)
- means of reference (sign/symbol/trace)
- articulation (science/art/religion)

and so on. The following will serve here as their most general level of articulation:

- modality of appearance (*representation/presentation/presence*).

Each differentiated social and spiritual world contains its own vision of the present; and each ontological region advances exclusive claims to being *essentially* modern and, therefore, distinguishes itself both from the premodern and from other 'illusory' conceptions of contemporary experience. Modern experience is trinitarian, that is to say, not in the historic theological sense of being three *in* one but, rather, in a radical separation of mutually incompatible experiences. Each region elaborates its own distinctive forms and modes of articulation and self-understanding, and eventually runs up against insurmountable obstacles to its further development, ending in indistinction.

The trinitarian character of modern experience may be characterized in terms of the leading philosophical positions that emerged with each; positions due, in turn, to Descartes, Leibniz, and Spinoza. All embrace modernity in grasping reality in terms of human autonomy, but each develops this theme in a particular manner. Descartes conceives the sensory world in terms of the point mass and develops a geometrical representation of reality in which reason operates as an immanent regulative principle that it is the task of philosophy to bring to self-consciousness. Leibniz is the philosopher of presentation and of willing; the monad is the enclosed, individuated soul of modernity, defined through immanence of growth, development, and the law of sufficient reason; an indwelling *vis inertia* rather than an external force. And Spinoza takes his point of departure in the simple presence of substance; experienced immediately in the passive receptivity of the subject for feeling.

Representation

Descartes states the predicament of modernity with admirable clarity: in *The World*, written around 1630, he remarks that 'although everyone is commonly convinced that the ideas we have in our mind are really similar to the objects from which they proceed, nevertheless I cannot see any reason which assures me that this is so' (1985, 2, 81). Sensations are like words which 'bear no resemblance to the things they signify, and yet they make us think of these things ... Now if words, which signify nothing except by human convention, suffice to make us think of things to which they have no resemblance, then why could nature not also have established some sign which would make us have the sensation of light, even if the sign contained nothing in itself which is similar to this sensation?' (1985, 2, 82).

Things

It is difficult for us now to recover the sense of symbolic interrelatedness within which things used to appear; the sensuous tip of a vast non-material reality. For modern society the thing stands on its own; indeed, reality is first of all a collection of things; an enormous still-life. The *thingness* of the thing is now taken for granted but, just because of this familiarity, its distinguishing criteria require examination. The thing is an empirical individual. While, in principle, it is never possible to isolate physical processes and interrelations so as to observe, standing out from a background flux of appearances, an object which is self-subsistent and remains unchanging, this ideal is the model that we continually apply to reality and through which we experience all externality. Reality seems to fall 'naturally' into just such observable entities; bounded in space and continuous in time. The ideal object is absolute and non-reactive, but we also know that, in fact, all things are subject to change, and to that extent are not constituted as 'things' at all. But this knowledge does nothing to undermine our practical experience of the world as composed of so many different things; we persist in viewing reality as 'the unity of the collection of something manifold into a representation of unity' (Heidegger 1967, 205).

The founders of modern thought were well aware of the novelty and radical implications of this world. By ceding being to things and, at the same time, withdrawing things to some remote region that could not be assumed to be identical with their representations, they created both the necessity and the possibility for the modern world of knowledge; a doubtful interpretive framework for the recovery of the world lost to immediacy.

We also suppose that things exist 'for themselves'; they do not, as they did within the medieval Christian-Platonic world view, *depend* on anything else. The characteristics of the thing became gradually simplified and clarified. Emile Meyerson, whose work remains fundamental to any adequate understanding of the character of modern scientific thought, insists that both for our everyday unreflective attitude to the world and for the emergence and development of scientific theories of reality we require 'an unshakeable faith in the existence of things' (1989, 21). And the thing can never be found in sensation: 'what distinguishes the thing from the sensation is that it is less fleeting, more *permanent*; but here again the theoretical being surpasses the thing of common sense, for it is considered to be immutable: energy, material mass, the atom, the electron are absolutely constant, eternal, whereas all that we perceive directly is, without exception, subject to the influence of time' (1989, 25).

Modern thought, thus, emerges primarily through an intensive and ultimately unsatisfactory reflection on the nature of thingness; and, first of all, thingness as *body*. But what is body? The beginning of modern thought is the coming into being of a new conception of body as the philosophical clarification of all experience of the world. In the pioneering works of Hobbes, Descartes, and Spinoza body plays a central role. In different ways their writings strip the body of its symbolism, its powers of reference, and its participation in a complex and immediately meaningful world that included human reality within it. In stark contrast both to the religious symbolism of the medieval world and, interestingly, to the animated cosmos of the Renaissance they advanced a view of body as simple material being that exists in itself. But we cannot experience body in its simplified and essential form, and to grasp its inert thingness we have to conceptualize it through the mind emptied of superstition.

The body as the representation of reality, and the representation of body, are condensed in the thing. To grasp the world as the thingness of the thing is the first radically modern conception of reality. And, though it is announced as a determined and principled monism, the notion of the thing, of body, involves the simultaneous application of two quite separate defining criteria; an elision that temporarily suppresses rather than overcomes a fatal dualism. Body is matter and can be grasped only in relation to what is non-body; that is both to *mind* and to *space*.

Body/mind

Descartes is associated with the categorical separation of body and mind that, in retrospect, is viewed as foundational to the entire project of modernity. The separation of reality into *res extensa* and *res cogitans* was not, he claimed, a voluntary conceptualization but a distinction which forces itself upon our attention as soon as we divest ourselves of false ideas and the traditions of premodern thought. So vital is this difference, not merely to the development of clear and distinct ideas on any subject, but to the right conduct of life and the ordering of society, that Descartes insists that it is the *only*, and not simply the most important, distinction given to us in a primordial sense. Spatial extension and immediate subjectivity define the two existing domains into which reality falls.

Body is here *defined* as extension; body and space are identical. There can be no body without space and space must be entirely 'filled out' by body; extension and body are one and the same. Descartes's insistence upon this point, an insistence that stemmed from his rigour and his philosophical ambition, also betray a lingering commitment to premodern modes of conceptualization, and led him to reject the possibility of 'empty' space. His followers thus became drawn into a prolonged and intensive dispute with Newtonians; a dispute which helped to shape the emergence of both an experimental/empirical and a rational/theoretical tradition in modern science (Shapin and Schaffer 1985).

Body/space

For Hobbes, on the other hand, our elementary notion of body is given as something related to, but distinct from, space. Hobbes argues that 'from feigning the world to be annihilated' (1840, 91) we can see that 'space is the phantasm of a thing existing without the mind simply' (1840, 94), and that 'body is that, which having no dependence upon our thought, is coincident or coextended with some part of space' (1840, 102).

Having imagined all things to be annihilated, body can be reintroduced into an empty universe, if not with divine foreknowledge of its ultimate nature, then at least with God-like simplicity and according to comprehensible principles. Reason, thus, destroys the world in order to comprehend it. It reconstructs from nothing, according to its own immanent laws, a model of the universe. This process, as it is elaborated and refined, does not so much mirror nature directly as simulate, in its own abstract space, the sensory effects to which real but unimaginable bodies give rise. Body 'in itself' remains unknown, but can be reconstructed, beginning at its simplest level as 'that which having no dependence upon our thought, is coincident or coextended with some part of space (1840, 102). And as 'being without the mind', body is conceived by the mind to be that which lies outside itself; it is the radically unthought, the objective.

Space/mind

It was Pierre Gassendi, rather than Descartes or Hobbes, who proved to be most influential in establishing the plausibility of the notion of an 'immense space existing before God created the world ... immobile ... incorporeal ... uncreated and independent of God' (Randles 1999, 126). An 'imaginary space' into which objects had been introduced.

Gassendi urges the reader to 'allow your thought to wander beyond this world to view another world – a wholly new one which I shall bring into being before your mind in imaginary spaces' (1999, 90). Into this space he introduces 'a real, perfectly solid body which uniformly fills the entire length, breadth and depth of this huge space in the midst of which we have brought our mind to rest' (1999, 91). He then differentiates body according to all possible forms, sizes and motions and from this recovers the world with which he began; an imaginary procedure through which the minimal and essential characteristics of matter can clearly be viewed.

Whatever their differences in method and assumptions, both empiricist and rationalist reconstructions began by acknowledging the muteness of body. And both traditions sought, not so much to speak on its behalf, as to create an entirely new language through which a world is made to reappear according to immanent laws; laws which have now been appropriated and attached to the human realm in spite of the unpromising truth that nature was unknowable, insignificant and detached from all human immediacy.

These radical thought experiments – the immediate descendants of the imaginative Renaissance 'flight' above the world to be found in Cyrano de Bergerac, Robert Burton, Johannes Kepler and many others – with their bold annihilation of all aspects of actual experience of an external reality sought to establish a clear starting point for scientific reasoning. At the same time these philosophical reflections on 'thingness' fed the development of a descriptive and empirical account of nature. For both traditions, the unresolved antithesis between, on the one hand, body and space, and, on the other, body and mind, played a fundamental role in developing scientific ideas. If both body and space, and body and mind, were radically distinct then it became (psychologically if not logically) almost irresistible to equate mind and space as 'non-body'. It thus became plausible to 'think' space as the *logical* structure of nature and, equally, to analyse the mind geometrically as 'mental' space (Young 1994). Many of the characteristic features, and especially the characteristic difficulties, of the modern scientific traditions in relation both to nature and to human experience, can be traced to this implicit but unfounded identification.

Separation

The modern representation of reality as 'things-in-space,' involving a radical separation of body from space and body from mind, finds its earliest and most striking development in still-life painting. Here, rather than in philosophical reflection or scientific investigation, a space of representation is defined in a new way.

After a long period of neglect, European still-life painting, which became established in a number of centres around 1600, is now recognized as an important and innovative pictorial form (Schneider 1999; Ebert-Schifferer 1998; Bryson 1990). Recent reappraisals, particularly of Dutch seventeenth-century works, have placed this tradition in a broader context of emerging modernity. It has been argued that still-life, far from being tied to earlier symbolic forms or to merely decorative schemes, should be viewed as an art that was 'the most philosophical of its day' (Segal 1988, 31). Still-life is significant, above all, in the uncompromising fashion in which it represented the world objectively, and the object in its self-sufficient concreteness.

Early Spanish still-life succeeds more than any other in isolating the single object and in depicting it in its self-subsisting objectivity. Where Dutch painting was to invest light with a certain metaphysical value as space, Juan Sanchez Cotán and Francisco Zurbarán focused light on the singular object, picking it out as if by a theatrical spotlight: 'isolating objects against their background of solemn darkness and revealing their hallucinating presence' (Sterling 1981, 94; Jordan 1985). Cotán and Zurbarán succeed in isolating the singular body-in-space; body glows against a black impenetrable background. There is a cosmological geometry in Juan Sanchez Cotán's harmonious compositions; works which are 'exercises in renunciation of normal human priorities' (Bryson 1990, 630). He focuses the viewer's gaze on the absolute singularity of contingent and valueless objects that, in spite of the monastic context of their composition, adumbrates a wholly secular modern objectivism.

In isolating familiar objects in space, torn from their domestic or natural context, they become unfamiliar and functionless; at the same time they acquire the dignity of a universal objectivity. Seventeenth-century Dutch paintings feature 'the thousand objects of everyday life' (Barthes 1982, 63); each object shown in its particularity is 'never privileged; it is merely there'. Every object has 'the detachment and the density of Dutch cheeses: round, waxed, prehensible'; it is 'the triumph of an entirely self-sufficient nominalism' (1982, 64).

In the world of the still-life, fundamental materiality comes into prominence in a new way. Just because paintings depict objects of little value, their value as representational objects becomes more evident; and just because the regular fate of such things is to be cut up, shredded, and cooked, the preservation of their visual form eternalizes their unique space-filling substantiality.

Cotán pays attention to detail. The outer cabbage leaves curl back as if anticipating the process of decay. Reduction of the momentary, contingent state of the object to its visual image, however, renders permanent this precise degree of curl in the leaf. A moment of transition becomes fixed; the object becomes absolute and in being rendered absolute becomes cosmologically remote, inaccessible, uncanny. The decontextualization of objects and their representation primarily as *things* simultaneously transform the human subject into a 'point of view'; an all-seeing God-like eye.

Painting gains permanence in return for the loss of sensible qualities. The flowers in a still-life do not have any aroma, but they do not wither. This simple observation, already made by Jan Breughel, remains fundamental to any understanding of the tradition of still-life painting. Even vanitas still-life paintings, which have so frequently been taken to represent the transience of all earthly life and a moral injunction to look to higher things, draw attention to the triumph of the artist *over* death (Chong and Kloek 1999). Surviving seventeenth-century texts suggest, in fact, that non-symbolic interpretation of still-life was commonplace. Contemporary commentaries frequently value paintings 'for their ability to preserve reality with a permanence that defies death' (Chong and Kloek 1999, 14), and there is little evidence that the popular emblem books, such as the *Sinnenpopen* of Roger Vischer or the collection of proverbial sayings and iconologies of Jacob Cats, were widely used to interpret still-life.

Qualities

Descartes's philosophy aimed to rid thought of qualities and to construct a model of the world from purely formal geometrical relations. Science, however, in claiming a privileged position as the unique provider of knowledge of nature, had to establish a real connection between any such logical system and the immediate forms of sensuous awareness in which reality appeared to the human subject. A distinction between primary and secondary qualities developed ostensibly to mediate the notion of body in relation to space and the notion of body in relation to mind, and for that reason was to prove decisive to the entire development of modern science. This notion already held a central place in Galileo's conceptions of nature. In a famous passage in *Il Saggiatore*:

> As soon as I think of a material object or a corporeal substance, I immediately feel the need to conceive simultaneously that it is bounded and has this or that shape, that it is big or small in relation to others, that it is in this or that place at a given time, that it moves or stays still, that it does or does not touch another body, and that it is one, few, or many. I cannot separate it from these conditions by any stretch of my imagination. But my mind feels no compulsion to understand as necessary accompaniments that it should be white or red, bitter or sweet, noisy or silent, of sweet or of foul odour. (Galileo 1967, 309)

John Locke subsequently made the distinction between primary and secondary qualities a general feature of the empiricist tradition. Qualities in objects have the power to produce in us certain 'ideas' by which we recognize the object. Primary qualities are 'utterly inseparable from the body, in what state soever it be' where successive subdivision does not deprive the remaining body of these qualities. Division 'can never take away either solidity, extension, figure, or mobility of any body'. Secondary qualities 'in truth are nothing in the objects themselves'. Ideas of primary qualities are 'resemblances', but not of secondary qualities; for them 'there is nothing like our ideas existing in the bodies themselves'.

Locke makes solidity and impenetrability the most fundamental of primary qualities; solidity is suggested from 'grosser bodies' but 'the mind having once got this idea ... considers it, as well as figure, in the minute particles of matter that can exist, and finds it inseparably inherent in body, wherever and however modified' (1975, book ii, ch. iv, section i). In Locke the primary qualities (essential, quantitatively measurable, commonly sensible) 'are utterly inseparable from the body in what estate soever it be', and secondly, in crucial respects are said to resemble their causes: 'their patterns do really exist in the bodies themselves, where in secondary qualities there is nothing like our ideas existing in the bodies themselves'. This view was consistent with Newton's: 'The qualities of bodies of bodies, which admit neither intensification nor remission of degrees, and which are found to belong to all bodies within the reach of our experiments, are to be esteemed the universal qualities of all bodies whatsoever' (1962, vol. II, 398). An appeal to experience of sensing, rather than a rigorous analysis of the conceptual preconditions of our idea of body, was taken to have established extension, shape, hardness, and impenetrability as the primary qualities of bodies.

Both empiricist and rationalist versions of modern naturalism, that is to say, were sustained by the conviction that primary qualities were the 'natural symbols' of the simple bodies that constituted the world and that, in the uniform space of representation, human reason could grasp the operative principles of nature. The world of experience could be analysed into constituent elements in which elementary bodies appeared as localized geometrical points endowed with mass, shape, and motion. And from the continuous interaction of these elementary units, and according to strictly intelligible laws of collision, reaction, combination and so on, a complete 'system-of-the-world' corresponding precisely to our original experience of reality, could be deduced.

The duality of reason

Leibniz, however, in his correspondence with Clark (Newton's mouthpiece in an important debate), makes the following important observation:

> The great foundation of mathematics is the principle of contradiction, or identity, that is, that a proposition cannot be true and false at the same time; and that therefore A is A, and cannot be not A ... But in order to proceed from mathematics to natural philosophy, another principle is requisite, as I have observed in my *Theodicy*: I mean the principle of sufficient reason, viz. That nothing happens without a reason why it should be so, rather than otherwise. (Leibniz and Clark 1956, 15–16)

This strikes at the heart of the project of modernity grasped as a process or *representation* that claimed to be both valid and intelligible. The implicit identification of mind and space apparently allowed reason to bridge the gap between the sensible and the intelligible, but on closer inspection it not only failed to recover what had irrevocably been lost, it could not clarify its own operation within the system of representations.

These antinomies and their concealment under a banner of uniform and universal reason remain the source of a general and still unresolved tension between theoretical and empirical traditions within modern science. As Emile Meyerson long ago argued in his powerful book *Reality and Identity* (which invokes Bergson as well as Leibniz), there remains a fundamental antagonism between the notion of rational science as an abstract model in which can be represented the underlying structure and forces of nature, and an explanatory science which seeks to elucidate observable events in terms of their antecedent causes. 'It is apparent,' he claims, 'that the postulate of causality is in no way identical with that of conformity to law' (1989, 30). 'In fact we only attain laws by violating nature, by isolating more or less artificially a phenomenon from the whole, by checking those influences which would have *falsified* the observation' (1989, 31). The laws are only 'the image of ordering'. Science assimilates cause to law and thus imposes a uniform and abstract empty time on the working of nature.

Thus, he argues, 'the principle of causality is none other than the principle of identity applied to the existence of objects in time' (1989, 43), which amounts to saying 'Things are thus because they were already previously thus', and theoretical statements and hypotheses 'are simple figurative representations, destined to serve as mementoes, to fix ideas' (1989, 52).

Scientific explanation seeks to unite space and body through a principle of conservation. The postulate of the identity of things in time leads to atomic theories; to 'objects of thought, capable of being considered as substances' and yet 'conserved amongst phenomena eternally changing' (1989, 215). 'The strange prestige of the principle of conservation' derives from its useful duality as both a logico-mathematical principle and a physical reality.

This principle implies the annihilation of time and makes space the fundamental explanatory principle of science. In rational mechanics, thus, 'all motions are reversible' (1989, 218). More is involved here than a necessary simplification: 'it is a tendency to transform a relation into a thing in order to see conserved, not only the law, but also the object, and this we know, is the true sense of the causal tendency'. Hence, 'to explain is to explain away' (1989, 222).

The mechanization of the world picture

The regulative principle of reason, Leibniz argued, lost itself in the empty abstraction of space, or the unintelligibility of body. Some of the fiercest philosophical debates of the seventeenth century were concerned with issues that had their roots in this insight. But the modern world view and the experience of the world as modern were only tenuously connected with such reflections. It was, in fact, an unsystematic and unclarified set of assumptions and analogies that came to represent modernity as the 'mechanization of the world picture' (Dijksterhuis 1961; Heidegger 1971).

This did not depend initially upon drawing an analogy between actual machines and the operation of nature, though subsequently modern technology was to provide an important concrete example of the possibility of 'self-regulation' (Mayr 1986; Poovey 1995, 38–9). It depended, rather, upon the linking of two quite distinct ideas; first, the abstraction and simplification in which nature is represented as a system of idealized bodies in a state of constant motion which, through interaction according to simple laws, attains an equilibrium state; and, secondly, the idea of efficient cause as the necessary effect of 'causes' which can be represented as physical processes, above all, collision. The whole operation of this system can be understood in terms of the universal characteristics of bodies – those things which are everywhere fundamentally the same – and some simple rules of interaction.

The contradiction of representation

The most determined efforts to conceive of reality in terms of body ended in contradiction or, rather, they gave rise to a flourishing tradition of empirical science that ignored this contradiction. Not only did the system-of-the-world remain undeduced from the body-in-space, but it required the arbitrary introduction of non-mechanical principles unfounded in the known characteristics of bodies or the geometrical intuitions of space; and, worse, the body itself remained inexplicably 'given' and thoroughly irrational. Thus, all rational reconstruction of a mathematical and logical sort was simply laid over the irrational singularities of nature rather than penetrating to their essential and hidden reality. The formalism of science was, nevertheless, a physical theory; a theory of an analogical kind which hinged on the 'identity' of the physical mass with the mathematical point. A quantity represented as an indifferent point could be entered into the formal system of equations and provide a coherent and systematic representation of observable processes – most notably the free movement of celestial bodies.

This contradiction is rooted in the embodiment of modernity; that is, in the experience of the body as *both* an architectonic plan of nature *and* an obscure heavy mass; as both a recognizable exteriority and a hidden interiority.

Presentation

Whereas representation links objects to other, ultimately identical, objects in an ideal, geometrical space, presentation links subjects to other, non-identical subjects in an ideal, recollected time: 'Time is *inner* space – space is *outer* time,' (Novalis 1997, 136). The elementary unity disclosed in presentation is the self, or soul; formed as a continuous process of striving and self-actualization. Representation is formed as a meaningful 'picture' of exteriority; presentation is the *expression* of an invisible interiority. Representation runs up against the contradiction between law and cause; presentation snares itself in the paradox of communication, the demand of selfhood to both express itself and conceal itself.

Soul

Modern human self-images were derived not only from the traditions of science and rationalism but also from new reflections on the nature of the soul.

A quite distinct tradition developed alongside and occasionally in opposition to that of the mechanical philosophy. This involved not only a shift in focus away from the hard-shelled 'individual' to a more social and relational conception of selfhood, but also a radical recasting of ideas about nature, humanity, and their interconnection (Gusdorf, 1948, 1095; Richards 2002).

The soul is not identical with subjectivity or with mind; nor is it defined as a residual category of the non-material. Where the perspective of body and representation begins with the isolated individual as the point mass from which to reconstruct a geometric model of nature and society, the perspective of soul and presentation begins with an already formed but immature inner world that can be grasped as an incipient process of *striving*. From the first the individual contains all the elements of humanity, and is linked to nature in terms of periodic appetite, and more generally to the world through the extension of itself in terms of intention, purpose, action and the appropriation of goods. The human soul is conceived in terms of its incapacity and inability for independent life; with both its freedom from nature and its dependence on other people as the precondition for that process of self-realization which is peculiarly its own.

This view has its roots in the same Renaissance revaluation of humanity that fed into the development of early modern science and the metaphysical transformation of modernity. In this case, however, modernity finds its roots in neo-Platonism and hermeticism, and in the understanding of nature as a *living* process rather than a pictorial scene. It is, of course, in late-eighteenth- and early-nineteenth-century Romanticism that this understanding of reality reaches its fullest development (Gusdorf 1985; 2002; Richards 2002).

Thus, just as scientific rationalism and metaphysical speculation are fundamental elements in western culture reincarnated in specific forms in each epoch of its development, so Romanticism undergoes a series of collateral transformations. Its specifically modern form, which includes within itself a characteristic revaluation of its own past, is distinguished by a novel topological relation to other fundamental western values. This might be described as a movement towards interiority and infinity. A subjective relation to the world increasingly came to be distinguished from practical life; it became redefined as an interior and private domain, a space extended in terms of personal 'depth'.

Self

Self, as distinct from body, is interiority, duration, freedom, uniqueness, finitude, and striving. The self is not separated from time, in the way body is separated from space, but is assimilated to temporality as an irreversible process of development and becoming. And unlike the self-sufficiency of body, the self experiences its own incompleteness as *desire* for another.

This view owes most, perhaps, to the writings of Jean-Jacques Rousseau, and it is to his distrust of society that the specific form of modern romantic detachment can be traced. It is in Rousseau that romanticism as a continuously present feature of western sensibility is given its decisive modern incarnation as an interior monologue. And, as a result, the movement which, to some extent at least, sought to overcome the scientific detachment of representation, introduced its own, equally isolating form of subjectivism.

In modern society we continually interact with strangers and, even with those we think we know, express ourselves through a series of conventional forms that seem to exist independently of our true feelings. We 'no longer dare seem what we really are' and as others must similarly wear a mask 'we never know with whom we are to deal'. In this regard we cannot help but become conscious of the distance between appearance and reality and justifiably suspect that 'Jealousy, suspicion, fear, coldness, reserve, hatred and fraud lie constantly concealed under the uniform and deceitful veil of politeness' (Rousseau 1973, 6–7). This is the negative side of the need for approbation, which is not, in fact, an aspect of our original social nature but, rather, an artificial desire characteristic of modern society (Starobinski 1988). In daily interaction 'I find only empty appearances of feelings and truth ... I see only ghosts and phantoms that are glimpsed for a moment, only to disappear when you try to lay hold of them. Until now, I have seen many masks, when will I see men's true faces?' (Rousseau 1973).

Rousseau's difficulty, thus, is to find a way of distinguishing between superficial selfishness, which is merely a reflection of modern society's 'web of deceit', and the authentic selfhood which is the soul's free expression. He attempts to solve the problem through two linked strategies. First, he renounced the spurious affections of others and 'sought to break the shackles of opinion and to *do* with courage what seemed to me good, without giving the slightest thought to the judgment of others'. And, secondly, he traced a route back through the 'train of secret emotions' that was his personal history from contemporary self-deception to primordial innocence. He recollects himself, successively reliving all the crucial experiences of his life. So that, while his story is one of misunderstanding and conflict leading to an irretrievable rupture with society, his recollection, up until the moment of his final solitude, reconfirms his essentially social nature and gives him back, and projects upon the world, the identity which his own radical pursuit of happiness has destroyed. Rousseau remains important primarily as the originator of an autobiographical form of literature that is ideally suited to express the peculiar identity of the modern soul; as such it is the most imitated of modern books (Rousseau 1970).

Rousseau's immensely influential writings, for all their inspiring modernity, yet remain in certain important respects conservatively backward-looking. The subjectivity realized in his personal literature holds fast to an essentially outmoded conception of representation. Rousseau, acutely conscious of the doubt which has entered philosophy and science, rediscovers a consoling certainty in inward self-certainty. It is as if the premodern notion of substance, dislodged from its place in nature, had found a new and proper place in which to reside. Rousseau's extreme, even pathological, passivity and love of self-revelation are at one with this metaphysical longing to discover within himself a permanent and incorruptible essence. It is sufficient to unveil this essence, to reveal himself by letting slip the mask of social conventions, for him to become transparent to others and for his honesty to be vindicated in the eyes of the world.

Self-development

Rousseau bared his soul, and bore upon it the marks of rejection and ridicule. His passivity before an unresponsive public, to which he nonetheless submitted his *Confessions* in order that it be accepted and validated, directed him backwards to ever deeper revelations of himself, until he discovered the paradisiacal, original state from which he had been ejected. However, rather than view the formation of a socialized ego as an obscuring veil draped over a primordial subjectivity, it became possible to view authentic selfhood as the future-oriented task of the ego itself. The soul was structured through the assimilation of human culture and expressed through social relations that expressed these internalized values. The self became a task, a duty of actualization imposed upon itself. It was only through a continuous process of assimilation, on the one hand, and expressive action, on the other, that the self realized itself in its inner uniqueness.

The goal of life was conceptualized as *Bildung*, as the formation of character and the cultivation of its values through education and the intimacy of freely chosen personal relations. This became a literary norm as well as a practical moral imperative and, much later, received its authoritative characterization by Wilhelm Dilthey:

> A lawlike development is discerned in the individual's life; each of its levels has intrinsic value and is at the same time the basis for a higher level. Life's dissonances and conflicts appear as necessary transitions to be withstood by the individual on his way towards maturity and harmony. (1985, 336)

Universal norms and cultural ideas are here inflected uniquely in the makeup of the individual, whose life is ordered and ultimately made meaningful in their terms. The task of revealing the self was simultaneously a duty to realize this inwardness, to form and express it in universal terms. The ideal of *Bildung* once again rendered the soul visible, though not transparent, but its authentic value now became a task to achieve, and not a primordial condition that had to be recovered. The soul was thus given a definite content and a certain solidity.

The ideal of *Bildung* as a significant human image was associated particularly with the development of German culture, which embodied this ideal in many of its exemplary characters. Wieland's *Agathon*, Hölderlin's *Hyperion* and, above all, Goethe's *Wilhelm Meister* provided the reader with concrete examples of the unfolding of a 'beautiful soul'. The *Bildungsroman* not only portrayed the formation and development through self-actualization of a central character but was intended also as a means of shaping and cultivating the reader (Norton 1995, 152).

However, even in its definitive incarnation, the *Bildungsroman* revealed itself as an unrealizable ideal. The inner contradictions in the conception of *Bildung* become evident as aesthetic and moral tensions in the novel. In Book Six of *Wilhelm Meister* a lengthy excursus 'Confessions of a Beautiful Soul' not only breaks the narrative unity and perspective of the novel (a formal imperfection to which Schiller unsuccessfully objected), but provides a detached and even ironic commentary on the basic theme of the whole work. Inner freedom and unity of character can be realized in the 'beautiful soul' only through a contemplative withdrawal from society. The harmonious social world, which is presumed to be the externalized counterpart of inner self-determination, in fact does not exist and, as Rousseau had discovered, interferes with the articulation of unity and fullness of character even as an aesthetic ideal. The *Bildungsroman* actualized a vision of selfhood that, in its completeness and perfection, proved incapable of carrying forward the long-term commitment to realism which fuelled the development of the European novel (Moretti 1987).

Aesthetic education

If the ideal of freedom, unity, self-expression and autonomous selfhood appeared to be *only* an aesthetic ideal, realized to the extent to which the individual could maintain an aesthetic distance from the cloudy reality of social life, then aesthetic values, however they were conceived, became central to the entire perspective of the soul. *Bildung*, thus, was associated throughout the second half of the eighteenth century and beyond with the emergence and rapid growth of a new philosophical interest in aesthetics. It might be argued, indeed, that where dynamics had been the science of nature, aesthetics became the science of the soul.

There was, of course, a long tradition of what might be termed practical aesthetics stretching back to antiquity; attempts to define ideal forms for the production of all types of images, including speech. Indeed, aesthetic interests had been fundamental to the Enlightenment, particularly in the work of Shaftesbury and Hutcheson whose work became increasingly influential throughout the eighteenth century. It was Baumgarten's *Theoretical Aesthetics*, however, which shifted the entire focus of interest to the subjective role in the creation of aesthetic value. It was the mode of receiving and appreciating beauty, rather than the formal qualities constituted in the beautiful object itself, which became the central interest. He defined the sphere of aesthetics in terms of both sensory psychology and 'higher' faculties of judgement, and provided an interpretation of the empiricist tradition of psychology that enhanced, rather than undermined, the autonomy of the human subject. His main influence, thus, was in creating the academic discipline of aesthetics as a central philosophical preoccupation.

This tendency reaches its fullest development in Kant, whose entire philosophy represents a deepening of subjectivity. He himself referred to a 'Copernican revolution' in philosophical consciousness and his second and third critiques in particular redefined the soul in terms of an enriched moral and aesthetic content. The autonomy of the soul is there revealed in the disinterested character of its judgements and in its free subordination under universal norms. This attempt to reconcile a principle of inner freedom, which is the source of our understanding, with a universal conception of reason, which is rooted in sensuous nature, is focused on the articulation of judgement as a synthetic faculty of the soul.

The aesthetic brings the soul into prominence; it is a particular kind of *self*-consciousness. Aesthetic judgement is the 'free play of the representative powers in a given representation'; it can refer to nothing else than 'the state of mind in the free play of the Imagination and the Understanding'. The beautiful, therefore, is the soul's self-awareness in the contemplation of an object that is 'free from all constraint or arbitrariness'. And it is, thus, through art rather than through nature that we become most wholly conscious of the synthetic power of the soul. Art, so to speak, freely creates, or recreates, images of a rule governed and humanized world. It expresses through its specific creations, above any particular significance, the human power to create its own world, its liberation from nature and free subordination under a 'second nature' of its own making (Kant 2000).

The soul is infinitely 'deep'; human subjectivity is inexhaustible. Beyond all judgement of beauty, thus, the aesthetic sense of the sublime expresses the soul's boundless interiority. The judgement of the sublime is not linked to any specific object or image; it is 'to be found in a formless object' and is, therefore, 'a like concept of Reason'. The sublime is an ambivalent condition, occasioned by a bewildered and dreadful aspect: 'the point of excess for the imagination ... is like an abyss in which it fears to lose itself' (2000, 107).

The sublime 'must be sought only in the mind of the judging Subject' (2000, 104). And, although in 'the immeasurableness of nature and the incompetence of our faculty for adopting a standard proportionate to the aesthetic estimation of the magnitude of its *realm*, we found our own limitation', this possibility of making such aesthetic judgements reveals a supersensible faculty of the soul 'which has that infinity itself under it as a unit ... and [we] so found in our minds a pre-eminence over nature even in its immeasurability' (2000, 111).

The centrality of aesthetics to modern experience and to the central philosophical and political issue of modernity was taken up by Schiller whose *On the Aesthetic Education of Mankind* immediately became a manifesto for Romanticism. Here the Kantian understanding of aesthetics as mediation between understanding and reason was given a characteristic inflection. For Schiller modern society had become dominated by the principle of utility and the self-sufficiency of reason in which it was expressed: 'Utility is the great idol of our age, to which all powers are in thrall and to which all talent must pay homage' (1967, 7). The representational conception of reason held sway over all others: 'Reason had separated itself off, disentangled itself, as it were, from all matter' (1967, 41). And this separation had stimulated, as a reaction to its soulless abstraction, the cult of immediacy and feeling that had come to prominence with Rousseau. The modern soul was fatally compromised:

> But will such a mind, dissolved as it were into pure intellect and pure contemplation, ever be capable of exchanging the rigorous bonds of logic for the free movement of the poetic faculty, or of grasping the concrete individuality of things with a sense innocent of preconceptions and faithful to the object? (1967, 43)

Schiller's answer is to develop a notion of aesthetic education as a mode of reintegrating the human in a domain of *freedom*. It is in the free activity of the 'play-drive' that human unity and totality is recovered; it is 'play alone, which of all man's states and conditions is the one which makes him whole and unfolds both sides of his nature at once'. Play is both ideal and sensuous and 'man only plays when he is in the fullest sense of the word a human being, and he is only fully a human being when he plays' (1967, 107). It 'sets man free both physically and morally' (1967, 97). The free creation of art provides objects of beauty which, in a similar fashion, provide a union between reason and feeling, between abstraction and sensuous immediacy, and return us to the preconceptual unity of the play-drive from which the two sides of human nature have been differentiated: 'By means of beauty sensuous man is led to form and thought; by means of beauty spiritual man is brought back to matter and restored to the world of sense' (1967, 125).

In Schiller, as later in the influential writings of Lessing, the totalizing power of art embraces the entire experience of life. It is not a purely psychological consolation for the progressive but dehumanizing condition of modernity; it is, rather, the foundation upon which a new and fuller expression of humanity can be actualized in social life. It is not the modality of individuated *Bildung* so much as the beginnings of a new form of collective life. The infinite depth of inwardness is transformed into an unlimited possibility for 'total freedom' and the foundation of radical claims for human happiness.

The musical sublime

Music, even more than painting or poetry, became the art that most adequately exemplified this new enlarged conception of aesthetics. Towards the end of the eighteenth century music asserted its autonomy from textual, ritual, and historical contexts. Instrumental music became, for the first time in western society, the highest and purest form of musical art and, at the same time, established itself as the Romantic art above all others (Dahlhaus 1989; Neubauer 1986; Chua 1999).

Familiarity with the modern development of instrumental music makes it difficult to recover the shock of its originality, which has the same revelatory power for the sphere of presentation as the still-life had for representation. What could music freed from textual and ritual context 'mean'? While the emotive power of music had long been recognized, its specific meaning had always been tied to an extramusical context. Music was a means of heightening or dramatizing a social practice that was conceivable (and frequently enacted) without 'accompaniment'.

In the early modern period, of course, music had already played a key role as an important cultural focus for the baroque age. This is nowhere more evident than in the spectacle of the opera, which might be viewed as a musical *Wunderkammer*. Music was 'opened as never before to the public – as the expression *par excellence*, of political or religious authority' (Bianconi 1987, 28). Opera was the first modern music and its reliance on sung text should not mislead; it was primarily and, in its earliest forms in Monteverdi, already an absolute music. The sung voice of opera is properly grasped as a musical instrument, rather than a medium for communicating words: 'Voice connects its bearers and hearers to ordinarily supersensible realities' (Tomlinson 1999, 4).

Throughout the eighteenth century instrumental music had been devalued just because of its mimetic ineptitude. But the emergence of music as autonomous art, and aesthetic reflection as the philosophy of the subject, gave a new dignity and significance to music. Indeed music came to be viewed as a uniquely privileged expression of the otherwise hidden world of subjectivity. From about 1800 instrumental music became a *sui generis* art form whose meaning was inherent in the pure relationalism of sonority rather than any contextual or mimetic function: 'Now, the entire effect of music ... consists in accompanying and making perceptible the inner movements of the spirit analogously through outer ones' (Rosen 1999, 127). Music, that is to say, came to itself as a modality of human self-expression; it was not to be grasped in terms of a theory of representation other than as the 'natural symbol' of feelings and emotions. Music was graspable as expressive immediacy. The history of music was suddenly revealed as a long preparation for human autonomy, an art in waiting, so to speak, for the moment when human selfhood broke free of nature and God and found its own voice; a musical voice. There was something primordial in music; not only could it express the specific character of modern experience, in its most profound and moving passages it revealed, as it were at a deeper and more historic level, the original character of humanity. The history of the subject, and not merely its contemporary appearance, provided the inexhaustible depths of musical exploration. This view leant heavily on the writings of Rousseau, particularly on his *Origins of Language* rather than his explicitly musical texts. The original unity of humanity and nature, a unity shattered by the artificial construction of society and the setting in motion of its corrupting images, was invoked and even regained in the experience of musical purity. Primordial self-presence, once felt directly in every aspect of life, in speech, in sense, in movement, in the very form of existence, had been broken and fragmented; but in music there resided a residual form of this unity, a vital connection to the original character of humanity.

This view of music was taken up not only within idealist philosophy which drew its inspiration from the Romantic movement – most notably in Schelling's view of music as 'pure form' – but in the first critics of Romanticism, including

Hegel for whom music was the 'abstract interiority of pure sound' (Goehr 1992, 154) and Kierkegaard who regarded music as immediate sensuousness. More recently it finds a spokesman in Adorno, for whom the 'incorporeity of music' helps clarify its specific quality as a form springing directly 'from the pure realm of the soul, free of the world of things' (1999, 112). It is no 'aesthetic illusion', 'no image for an other, but a spiritual entity in its own right that does not point *a priori* to something else' (1999, 108). And in the remarkable work of Ernst Bloch absolute music is consecrated as the carrier of the utopian vision in western culture (Bloch 2000).

Desire

The internal world of the soul is conscious of its own insufficiency. Infinite depth, like infinite extension, is acosmic; that is to say, the character of inwardness as selfhood cannot be grasped as a totality or structure. Acosmic relations can only be grasped as a continuing process. But, whereas the universal laws held to govern the interaction of objects in the exterior world are indifferent to time and space, universal interiority is grasped as a unique process of self-expression, which is sensitive to both temporal and spatial displacement. The where and, above all, the when of selfhood is a fundamental aspect of its constitution. And while movement of body through space is given with the very notion of body, as *inertia*, all interior self-development is experienced as *striving*.

All forms of self-development seek validation through adequate forms of expression; the self, in its essential character as selfhood, is compelled to *present* itself. The self is self-presentation. The Romantics understood this and made it central to their narrative of modernity. The youthful hero of the *Bildungsroman* begins in melancholic self-enclosure; like Wilhelm Meister, 'shut up within himself' (Goethe 1982, vol. 1, 63). Typically he is torn from lethargy by restless longings that stem from soulful wants rather than bodily needs: 'At one time he wished for a horse, at another for wings … A secret fire was gliding through his veins; objects distinct and indistinct alternated within his soul, and awoke unspeakable desire' (1982, vol. 1, 208). He 'suffered and loved' his unquiet soul, once roused, putting beyond his reach 'mere corporeal cheerfulness' (1982, vol. 1, 312).

All striving, all desire, is really a longing of the self for the self. As distinct from the spatial perspective of representation, in which the self is conceived as a pre-existing subject and the foundation of intentional action, the self, in the presentational perspective, appears as a continuous process of self-expression. Desire is a self-expression of incompleteness. It is because the self cannot fully form itself inwardly that it is stirred by desire; and expresses its incompleteness as the longing for something beyond itself. Desire is the want of something, an absence and emptiness that appears, first of all, as restless melancholy.

Hegel, though he rejected the Romanticism of much post-Kantian idealist philosophy, expresses very clearly this infatuation with the self as the inexhaustible depth of the soul. For Hegel 'self-consciousness is *Desire* in general' (1977, 105) and desire he takes to be a striving towards, and expression of, inner unity.

But for Hegel self-consciousness is wholly itself only when it exists for another self-consciousness. He discusses this relation in a famous passage in the *Phenomenology of Spirit* as the dialectic of lordship and bondage, in which the formal conditions of self consciousness are clothed in a historical narrative of the emergence of a specific social relation. This allows a somewhat clearer statement of the process of emerging self-consciousness as the infinite expansion of the interior world: 'Self-consciousness is, to begin with, simple being-for-itself, self-equal through the exclusion from itself of everything else. For it, its essence and absolute object is "I"; and in this immediacy, or in this (mere) being, of its being-for-itself, it is an *individual*. What is "other" for it is an unessential, negatively characterized object' (1977, 113).

But this 'other' is a similarly self-conscious being: 'Each is indeed certain of its own self, but not of the other, and therefore its own self-certainty still has no truth.' Self-consciousness develops into a higher form in an act of mutual self-recognition. Above all, thus, desire is focused on the desire of another. Rousseau's distrust of society is transformed into the necessary condition for the emergence of a fully human being. But this cannot be done by fiat; trust and mutuality cannot replace suspicion and false objectivity of the other as a result of philosophical argument. The discourse that can bring about reconciliation and establish authenticity is the social process of differentiation and conflict through which mutual self-recognition in fact takes place and which Hegel's dialectic seeks to follow.

The conception of humanness as the expression of self-consciousness and particularly of rational self-consciousness was, so to speak, tagged on to the Enlightenment project and announced as a living reality. Hegel became the 'official' philosopher of modernity and his name was appealed to in justification of the status quo; a secular authority for an authoritarian state and an intellectual counterweight to the radical implications of Romanticism.

Nature

Just as, for any view of reality as a system of representation, the human subject appears as a particular kind of 'object' endowed with reason, so, for the world of presentation, nature appears as a particular kind of 'subject'. The Romantics, of course, were not simply sensitive to the beauty and terror of nature; many of them were scientifically trained, and the most 'soulful' insisted that an understanding of nature was fundamental to human self-knowledge as well as practical life. Novalis, for example, describes two paths which together lead to authentic human understanding:

> The first step is to gaze into the Interior – secluding contemplation of oneself. Whoever remains here has attained only half. The second step must be to actively gaze outward, in steady, spontaneous observation of the outer world. (1989, 28)

For Novalis, indeed, life's mission is not simple individual *Bildung* but more generally 'cultivating the earth'. Significantly, in fact, the Romantics accused Newtonian science of an unrealistic representation of nature; that the essential unity and totality of nature were misrepresented as a mechanical system, and that a valid approach to a *scientific* understanding of the world required a philosophical and emotional transformation. Romanticism was not a rejection of scientific method, but an attempt to harness it to the broader understanding of nature as life, which they espoused (Gusdorf 1985; Richards 2002; Starobinski 2003).

The fundamental starting point for any 'soulful' conception of nature was the idea of the formative and shaping power of life; a shaping power that was directly felt in human experience and flowed into the extraordinary variety of other living forms. The phenomena of growth, reproduction, adaptation, and form were the fundamental issues for any such science. New sciences of biology and chemistry became the central ground upon which such concepts were explicated and tested. The science of mechanics, dealing with inert matter, could never properly articulate the simplest phenomena of life which were, in fact, inherently more comprehensible as we directly experienced its most complex and developed forms. This was a properly intuitive science; but intuition had been fundamental also to the first scientific revolution, albeit it in a disguised manner (Lenoir 1982; Larson 1994; Müller-Sievers 1997).

Thus Kant, for example, shifted the notion of space from being an 'absolute true and mathematical' description of empirical extension to being a property of the soul, an essentially inner space of intuition without which 'nature' could not be conceptualized in terms of mechanical forces at all. The intuition of space was prior to and an *a priori* condition of nature as conceived within the 'body' perspective. This insight prompted a rapid development of both a new philosophical approach to nature, the *Naturphilosophie* of Schelling, and new research traditions within the sciences that concentrated particularly on the diverse manifestations of life.

Schelling's attempt to provide a general framework for such an approach focused on an attempt to 'dematerialize' the body perspective and render its insights in terms of the interaction of non-material 'forces' of attraction and repulsion. Thus, where Newton's mechanistic critics had accused him of entertaining hypotheses of an occult type to 'explain' his laws of gravitation, Schelling argued that he had failed to look sufficiently beneath the phenomena to grasp the totality of nature as an interplay of just such forces: 'Matter and bodies,' he argued, 'are themselves nothing but products of opposing forces, or rather, are themselves nothing else but these forces' (Schelling 1988, 156). Body was not simply the indifferent carrier of forces but dissolved into these forces such that 'attractive and repulsive forces constitute the *essence* of matter itself' (1988, 165). Schelling felt that new studies of electricity provided data irreducible to mechanism, and encouraged the belief that nature as a totality was composed of universal forces. The 'swift evanescence of electrical phenomena' was one of the 'life forces' that formed and animated nature.

Schelling directly inspired a considerable shift in the focus and character of much scientific work, even among those who rejected his speculative philosophy. Some, of course, such as Oken and Blumenbach, embraced his entire system. Blumenbach, thus, attempted to unify the life sciences under a concept of *Bildungstrieb* (life force); which 'is not born of matter but is a life force expressed by the indomitable reality of the organisation of matter itself. The organisation cannot thereafter be broken down into its material elements, and thus it cannot be explained in physical, mechanical, or chemical terms' (Poggi and Bossi 1994, 104). Indeed, following Schelling's dictum that 'Nature should be Mind made visible', the 'architectural structure' of the organism is here understood as a spatial representation or manifestation of *Bildungstrieb*.

This whole approach additionally had been encouraged in Germany by the authority of Goethe, at once the most virulent and least well-understood critic of Newtonian science (Amrine et al. 1987; Bell 1994). Goethe's early education included works in the alchemical and hermetic tradition 'in which nature, though perhaps in fantastical fashion, is represented in a beautiful combination ... [we] were more delighted with these secrets than we could have been at their elucidation' (1971, 370–1). This early mysticism coloured his many-sided development such that his diverse activities expressed an inner unity; a conception of life brought out with striking clarity by Dilthey in his *Poetry and Experience*, as a continuous liberation of *images*. He, thus, felt the inadequacy of an analytic and empirical tradition that isolated sensations and objects from each other and from the subject:

> it seemed strange to me that I had to tear asunder, isolate, and, as it were, destroy, those operations of the mind which I had performed with the greatest ease from my youth upward, and this in order to see into the right use of them. (1971, 265)

Goethe claimed that nature as a whole could be grasped morphologically and that, through appropriately receptive viewing, it revealed its 'primordial phenomena' (1989, 284). During his travels in Italy Goethe became convinced that the diversity of plant forms could be understood as a series of transformations of a single 'supersensuous plant type'. The primordial plant form, *Urpflanz*, is realized in the leaf, from which all other plant structures are derived: 'everything is leaf, and through this simplicity the greatest diversity becomes possible' (1989, 7). Indeed, 'if all plants were not molded on one pattern, how could I recognize that they are plants?' (1989, 14). Thus, 'metamorphosis is the key to the whole alphabet of nature' (1989, 13).

Thus, we find that 'everything is ceaseless flux' (1989, 23). To grasp these forms, not just in themselves but as expressions of the unity and wholeness of nature, requires that we remain 'as flexible and pliable as the example she herself provides' (1989, 26). There is no 'natural system' of forms or 'system' in nature; nature rather '*is* life and its progress from an unknown center toward an unknowable goal' (1989, 116). His notion of metamorphosis, thus, does not lead to a deductive and systematic knowledge, but reveals the true heart of nature as a continuous flux in which 'nothing is unconnected with the whole'.

The paradox of presentation

The identity of nature, as, similarly, the self-identity of the individual human being, strives for expression and actualization in an authentic form. The self is identified both with absolute interior freedom and with self-determination through self-expression. As authentic selfhood, however, pure interiority must seek expression in external forms, which binds it to the limiting and illusory world of representations. At the same time selfhood cannot remain quiescently within the body as empty possibility; its being requires presentation. The self, thus, is driven to express itself in inauthentic forms. It can neither express itself authentically, nor resist expressing itself inauthentically. Selfhood in the modern era, as Kierkegaard recognized, is a paradox; it is both intersubjective and incommunicable.

Presence

For modernity presence was, first of all, identified with the unreality of everything transcendental in a religious or metaphysical sense. It was viewed as something radically outside experience and belonging fantastically to the past; that is to say, it was abolished. However, as modernity developed its own reality and constituted itself as an autonomous world, everything transcendental flowed back towards immediacy and broke into mundane existence, suffusing it with mystery. Presence thus becomes simply what is, anything that is 'there', and is no longer to be thought as something spiritual in an older sense. Modernity makes presence present in a new way; once again the spirit is made *flesh* (Henry 2002).

Immediacy

Husserl's phenomenology may, in fact, be viewed both as the denial of *metaphysical* presence and as the affirmation of *self*-presence. This is just another way of expressing the dictum that 'consciousness is always consciousness of something'; and its corollary that consciousness cannot be its own object. Consciousness continually withdraws from itself and hides in contingent and partial objectivities. This reticence, however, is by no means an infinite regress and comes to rest in the effortless self-certainty of the living person; that is in the real *presence* of human subjectivity that founds and makes itself felt in the assurance of apodictic truth. A central theme in the development of Husserl's thought, and of subsequent phenomenological reflection, has focused on the status of this subjectivity and the practical, and philosophical, effort to secure it from its own undermining despair. An elaboration of the transcendental standpoint is driven by this concern. Husserl's development has frequently been misunderstood and, from non-phenomenological standpoints, condemned as 'idealist'. But this is not just to misconstrue Husserl's thought; it is, more seriously, to distort the historical context within which phenomenology becomes meaningful. For the premodern western world view the transcendental is outside the cosmos, non-empirical, and infinite; but for modernity it is the finite, empirical and determined that is transcendental. Consciousness, that is to say, is an *encounter* with the particular; and experience, which has the appearance of facticity, points outside itself to the essentially ungraspable presence of consciousness and its object. Consciousness, thus, is both the inescapable and the endlessly elusive foundation of experience. And, as for modernity the transcendental is just what lies outside consciousness, it is, paradoxically, the world of *experience* that is transcendental. Experience is that which appears before, but is not identical with, the receptive and constituting consciousness. Presence is the self-assurance of existence rather than objectified acts of consciousness.

Ernst Bloch, an unorthodox Marxist whose work demonstrates strong affinities with phenomenology, recognizes the historical and conceptual difference between the experiential limit of an artificially demarcated 'moment' and '*the darkness of experience itself*' (1999); an experience he, nonetheless, succeeds in characterizing:

> For without distance, right within, you cannot even experience something; not to speak of representing it, to present it in a right way ... all nearness makes matter difficult, and if it is too close, then one is blinded, at least mute. This is, however, only in a strict sense true for a precise, on-the-spot experience, for the immediate moment that is still in the dark as a 'right-now' that is lacking all distance. But this darkness of the moment, in its unique directness, is not true for an already mediated right-now, which is of a different kind and which is a specific experience called 'present' ... Nevertheless, something of the darkness of the immediate nearness is conveyed. (1999, 207–8)

Our own presence eludes both representation and presentation: 'We do not really know what absolutely "is"' (1999, 199). Presence appears, or rather leaves a trace of its evanescence, in retrospect, when it is no longer presence at all:

> Only immediately afterward can I easily hold it, turn it before me, so to speak. So only my immediate past is present to me, agrees with what we experience as apparently existent. So this is what it means to live? ... Never to be there ... When does one really live, when is one consciously present oneself in the vicinity of one's moments? As urgently as this can be felt, however, it always slips away again, the fluidity, darkness of the respective moment, just like this other thing that it means. (1999, 187–8)

Husserl's phenomenology relentlessly pursues both the constituting acts of consciousness *in* experience, and the character of subjectivity *given* as presence. Importantly, human subjectivity is equated by him not with the empirical ego but with a genuinely intersubjective reality. The elusive character of consciousness is a measure of the abyss between the empirical ego and the transcendental subject and provides essential insight into the *social* character of experience in its interior and individual as well as its more openly collective aspect.

What is given in the givenness of presence is not a self-constituting ego but the intersubjectivity of the immediate 'I' in its ceaseless interaction with the equally intersubjective appearing of the world. Presence, that is to say, is never presence of something; it is a *relation* between two mutually irreducible and equally incomprehensible modes of being. Consciousness is not the same as the world it constitutes as experience; but *that* there is an apprehending consciousness, which cannot apprehend itself, and *that* a world other than consciousness is apprehended, is simply given.

Where the representational and presentational standpoints seek to overcome dualism of subject and object by a reductionist tactic, in fact by fiat, the monism of presence conceals a duality in its elemental givenness. Presence is *both* 'here' and 'there', present and absent, consciousness and world; it is sheer immediacy. *Pathos* is the more specific form in which the givenness of the given appears to us; and the mode in which this duality submerges itself. The distinctive quality of feeling, as feeling, makes evident the radical difference between, on the one hand, presence and, on the other hand, the object–subject relation embodied in every objective representation and self-presentation. Pathos is not given in spatio-temporal forms; it is not objectified as things or as the self. In a quite specific way pathos is eternal; it is given without reference to time. We cannot become aware, that is to say, with our own birth or death. Presence, alluded to in the mysterious welling of feeling, as pathos, is grasped magnificently by Kierkegaard in his *Concluding Unscientific Postscript* as a *readiness* for experience of a particular kind; for affection, love, suffering and, at the same time, the essentially 'upbuilding' of patience (Ferguson 2003).

Feeling is irresistible subjectivity and always appears to us transcendentally, as something that sweeps over us, carries us away, takes possession of our soul; something that we are powerless to prevent or resist. That is to say, feeling is given *to* us, and appears *in* us.

Seizure

Presence *awakens* and *seizes* the subject; it takes possession of us (Nancy 1993). We cannot grasp presence deliberatively or intentionally, and it cannot be the aim or object of action. To be seized is to surrender to the given as something eternal; something for which transformations of space and time are irrelevant. The eternal, however, is no empty form. Love, for example, is carried in us as pure immediacy. This does not mean that it will persist; the eternal is not the permanent, unchanging, or infinite. Rather, *when* we are in love we are so *absolutely* and are seized by its presence. Similarly we may be seized by something we know, at other times, to be evanescent;

an intense pain, or an epileptic attack, or a dream for example, have the character of overwhelming the spatio-temporal world for which a particular past and future are constitutive aspects. Similarly, falling in love is something that *happens* to us, although it may coexist with 'ordinary' life. The eternal is, in a sense, *absolutely* mundane and, therefore, quite distinct from the everyday life of representational and presentational structures and processes. Play, love, dreams, happiness, disgust, shame and so on, as well as diffuse states of affection, detachment, longing, and so on, share with fully demonstrated logical and scientific truth an overwhelming sense of immediate certainty; they bring, so to speak, their own reality with them. Waves of feeling come to us, sweep over us, and through us, with the quality of apodictic truth that so impressed Husserl as the essential accompaniment to every pure phenomenon.

The seizure, in another sense, is also that which is taken, especially that which is taken by force. The medical and spiritual sense is related to the legal meaning. It is at once total surrender and absolute imposition. Presence resists objectification but seizes the object already there; the found object that is the privileged exhibit for many contemporary artists following Marcel Duchamp's inspired exemplar. By seizing we make the pre-existing object our own; by seizing the artist brings externality into a new relationship with the self and its creative powers. We seize only that which is remote from us, foreign, alien, and threatening. Seizure does not inaugurate a train of exchanges; it does not hint at reciprocity. It is at once the powerless and the powerful; in the seizure everything is brought to a halt.

Pulse

Presence is subjectivity outside, and otherwise than, experience (Levinas 1998b). It is given not as thing or self but as ceaseless streaming of now-ness. It is eternal immediacy. Presence, clearly, cannot be grasped in a positive concept or act; it recedes from enquiring attention and eludes focus. Presence does not show itself; it neither appears directly as an expressive presentation, nor arises indirectly in an arbitrary representation, but, rather, makes itself *felt* in the enigmatic character of passion. Presence is not grasped or understood, but stands mutely before us and within us as the non-rational; the unconscious.

It is perhaps unsurprising that many gifted writers and philosophers have been drawn to phenomenology precisely because of its apparent rehabilitation of the non-rational and its affinity with the premodern religious language of the significant but now neglected western mystical tradition. Phenomenology makes negative theology once again respectable. Equally, of course, this association, for others, taints phenomenology with the residue of a justifiably discarded world. Yet, in surprising ways and in writers of impeccable modernity, presence works its way, so to speak, unspectacularly into the secular, the mundane, and the everyday. In modernity presence makes itself felt in the relentless pulse of *moodiness*.

Mood is generally understood as the *background* to experience but it belongs just as much to the foreground. Krueger, an interesting phenomenological psychologist who worked in Leipzig during the 1920s, asserts that 'Feeling is the matrix of the other modes of experience and their richest culture-medium' (quoted in Strasser 1977, 91). However vague and indeterminate, the recalcitrance of mood shares its pathos with the more conspicuous phenomena within the experiential field. Mood suffuses consciousness and colours its totality. And mood essentially alters; it is the continuous modulation, the music, of feeling. The moodiness of experience is an ever changing tonality; a continuous, irregular pulse running through every more particular qualification of sensing and willing. Modernity is dynamic even, and perhaps especially, in this respect. Mood appears as an ebb and flow of feeling; a continuous swell that breaks out in never quite predictable ways into a superficial emotional spume. A pulse of intensity runs through every mood, tensing and relaxing, crossing and recrossing immanent transformations of quality. The indeterminate modulations of mood remain obscure. They are indicated by the most general descriptive terms rather than by name; moods are 'good' and 'bad,' 'low' and 'high'; you are 'up' or 'down', 'calm' or 'touchy', 'positive' and 'negative'. And, significantly, mood is frequently referred to as an enshrouding 'spirit' that incomprehensibly descends and, equally inexplicably, lifts. The movement of mood moves us. We are always at one with our moods, 'carried along' in their stream; the stream of consciousness is the oscillation of mood. Krueger suggestively claims that it is the vagueness of mood in which the wholeness of the experiential world is apprehended: 'The experiential qualities of this gathered whole are matters of feeling' (Strasser 1977, 181). Moody presence, 'being-in-a-mood', is the 'twilight consciousness where life becomes experience' (1977, 181). Thus, 'it is disposition, and not perception, which constitutes the elementary foundation of experience' (1977, 182).

The shaping and forming of mood are also obscure. Particular qualities of feeling are distinguished and differentiate one from another, seemingly in response to 'objective' features of situations and the conditions of experience. Yet, even strong feelings such as anger, jealousy, fear, and so on remain at best tenuously connected to actual events in the experiential field. Pascal points out that we are at times happier, and at other times sadder, than any circumstance in our life 'reasonably' warrants. Feeling seems always to break over us and in us without regard to circumstance; there is something profoundly unexpected in every pulse of feeling. Its primary reference is to the unconsciousness, precisely to that which cannot be an object of knowledge or action because it is not in the first place externalized. There is no distance between ourselves and our feelings and no point of view from which we can observe them as a spectator; dispassionately. It is the closeness of feeling, an indivisible unity with our feelings, which precludes any 'rational' understanding of their movement.

Rhythm

The ebb and flow of presence, the periodic oscillation of its specific feeling tone, is established as rhythm; above all as bodily rhythm. From the second half, and particularly towards the end, of the nineteenth century and into the early years of the twentieth century a new awareness of bodily rhythm and its significance becomes evident in European and American culture. Physical education and training, sport, outdoor recreation, and especially dance became a new focus for cultural development (Haley 1978; Toepfer 1997). This was in large measure, of course, a response to the exhaustion of the working class that resulted from intensive industrialization and the increasing physical constraint of mechanization (Rabinbach 1990). Indications of physical deterioration, as well as moral corruption, in the working population provoked alarmist discussion of 'degeneration' (Nordau 1994). The British authorities rejected a large numbers of recruits for the Boer War on medical grounds, prompting the introduction of compulsory physical training in all schools and the encouragement of active leisure pursuits (Bourke 1996). The political aims of movements espousing 'physical hygiene', 'Christian manliness', and the like are evident, but what is of particular interest here is the way in which the physical culture of the late nineteenth century became the focus for, and further stimulated, a new sense of corporeal presence.

A utopian 'return to the body', which is associated with the sudden appearance and rapid development of modernism in popular and professional dance, has its theoretical origin in François Delsart's *Cours d'esthétique* (1840), which elaborates a general theory of gesture. But it was later, through the influential writing and teaching of Émile Jacques-Dalcroze (1921), that the new sensibility was fully articulated. His system of rhythmic movement inspired enthusiastic followers and imitators throughout Europe. In Russia, for example, the poet and literary critic Osip Mandelstam was seized by its unlimited possibilities: 'Harmonious, universal, rhythmical acts, animated by a common idea, are of infinite significance for the creation of future history' (1991, 111). This is not merely 'bourgeois esthetics', or 'hygiene or gymnastics'; it is, rather, 'a synthesis of the spirit and the body, a synthesis of work and play' (1991, 110). In America Isadora Duncan, Ruth St Denis and Ted Shawn, similarly inspired, introduced modern dance as practical corporeal liberation rather than spectacle. Dance was embraced as pure rhythmic movement in which the body recovered its energy and freedom as well as its real presence. And, in Rudolf Laban's highly developed form, these ideas found their way back into educational practice as well as classical ballet (Laban 1963; Maletic 1987).

As distinct from the ideal of the weightless body that had dominated nineteenth-century classical ballet, these modern innovations celebrated the 'grounded human body' as a 'heavy mass'. The body here is moved neither as an instrument nor as a medium of expression, but as a participant in the theatre of being. Dance is a corporeal kinaesthesia through which flow the collective currents of modern life. The body is the primary reality, and contemporary dance is its elemental medium, its specific mode of being. Dance is movement; voluntary but effortless, oscillatory and rhythmical, neither rectilinear nor developmental; it is a surrender to and seizure by/of corporeal presence.

At the same time classical ballet was radically transformed from within its own traditions by Serge Diaghilev and the Ballets Russes, whose performances in Paris in 1907, and for several years following, electrified highly cultivated audiences. Here 'pure dance' was formed out of the decaying conventions of an older art. Jacques Rivière, thus, appreciates the radical character of *Le Sacre du Printemps*: 'Here is a work that is absolutely pure ... Nothing is blurred, nothing obscured by shadows; there is no veiling or poetic mellowing, no trace of aesthetic effect' (Copeland and Cohen 1983; 115).

The Russian ballet set itself against artifice; the unobscured body stands out sharply from its surroundings, and adheres more closely to its natural movement. Rather than continuous fluidity, the dancer aims at something more complex:

> as many propensities and occasions as are offered by the body, as many times does the movement stop and start again; as many possible points of departure the dancer discovers in himself, as many times does he rise again. He regains possession of himself at each instant; like a source that must successively drain all its fountainheads, he recovers his strength, and his dance becomes the analysis, the enumeration of all the body's inclinations toward motion that he can find in it. Here we discover in Nijinsky the same preoccupation as with Stravinsky: to approach everything according to its own orientation. His aim is to follow all the inclinations of the body very directly, regardless of their divergence, and to produce movement only through them. (Copeland and Cohen 1983, 118–19)

The movement does not directly express feeling as if, so to speak, feeling could flow from it, rather, presence is captured and contained within it: 'The body no longer is a means of escape for the soul; on the contrary, it collects and gathers itself around it; it suppresses its outward thrust, and, by the very resistance that it offers to the soul, becomes completely permeated by it, having betrayed it from without ...' Just a century after the advent of 'absolute music' Paris witnessed the birth of 'absolute dance'. Modern dance, an 'intense festival of the body' (Valéry 1989, 59), rather than sport or games, is continuous with the pure corporeal presence that constitutes the phenomenon of play (Caillois 2001; Turner 1982; Melucci 1996; Spariosu 1997).

An insightful critic, Paul Valéry, remarks that 'Every epoch that has understood the human body and experienced at least some sense of its mystery, its resources, its limits, its combinations of energy and sensibility, has cultivated and revered the dance' (1986, 55). Along with Stéphane Mallarmé he recognized dance to be the most modern of modern arts; the art in which the essential quality of contemporary experience was lodged as its animating presence (Mallarmé 2001).

Pleasure

The pathetic seems to be the least orderly and regulated of the major ontological regions of experience. The powerlessness of intellectual reason or ethical choice in the face of passion, acknowledged by all modern philosophers to be the real limiting condition of their own reflective efforts, encourages the conviction that modernity triumphs only to the extent that feeling is suppressed. The project of Enlightenment, securing the world of experience for humanity, is often understood as involving a renunciation of feeling; a stern rejection of mood as something equivocal and even threatening. It is in this framework, indeed, that Freud's psychology has frequently been interpreted. Modernity is then viewed as the progressive repression of feeling. The self-regulating character of modern life apparently depends, in fact, on the extent to which the entire realm of feeling is systematically excluded as a real content of experience.

Such a view, however, seriously distorts Freud's writings and, more seriously, ignores the significant regulative processes immanent to the sphere of feeling itself. What effectively domesticates radical presence – immediacy – is the constitution of pleasure as a particular kind of experience. This is, more precisely, the import of Freud's theory of repression, which finds precursors in Schelling's radical essay on freedom and Nietzsche's psychology of ressentiment, and might better be understood as the *critique* of pleasure (Žižek 2000). The *possibility* of the experience of pleasure, that is to say, is founded upon the process of repression. Pleasure emerges, along with the ego, in the process of forgetting the ecstatic flux of the 'primary process'. On the insecure boundary of the human it is not pleasure but the anarchic monism of feeling that the emerging ego pushes from itself. Pleasure *depends* upon repression (Whitebook 1996; Ferguson 1996). In the primary process there is no pleasure, no liking and disliking; here subjectivity is entangled in an imperative and impersonal pulse of indeterminate feeling.

Repression, furthermore, transforms rather than rejects the primary process. It is nothing other than the setting out of an ego *from* the primary process, which remains as the hidden source of its psychic energy. This is also a process of differentiation. Ecstasy is broken up and parcelled out, inhabiting and linking every mood with its shadowy, nostalgic presence. A specific region of feeling is defined, named, distinguished, and ordered. The ceaseless ebb and flow of mood is replaced by a restless transition from one feeling to another, a succession of distinct states replaces the nameless pulsation of sheer moodiness. Repression is *self*-repression, which is at the same time self-creation; the manner in which the self generates itself from its own indeterminacy.

Pleasure is the specific *value* gained in this process and the reward that comes to motivate and regulate the psychic life of feeling. Rather than being possessed or seized, the psyche actively orients itself towards pleasure and self-enjoyment. The oscillation between gathering tension and periodic release qualifies the ebb and flow of mood with a new directionality.

Internal horizon and perspective are established. Pleasure replaces happiness; sexuality colours eroticism; fear domesticates anxiety; religion orders the sacred.

It is not simply the case that *what* gives us pleasure is altered and comes to occupy a specific place in our experience, for example as fashionable commodities or leisure time; but, more fundamentally, it is *that* pleasure becomes for us a specific psychic value that characterizes modern experience. Our *liking* for pleasure seems altogether self-evident and unremarkable. Yet, in a larger historical context, this is far from being a given condition of experience. It is only gradually and in a faltering development that liking and pleasure become synonymous, and finally obscure the gulf between the ego satisfaction of the modern, individuated, embodied subject and the self-shattering transcendence of immediacy. Pleasure is both the *trace* of happiness and the *sign* of utility. The seemingly automatic and natural orientation of the psychic economy towards historically validated forms of self-aggrandizement and the satisfaction of wants is, consequently, experienced as the peculiar *dissolution* of embodiment that we call pleasure. Remarkably, pleasure spans the gulf between the immanence of representation and the transcendence of presence and, thus, introduces a regulative principle into the indeterminate zone of feeling.

Pleasure makes presence familiar and, seemingly, demystifies transcendence. It plays the role of mediator by pretending to combine, in its mundane otherness, experiential forms that strictly speaking remain incommensurate. What meets in pleasure, in embodied feeling, never genuinely merges or combines. In making pleasure the 'natural' orientation of contemporary embodiment, immanence and transcendence, time and eternity, indeterminacy and determinacy, finite and infinite are simply run together under a common label. Pleasure, which is experienced 'in the flesh', remains both incarnate spirit and ensouled body. Gabriel Marcel, following Pascal, makes the point: 'Certainly, it would be rash to attempt to put one's finger on some spot in history when the unity of the world was something directly felt by men in general. But could we feel the division of the world today, or could some of us at least feel it so strongly, if we had not within us, I will not say the memory of such a united world, but at least the nostalgia of it?' (1949b, vol. 1). And Paul Ricoeur, equally influenced by Pascal, points specifically to the duality of pleasure, its symptomatic character in simultaneously concealing and revealing presence: 'The repose in pleasure threatens to bring the dynamism of activity to a standstill and screen the longing of happiness' (1986, 94).

Pleasure plays the same role within the domain of presence that reason performs in relation to representation and selfhood to presentation. Regulative principles bring together and conceal the disjunction between law and cause, expression and communication, immanence and transcendence.

How are the 'unruly passions' to be controlled? Just by 'giving way' to 'selfish' pleasure. Indulgence, rather than ascetic denial, is institutionalized as the spiritual genius of contemporary society. And as contemporary spirit is embedded in objects, in commodities, access to pleasure is controlled through the market mechanism that orders the production and circulation of those same objects. Pleasure is normalized as a psychic equilibrium; the periodic accumulation and release of tension are held within strict limits, the amplitude of oscillations is gradually reduced and brought within a safe and predictable zone of mundane enjoyment. Pleasure is always moderate; and appetite is cultivated rather than forceful, satisfied by an adequate and acceptable object.

Trust

Trust, rather than truth or authenticity, is the criterion of presence; and the rock upon which it founders. The issue raised by every incipient feeling is just its 'reality'. Can we trust our own feeling? Does the strange visitation that grips us hint at some real presence to which we should surrender, or is it an alien and artificial state that we should reject? We are immediately suspicious that our feelings may not be genuine, they may not be 'our own', and that circumstance and convention have conspired to plant in us guilt, or grief, or ambition where none spontaneously awakens. And, of course, sociologists are justified in pointing to the transformation of social relations in the emergence and development of the modern world that encourages and even makes possible certain feeling states. The intimacy of love, jealousy, and hatred certainly have a social history, but the association of particular relations with specific feelings can be deceptive. The social relations of intimacy offer themselves as locations rather than causes of the feelings that accompany and are seemingly roused by them (Giddens 1992; Bauman 2003).

In whatever context presence manifests itself as presence, it confronts us with a challenge. The background assumption that makes pleasure 'safe' is, in fact, a general distrust of the intensity and extremity of *any* feeling. Pleasure is to be trusted because any pleasure is, by definition, moderate in feeling. But this resolution is unstable and superficial. It acknowledges that our relation to all ultimate values should be governed by insincerity and hypocrisy, rather than truth and authenticity. Presence, however, wherever it is manifest, is so absolutely and thus insinuates a spirit of transgression into the most 'innocent' forms of enjoyment. A spirit of happiness, eroticism, anxiety, danger and so on finds its way back into the stream of life and wrecks even the moderate satisfaction pleasures are designed to confer.

The mystery of presence

Marcel openly accepts the obscurity of existence, admitting that 'my life is essentially ungraspable'. The radical secularization of modern knowledge ultimately fails to clarify the newly reclaimed world of human experience. The mystery of presence lies precisely in our unavoidable encounter with what remains ungraspable in our experience of ourselves. What we recognize as experience is always a relation between self-clarifying processes of practical and theoretical reflection on the one hand, and the utter darkness of human being on the other. In modern society and modern culture reality becomes synonymous with body, but, either as embodied soul or as incarnate spirit, body remains fundamentally obscure. Presence flows into modernity from its premodern extramundane exile and gives to objects, to bodies, a supreme sense of reality. That, for the modern world, there is nothing other than body does nothing to dissipate the mystery in which reality had always been shrouded. Modern embodiment – which is the embodiment of modernity – bodies forth mystery; it becomes aware of itself in terms of an unfathomable movement of feeling; 'I *am* my body only in so far as for me the body is an essentially mysterious type of reality' (Marcel 1949b, vol. 1, 103).

7

Society: Sociological Reductions

> In its historical development, the formation of concepts referring to lived
> experience is at the same time founded on understanding, which is in turn
> grounded in lived experience.
>
> Dilthey, *The Formation of the Historical World in the Human Sciences*

A historical sociology of the natural attitude provides an important corrective
to the tendency within phenomenological philosophy, in spite of its protest-
ations to the contrary, to deal in abstractions; to derive concepts from phenomena rather than to reduce experience to phenomena. An ethnography
of modernity, furthermore, complicates the situation by revealing three natural attitudes rather than one. The natural attitude with which Husserl
began is that found within the region of sensing/representation; but in the
elaboration of his philosophy, willing/presentation and feeling/presence
become increasingly prominent. Phenomenology explores these regional
ontologies in their own terms, as irreducible data of consciousness. But we
may well ask how this is possible. If these phenomenological regions are
genuinely distinct, how can they appear together in a singular consciousness, and how can they be interrelated? How is a general phenomenology
possible at all, given that it must be articulated within the limits of a com-
municable discourse? Phenomenology, after all, as a philosophical project
exists in writing and speech and forms itself, furthermore, as part of the
very cultural development it seeks to anatomize.

The common responses to such difficulties, in accordance with preconceived notions, are either to reject phenomenology as inconsistent or to
reject criticism of phenomenology as an unjustified imposition of narrowly
rationalist criteria of adequacy. However, it is worth putting the matter differently, even if it serves only to delay the moment of decisive choice.
Rather, *given* that phenomenology has brought to light, through its own
unclarified methods, the essential trinitarian structure of experience, how
has this been achieved? Phenomenology's ultimate appeal is to direct experience and self-evidence; is it not self-evidently the case that our experience, whatever else might be said of it, is constituted through sensing,
willing, feeling and appearing in representation, presentation, and presence?
These terms refer to essentially different *kinds* of experience; irreducible
one to another, and irreducible (even by way of explanation) to any non-
experiential, singular, and putatively 'ultimate' level of reality as a whole.

This delaying tactic – for the time being to suspend doubt in relation
to the phenomenological project as a whole and temporarily to place its

discourse 'in brackets' – was employed throughout the previous chapter. *Assuming* the general phenomenological description is accurate, what insight does it afford for a historical and critical sociology of modernity? Now we can turn the question round. *Supposing* the historical-sociological description of the development of modernity outlined above is broadly accurate, what insight does this provide into the phenomenological approach to philosophical issues?

Any attempt to answer such a question must begin with a reconsideration of Husserl's own account of the phenomenological method. From this point of view the *phenomenological reduction* should be viewed as a description of the *actual development* of modern society. The philosophical difficulty of Husserl's *method* should not obstruct the path opened by phenomenology toward gaining essential insight into modern society. The development of modernity, that is to say, is best grasped as a process of *reduction*, in which 'society' clarifies itself and constitutes itself in new and essential ways. The *social reduction* – the reduction of society to itself – may be characterized as a process of institutional differentiation that replicates the separation of regional ontologies outlined in the preceding chapter. The historical-social process, analysed and described in different ways in the classical sociological literature, should not be regarded as the 'foundation', far less the 'cause', of these distinctive experiential domains. The recognition that consciousness *is* a social phenomenon, and that society is institutionalized *as* experience, is the shared insight at the root of both phenomenological and sociological investigations of modernity and precludes any such prejudicial judgement. The process of institutional differentiation, the parallel development of various autonomous forms of culture, and the separation of distinct regions of experience, however, unfold over a lengthy period and only in retrospect offer themselves as a coherent development.

Throughout the modern period, therefore, from about the beginning of the seventeenth century to the end of the nineteenth century, the notion of society emerged in distinctive ways *within* each of the perspectives given as representation, presentation, and presence. Society, that is to say, as with experience, nature, history, humanity, and so on, appeared in trinitarian abundance, performing its work of synthesis not once only but three times over and in different ways. Of course, from within each of the worlds constituted by modernity, society, like experience, nature, humanity and so on, appeared to be singular and coherent. The 'closed world' of the premodern west did not give way immediately to the 'infinite universe', rather, it was superseded by three new and distinctive worlds each claiming, in its own fashion, to be infinite. The clarifying insight of a genuinely phenomenological sociology had to await the further transformation of modernity wrought by the dismal history of the twentieth century. Thus, to bring this insight more fully into the open, the demarcation of 'society' must first be considered in relation to the regional ontologies immanent in its modern development. The social relation, institutional framework, form of authority, and so on, that appear to be essential to modernity are constituted, in turn, in ways that correspond to the immanent development of representation, presentation, and presence. In contrast to premodern societies that may be grasped in terms of the polyvalence of 'total social phenomena', modern society may be characterized primarily in terms of processes of *circulation*, which is institutionalized as a free market (representation/sensing); *production* in the collective experience of the factory, enterprise, and office (presentation/willing); or *consumption* in the family and community (presence/feeling). And the impasse that, variously articulated in each of its regional ontologies, obstructs the internal dynamics of modernity reappears here as the conflict, in turn, between libertarian individualism and the authoritarian state in early modern political theory; the struggle over class and nation as the primary locus of social identity throughout the era of high capitalism; and the opposition between community and crowd in the emergence of contemporary society towards the end of the nineteenth century.

The Phenomenon of Society

The specificity of modern society lies in its phenomenal character. Society becomes a phenomenon. Society undergoes a series of *reductions*; it comes to itself in and as experience. Modernity appears, that is to say, first of all as the consciousness of society; the consciousness of life as the life of society. For the modern age society is not a concept. The focus of modern philosophy, and other forms of discourse, does not betray a negligent idealism, so much as indicate the extent to which reality is crystallized in consciousness: the consciousness of society.

Husserl's central methodological dictum is to follow phenomena themselves. Philosophy must wait upon appearance. Every appearance is an act of consciousness; that is to say it appears exclusively as an *experience*. Appearances are just that; just what they seem. Normally, and without reflecting upon the matter, we interpret appearances as things having an independent existence outside our consciousness of them; but appearances carry no guarantee of the validity of such a view. Phenomenology, therefore, begins by systematically excluding all such interpretation. Appearances are not things; nor are they self-evidently symbols, signs, or representations of things. Phenomena should be grasped in their nakedness, just as they are. This requires that we 'suspend belief' in the exterior actuality of the world of appearances and take them as appearances and nothing more. Our normal orientation to the world has to be temporarily 'placed in brackets'.

This simple rule proves to be peculiarly difficult to follow. It is, first of all, difficult to dislodge the natural attitude, which infects both everyday and philosophical language. It is, moreover, a task that requires extraordinary patience; there are no short cuts, deductive chains of reasoning, conclusions, axioms, or systems to provide ready-made conclusions. Following the phenomena is an infinite task; appearances and their modalizations ceaselessly succeed one another. This seems to be a new and extreme kind of

161

empiricism; the vital human interest in the world, what has been bracketed, it seems, will never be restored. It is just this difficulty that persuaded many of Husserl's early followers to depart from his rigorous method and establish their own brands of phenomenological philosophy.

But phenomenology loses everything if it abandons this method and becomes indistinguishable from the impressionism of so much contemporary cultural studies. What is suspended, or bracketed, is just our everyday effortless belief in the exteriority of the world. From another point of view, however, what is removed to the limbo of frozen consciousness is the systematic *doubt* that propels modern rational discourse. The phenomenological method is the suspension of doubt, the suspension of disbelief. This, however, is just the convention that inaugurates one of the key elements in the emergence of modernity itself; the theatricality of baroque culture. Before it was discovered as a methodological trick, bracketing had already become an established practice for the everyday world of modernity. In the novel, in the *performance* that staged modernity in demonstrative and authoritative form, in the transformed carnival of the anatomy theatre, and the conventions of pictorial display, just such a suspension had occurred. The enabling assumption in all these new cultural forms involved an *actual* reduction rather than a methodological standpoint. The performance defines and confines reality – for the purposes of the performance reality is defined as nothing other than what is taking place on the stage. It is a world that is in many ways like the everyday world, but it remains quite distinct from it and nobody confuses the two (Bouwsma 2000; Maravall 1986; Agnew 1986).

Both kinds of reduction – the performative and the phenomenological – require a particular act of attention. And like all acts of attention it serves to isolate specific features within the field of consciousness; it brings them into the foreground, allowing everything else to fall back into an indistinct background. The performance accomplishes this by declaring itself in a spectacular fashion; it literally draws attention to itself in such a way that, as the performance gets under way, the audience 'lose themselves' in the action and cease to be aware of their ordinary surroundings. They 'live through' the actors' performance. A complicated ontological game is involved here. The actor is also 'living through' a character he is temporarily playing.

Modern culture, quite generally, developed by way of such reductions; specific fields of practice were, in principle, established as independent of others and were constituted according to consciously articulated internal relations. Artistic work, for example, came increasingly under the control of aesthetic and representational conventions that viewed the world, first and foremost, as a visual image. Of course the world of immediate experience was not *only* a visual image, but in treating it as *essentially* a visual form the rich complexity of actual experience could successfully be invoked. In another context Descartes considered reality exclusively in terms of the essential characteristics of substance; of material or extended substance (*res extensa*) and thinking or spiritual substance (*res cogitans*). And Galileo

162

considered the physical universe in terms of the reduced primary qualities of a uniformly constituted matter. All such procedures reduce experience to some specific aspect or quality of the world and ignore everything else. The advantage of this draconian method of simplification is that we can more readily grasp and manipulate, practically and conceptually, a reality made up of just one or two components than we can the overwhelming contingency, complexity, and sheer messiness of immediate experience. Reduction is by no means a demeaning of reality; an arbitrary and pointless splitting apart. The simplification achieved is intended (and believed) to be a clarification; the reduction of reality *to* what the reasoning and/or sensitive person is forced to regard as its essential characteristic. The technique of reduction in a dramatic way wrenches these essential aspects of reality out of the context of their everyday appearance, removes them from their phenomenal setting, and places them in a new reality liberated from the contingency of time and space. The visualized and painted object is deprived of the sensuous presence of its secondary qualities, but in its reduced form enters a realm of imperishable images. Reductions that both simplify and eternalize aspects of the emerging modern world, including still-life painting, theatrical performance, and natural science, appear around 1600.

The phenomenological reduction, similarly, requires a particular act of attention that brings phenomena to the foreground. That is to say, the ordinary interest in objects and events is temporarily neglected in favour of the (unusual) focus of attention on phenomena as *nothing other than* phenomena. There is nothing especially 'philosophical' about this process. We continually reduce the field of consciousness by attending to some specific aspect of it. Given the unbounded nature of this field we cannot do otherwise. This, in fact, is just the insight that phenomenology secures by attending, in the peculiar fashion it does, to every content of consciousness exclusively in its *phenomenal* form.

Unsurprisingly, discussions of Husserl's method, both critical and supportive, have tended to emphasize the distinctiveness of this approach. In terms of a philosophical perspective, of course, it is unusual but as a *social process* reduction is (or, rather, reductions are) central to the emergence and development of modern society and its culture. It is not only the various cultural and intellectual practices of the modern world that emerge through specific processes of reduction; *society* undergoes a series of reductions in which the 'total social phenomenon' (Mauss 1970, 76) is broken up and distributed among a series of orders, each characterized by distinctive immanent principles. These orders are then recombined fictively into an *image* of a now absent totality. Society becomes the imaginary *sum* of political, religious, economic, aesthetic, family, community, and so on, relations. The social as distinct from any specific set of institutional or private activities then refers to a general unifying framework of some sort, variously identified, broadly speaking, as human nature, the state, or values. And specific institutional arrangements, settings, and forms of representation are developed to express this putative wholeness.

Sociology developed, in part, by way of criticizing such views and sought to establish a more critical and analytically precise notion of society. Rather than arrive (or fail to arrive) at society by a process of aggregating given parts and elements, sociology sought to elucidate the *relations* and relational forms that imparted to these institutionally differentiated activities both their specific and, more significantly, their common characteristics. In phenomenological terms it might be said that society was ubiquitous but hidden; it was in every particular way of acting and being that characterizes modern life but had, so to speak, receded into the background of social consciousness. Society, which remained the precondition for any and all more delimited relations and actions, was inconspicuous and recalcitrant in comparison with the foreground interests of modernity. And what stood out from the social field was not one particular activity or kind of activity, but a whole series of seemingly quite different activities, depending on the specific interests of those constituting the activities themselves.

As modernity was established, that is to say, society as a whole receded into the background of the experiential field, and ceased to play the key constituting role for the natural attitudes that unreflectively took the world to be identical with activities defined and ordered within specific institutional domains. Society was no longer even the surplus or remainder to activities that had their own interests, principles, aims, mechanisms and so on.

In this perspective, it might be argued that the classical sociologists, in reestablishing the *reality* of the social in terms of what was *essential* to modern society, were already critical phenomenologists. For them the eclipse of society as the self-evident collective life, replicated in the microcosm of community and functional order, was not an error or illusion but the consequence of the historic transformation of society itself. To grasp how this had occurred sociologists, in effect, described a series of actual social reductions. If we learn to look at the social world in the right way, they claim, we can see what the complexity of everyday life modestly veils, the presence of society itself.

It is tempting to read the classics as offering variants on this phenomenological theme. In different ways Marx, Simmel, Weber, and Durkheim describe the social reduction of modernity – the transformation of society into the reality obscured by the hectic variety that is *also* part of this transformation. Max Weber and Georg Simmel describe the social process of reduction to circulation, Marx characterizes the reduction to production, and Durkheim delineates the reduction to consumption. That is to say, as with Galileo or Cotán, the rich context of everyday life is systematically ignored in favour of a perspective that isolates a particular aspect of these practices; the aspect, of course, that the sociologist intuits to be just that which is *essentially* social.

Reduction to the Gift

The gift, or gift relation, is often construed as being the primal form of society; the first and most fundamental manner in which society is both given and makes its appearance. And since the pioneering essay by Marcel Mauss the notion of the gift has entered into the foundation not only of anthropology, but also of philosophy and literary criticism (Hyde 1979; Derrida 1996; Horner 2001; Wyschogorod et al. 2002; Davis 2000; Caputo and Scanlon 2001). In spite of its thematic prominence, however, both Mauss's essay and, more importantly, the real character of the gift are often misunderstood and, in fact, remain obscure. Each theoretically self-conscious perspective on society includes a specific and appropriate view of the gift. Gift giving, receiving, and returning have been seen, for example, as an archaic form of exchange and the prototype of all developed market relations (Gregory 1982). The gift in this context is the original, spontaneous form of social life which bears a distant and equivocal relation to contemporary society, in which depersonalized economic exchange has supplanted it as the primary modality of satisfying everyday and every other need. A continuous development is, nonetheless, assumed to link gift exchange to modern utilitarian, market relations.

The most common understanding of the gift, however, comes, from Malinowski rather than Mauss, an analysis that is conceived in direct opposition to utilitarianism and any rational economic model of human activity (Malinowski 1978). Here the gift is viewed as the social fact above all others, and the presentation which sets in train all those complex interrelations that constitute more developed social structures. Fundamental to the notion of the gift, in this schema, is the norm of reciprocity. To receive a gift obliges the recipient to make a gift in return, thus establishing a reciprocal bond. The gift is simply an occasion for the demonstration of that egalitarian spirit that is held to animate social life in its simplest and most universal form. Here the original giving (prestation, or presentation) is an instance of the continuously present total social phenomenon; society itself.

But, as Mauss himself makes clear, reciprocity is not the guiding norm of gift giving and returning and, in fact, is not really a form of exchange at all. The gift is not to be confused with the commodity; it is governed not by a law of equivalence, but by the striving for domination. Gift giving is driven by an ambition to present the gift that *cannot* be reciprocated and thus establishes a relation of inequality. The original act of giving is, thus, an attempt to impose upon the other, to impose an obligation that cannot be repaid and therefore subordinates the receiver. And as 'Originally ... things had a personality', the gift carries the spirit of an identifiable donor and makes them present at a remote time and place. Gift giving, therefore, was a way of accumulating and extending power. Further, this domination is not entered into with any utilitarian motive or calculation of future gain, but simply in pursuit of an ever wider domain of personal power; it imposes the personality of the giver, individual or collective, extends their dominion, and seeks to incorporate and assimilate the receiver into the personal or collective identity of the giver:

> in this system of ideas one gives away what is in reality a part of one's nature and substance, while to receive something is to receive a part of someone's

spiritual essence. To keep this thing is dangerous, not only because it is illicit to do so, but also because it comes morally, physically, and spiritually from a person ... The thing given is not inert. It is alive and often personified, and strives to bring to its original clan and homeland some equivalent to take its place. (Mauss 1970, 10)

The norm of reciprocity, thus, emerges as an aspect of social conflict rather than a sign of moral consensus. Returning a gift is not just a way of discharging an obligation incurred by receiving the gift, but a way of freeing the original receiver from the power of the giver (Strathern 1971).

Mauss's original view of the gift has been taken up in a challenging way by Georges Bataille, who views the emergence of 'general economy' founded on superfluity, display, and excess as emerging through the process of gift sacrifice. This inverts the standard functionalist and historical accounts of archaic societies as more or less isolated communities of self-sufficient households constrained, above all, by scarcity. Bataille describes the large-scale structure of ancient societies in terms of overabundance and the gift as originally a way of 'getting rid' of a surplus; a process in which material 'goods' could be converted into usable reservoirs of political power (Bataille 1991).

More recently Derrida has reconfigured the idea of the gift, placing it altogether outside the economy of exchange and reciprocity. In his view the gift is just what cannot be given or received: 'For there to be a gift, there must be no reciprocity, return, exchange, countergift or debt. If the other *gives* me *back* or *owes* me or has to give me back what I give him or her, there will not have been a gift, whether this restitution is immediate or whether it is programmed by a complex calculation of long-term deferral or difference' (1992, 12). That which is given as a gift must be given without expectation of return, and the very idea of a counter-gift is incoherent: 'These conditions of possibility of the gift (that some "one" gives some "thing" to some "one other") designate simultaneously the conditions of the impossibility of the gift ... these conditions of possibility define or produce the annulment, the annihilation, the destruction of the gift' (1992, 12). Viewing the gift within the logic of exchange leads to the notion that the gift incurs debt; that at least we thank someone for the gift; but this acknowledgement is already a return, which destroys the gift. The genuine gift would have to be anonymous or immediately forgotten: 'If there is a gift, the *given* of the gift ... must not come back ... It must not circulate, it must not be exchanged ... It is perhaps in this sense that the gift is the impossible. Not impossible but *the* impossible' (1992, 7).

Such views indicate, beyond the centrality of the gift as a *topos* for sociology, the systematic character of the divergent positions; each of which includes accounts of the other leading viewpoints *within* its own perspective. That is to say 'society' is not a simple phenomenon, but a number of quite distinct, simple phenomena. This is not because society is composed of a number of *different* phenomena but, rather, because it is given in a variety of distinctive, but mutually exclusive, ways. The trinitarian structure of modern society, that is, includes its modality of appearance. Society as society may be experienced in a number of different ways; most significantly as exchange, production, or consumption. But *if* society becomes phenomenally real as any one of these forms it cannot simultaneously appear in any other.

Reduction to Exchange

There is no necessary continuity between the gift and the relation of exchange and, where the gift has, in one way or another, been grasped as a primal social phenomenon, exchange is most commonly viewed in the context of the historical development of complex societies. Exchange is an expression of the process of differentiation, which is the most general of all historical processes; and exchange can be viewed, thus, as the essential form of modern society. In modern society it is exchange in which the process of representation takes root; a relation in which one thing stands for or in place of another, quite different object. The natural attitude that emerged in modern society and was authoritatively expressed in the natural sciences and in political economy was an orientation to reality as the reality of exchange. And, as sociological thought emerged and gained its coherence through a critical reinterpretation of that attitude, a transformed conception of exchange continued to play a central role in its understanding of modernity. Exchange relations are significant, for example, in Durkheim's characterization of organic solidarity and in Marx's understanding of commodity production; themes which will be taken up in the following sections. In Weber's comparative historical sociology of modern society, however, exchange plays a more substantial role, and Simmel's sociology might well be characterized as a sociological reduction to exchange; a view of modern society, that is to say, in which exchange is viewed as the *essential phenomenon* of society.

Max Weber views modern society from the perspective of a rational system of exchange and the large-scale processes of institutional change in which it was implicated. The process of generalized exchange of commodities – the institution of the market – is in a practical form a reduction that bears a direct relation to the radical simplification of reality effected by the still-life painting or the theoretical constructions of the natural scientist. It removes the object from the context of daily life, considers it in isolation, and values it in terms of other, similarly decontextualized objects. The market overcomes the immediate constraints of time and space. Commodities produced at different times and in different places can be brought together in an ideal space to effect an exchange. Modern accounting practices and the precise calculability of profit, Weber stresses, emerge as the arena of exchange itself comes to be identified as society. The character of modernity is just that the region of transparently contending interests becomes increasingly dominant as the foundational institution and architectonic model of society. The 'iron cage' of modernity is the actual coming into existence in a practical sense of the notional rationality of exchange and its hypostatization as an imperative reality. The use of money as an intermediary enormously enlarges the scope of such exchanges and their relative independence of the contingencies of time and space. Economists are not wholly deluded, thus, in treating the market as a general and timeless mechanism; in a quite real sense objects appear in market exchanges as 'things-in-themselves', as bodies without a past or future, distinguished one from another simply by their value, their relative equivalence in the process of exchange itself.

Weber insightfully draws attention to the importance of accounting and book-keeping as illustrating and facilitating the practical idealization of market processes. During the Renaissance accounting procedures and simpler arithmetical notation, both of which developed in close association with geometric formulations of rules of perspective drawing, and new rationalizations of musical notation, were used not only to keep track of all transactions on a daily basis but to record and compare different sorts of market activities (Crosby 1997). Accounting procedures *reduced* complicated and multifaceted social encounters to simple economic exchange. Then, in transferring the record of such transactions to a ledger, these simplified phenomena were codified in terms of type and value rather than time, place, personal relation, circumstance and so on. There emerged from this procedure an effective model or representation of the entire social process stripped of its rich contingency; an ideal, timeless realm governed by lucid economic 'laws' and the simple arithmetic of profit and loss (Poovey 1998). Accounting was a systematic reduction that represented in a clarified manner the very process in which, and through which, society was constituted. It was just in this process of exchange that modern society had taken root and existed in its most elementary and essential form. The rationalization of the market, that is to say, consisted precisely in the reduction of society to the timeless interaction of ideal objects.

Of course, just as observation of, for example, the acceleration of falling bodies in any particular case seems to violate Galileo's laws, so actual market relations remain complex, contextualized events in which an indeterminate variety of factors plays a part in determining the outcome. But the inverse relation becomes ever more evident and significant. The essential character of society and the social relation that, to an increasing degree, 'accounts' for *all* aspects of everyday life and its institutional structure *is* nothing other than market exchange. And, to an increasing degree, actual market relations correspond to the accountant's model. The everyday, living context as well as the purely economic aspect of the exchange are defined by anonymity, impersonality, monetary value, and the idealized consideration of value.

Weber himself explicitly relates this process to the long-term development in western society of rational technology, rational science, rationalized law, bureaucratic regulation, and so on. That is to say, Weber provides a sociological view of the phenomenological reduction to representation/sensing and the emergence of the natural attitude in relation to it. Weber, famously, views the origins of capitalism in terms of the growth of a spirit for which this activity can take on the significance of being a fundamental and ultimate reality; a spirit for which rational calculation and an economic view of the world are not an impoverishment of the texture of social life so much as the decisive grasping of its pure and elementary form: its *essence*.

More recently historians, following Fernand Braudel's impressive lead, have taken up Weber's insight and extended our knowledge of the global character of trade and its transformative impact on the emergence of modernity in the west (Braudel 1982, 1984, 1985; Chaudhuri 1985; Curtin 1984; Pomeranz 2001; Pomeranz and Topik 1999). Trade prior to the modern period was primarily small-scale, local, and limited exchange. The importance of long-distance trade in luxury goods, including foodstuffs (Mintz 1985; Schivelbusch 1993), might well be viewed in light of the subsequent differentiation of impersonal and rational market relations and their hypostatization as 'society'. Where exchange was conducted by intermediaries, over large distances, among people who had little or no knowledge of each other, the purely economic aspect of the relation came into prominence and provided a model for the rational transformation of local market relations.

Within Europe books and pictures were among the first novel objects of a purely economic system of exchange. They were detached from any traditional sites of production and circulated freely as emblems of a new society; as commodities (Febvre and Martin 1976; Martin 1994; Honig 1998). In time every kind of good followed, and society came more and more to resemble the ledger.

Approaching exchange in a yet more general way, Simmel provides the most compelling account of society as an actual process of reduction. In his writings, society emerges as something 'given' in a wholly objective way. The 'psychic contents' of individual experience 'in the form of drive, interest, purpose, inclination, psychic movement' enter into society as the 'material' of sociation, but:

> In themselves, these materials with which life is filled, the motivations by which it is propelled, are not social. Strictly speaking, neither hunger nor love, neither work nor religiosity, neither technology nor the function and results of intelligence, are social. They are factors in sociation only when they transform the mere aggregation of isolated individuals into specific forms of being with and for one another – forms that are subsumed under the general concept of interaction. (Simmel 1950, 41)

Sociation, or interaction, is the most fundamental form of exchange, which is not to be understood simply as a generalized social means to the realization of non-social purposes; nor should it be identified, even as an originating model, with market relations. Rather, modern economic relations and the utilitarian calculus they engender are a specifically modern development in the *formal* character of sociation. On this view, and strictly speaking, 'society' is something 'outside the subject' and, consequently, does not constitute itself as a phenomenon at all. However, the forms of sociation are given in such a way that they also and essentially enter the conscious stream of life as so many possibilities, constraints, and opportunities. Thus, for example, where exchange is essential to society as such, sociability, which Simmel describes as the 'play-form of sociation', is the pure phenomenon of interaction. In sociability the form of sociation is 'freed from all ties with its contents. It exists for its own sake and for the sake of the fascination which, in its own liberation from these ties, it diffuses' (1950, 43). But the 'artificial world' of sociability with its various experiences itself becomes a psychic content motivating interaction. This is most generally realized in contemporary society through everyday conversation, which 'with the possible exception of looking at one another … is the purest and most sublimated form of two-way-ness. It is the fulfilment of a relation that wants to be nothing but relation – in which, that is, what usually is the mere form of interaction becomes its self-sufficient content' (1950, 53).

The sociological reduction to exchange is not a theory or concept, but describes the actual process in which society is 'crystallized': 'Exchange is the objectification of human interaction' (1950, 388). Significantly, Simmel recognizes that forms of sociation tend to persist. In an insightful essay Simmel remarks that 'Faithfulness might be called the inertia of the soul' (1950, 380). And, more generally, that 'Sociological connectedness, no matter what its origin, develops a self-preservation and autonomous existence of its form that are independent of its initially connective motives. Without this inertia of existing sociations, society as a whole, would constantly collapse, or change in an unimaginable fashion' (1950, 380–1). It is just the character of society, as distinct from the inner fluidity of psychic contents, to 'become crystallized … in formulas and fixed directions'. However, these forms 'do not express or shape an ideal, a contrast with life's reality, but this life itself' (1950, 386). In the phenomenon of faithfulness 'this sociological fixity, which remains outside life's immediacy and subjective rhythm, here actually becomes the content of subjective, emotionally determined life … Faithfulness is that constitution of the soul (which is constantly moved and lives in a continuous flux), by means of which it fully incorporates into itself the stability of the super-individual form of relation' (1950, 386–7).

The general tendency towards objectification in the forms of interaction is given a distinctive character in modern society in the phenomenon of money as a generalized expression for all forms of exchange: 'The function of exchange, as a direct interaction between individuals, becomes crystallized in the form of money as an independent structure.' We should not regard money as an indifferent medium for a process of exchange that has its foundation in a pre-existing state of society. Rather, exchange, which money objectifies, is the active synthesis which *is* society: 'exchange is one of the functions that creates an inner bond between men – a society, in place of a mere collection of individuals. Society is not an absolute entity which must first exist so that all the individual relations of its members … can develop within its framework or be represented by it: it is only the synthesis or the general term for the totality of these specific interactions' (1978, 175). And although, in principle, there are innumerable functions other than exchange, including super- and subordination, imitation, cohesion and so on, for modern society it is increasingly the case 'that most relationships between people can be interpreted as forms of exchange. Exchange is the purest and most developed kind of interaction' (1978, 82).

Initially there is no need to assume that exchange takes place *because* different objects are viewed as equivalent values. Values are determined in the process of exchange itself. However, the objectification of exchange realized in the use of money creates the overwhelming conviction that values are immanent in objects themselves. The complexity of exchange in modern society, the increasing length of 'teleological chains' sustained through money transactions, and the extraordinary variety of qualitatively distinctive contents that enter into such transactions, all serve further to emphasize the 'objectivity' of money as a measure of value. The radical decontextualization and reduction of all exchanges to money values also serve to encourage modern tendencies towards impersonality, anonymity, and an attitude of calculation. Money becomes the most extreme example of the transformation of means into ends. The growing abstraction of modern society is the counterpart of the pure objectivity of money. Where all values can be expressed in money, then every activity is conceivable as an economic exchange.

Simmel and Weber, in their distinctive ways, delineate the modern sociological reduction to exchange; that is, not as a theory of society but as an account of the real process in which modernity realizes itself as society.

Reduction to Production

Marx focuses attention on the reduction to production; on the emptying of society into the process of producing commodities. This associates Marx with the ontological region of willing/presentation rather than with sensing/representation or feeling/presence and their attendant regional qualities. Marx's close relationship to Romanticism and to the revolutionary spirit of Fichte and Schelling is evident particularly in his early works, which centre on establishing a valid critique of Hegel's later philosophy. Marx's rejection of that development, like Kierkegaard's contemporaneous attack, focused on its abstract and systematic character (Löwith 1964; Thulstrup 1980; Westphal 1996). In Marx's view, Hegel's thought was the apotheosis of the German ideology; that powerful tendency in modern thought that, in the wake of Kant's characterization of pure reason, had detached itself from the historical-social character of the living present and, consequently, lost itself in reckless pursuit of the absolute (Beiser 1987; Bowie 2003). Marx grasped the significance of the German ideology as a reflection of, as well as a reflection upon, the world it had forgotten. There was, in Hegel's philosophy, a compelling but distorted account of the real character of modern society. But Marx was determined not only to 'turn Hegel back on his feet', and reconnect thought with the world of *appearances* from which it had departed, but to turn thought towards the genuinely *phenomenal* character of modernity; that is to production. Hegel's thought could only become abstract and systematic because it had, thoughtlessly, taken the general process of exchange for the essential character of modern society. Hegel's philosophy is, thus, doubly misleading; it translates historically contingent aspects of the present into eternal relations and it selects for translation just those aspects of modern society that are superficial. By a process of abstraction and simplification Hegel, in fact, has rendered absolute the natural attitude that characterizes modern consciousness; Marx's aim is to historicize the critical understanding of modern society that results from a sociological reduction of that consciousness. An 'essential viewing' of modern society means 'seeing through' Hegel, *and* through the generalized process of circulation of which it is a reflection, to the process of production that constitutes its pure phenomena. And, of course, this 'essential viewing' brings out the *historical* character of that process.

The critique of Hegel, not surprisingly, was fertilized by insights native to the Romantic movement in opposition to which Hegel's thought had arisen and in relation to which it retained equivocal links. Recent scholarship has emphasized the centrality of developments within later Romanticism, and particularly in the thought of Schelling and Holderlïn (who as students both shared accommodation with Hegel), for the emergence of Marx's historical method and, equally, for the origins of European 'existential' thought (Žižek 1996; 2000; Bowie 1997). And it is in this context that Marx's sociological reduction is best understood. The affinity between Marx's reduction of society to production and the Romantic movement's reduction of humanity to creativity becomes more evident in the light of the subsequent, and now influential, writings by a number of iconoclastic Marxist writers. Particularly in the highly varied and unorthodox work of Walter Benjamin, Ernst Bloch, Theodor Adorno and the members of the Frankfurt School, Romanticism plays a key, if ambivalent, role both in their reception of Marx's insights and, more significantly, in their development of interpretations of modern culture as central to the fully developed modern mode of production. And, more particularly, the original and suggestive writings on music found in the work of Bloch and Adorno focus on the creative process in a Romantic manner; for the Romantics, after all, music was the privileged aesthetic form.

For Marx the constituting activity of society, of all social reality, is human *labour*, which is the dark matter of human creativity. *Productive* labour is the distinguishing character of human beings who, living outside the, real or imagined, primal condition of simple unity with nature, form and transform themselves in the process of securing their own survival. A *mode* of production is not only a historically developing means of transforming nature into the materials required for human life, it *is* that life activity. Humanity makes itself through its labour, producing itself in new ways and as a new being with the production of a world that sustains this inner transformation:

This mode of production must not be considered simply as being the production of the physical existence of the individuals. Rather it is a definite form of activity of those individuals, a definite form of expressing their life, a definite *mode of life* on their part. As individuals express their life, so they are. What they are, therefore, coincides with their production, both with *what* they produce and *how* they produce. (Marx 1970, 42)

Production, that is to say, is the sphere of self-expression as well as self-creation; both life and the means to life. Society is essentially production; that is to say, Marx locates the *phenomenon* of society (the social as distinct from the political, economic, religious, military and so forth) in production. This is easily misconstrued as the claim that economic production is the 'prime mover' of the historical process. Marx himself was occasionally guilty of expressing his ideas in language that, inappropriately, drew its meaning from the ontological region of representation, exchange, efficient causality, and the natural sciences. Thus, famously, in the 'Preface' to *A Contribution to the Critique of Political Economy* he writes:

In the social production which men carry on they enter into definite relations that are indispensable and independent of their will; these relations of production correspond to a definite stage of development of their material powers of production. The sum total of these relations of production constitutes the economic structure of society – the real foundation, on which rise legal and political superstructures and to which correspond definite forms of social consciousness. (Marx and Engels 1969, 43)

But 'the preface has nothing to do with the text' (Derrida 1981), an observation already made by Hegel in his own 'superfluous' preface to the *Phenomenology of Spirit*, which had warned of the possibly 'inappropriate and misleading' character of all material forcibly annexed to the ideally self-contained work. And while it is certainly the case that the major works of Marx's maturity pay close attention to the development of manufacture as well as to economic production generally, and his *Critique* shifts from philosophy to political economy, they do so in order to throw light on the peculiar manner in which labour is institutionalized in modern, capitalist society. The significance of production is viewed throughout in terms of its general character; as the process in which society generates, regenerates, and transforms itself. It is not confined to 'economic' relations; nor, importantly, is its pre-eminence understood in terms of causal effectiveness.

In the *Grundrisse* (the 'Introduction' as distinct from the 'Preface' to the *Critique of Political Economy*) he treats exchange and consumption as 'moments' of production. The *actual* process of social and institutional differentiation that gives rise to the conceptual trinity of production, exchange, and consumption 'all reduce themselves in the last instance to the role played by general-historical relations in production, and their relation to the movement of history generally. The question evidently belongs within the treatment and investigation of production itself' (1973, 97). The 'last instance' is not the mechanical 'cause' of the characteristic pattern of modern social relations but the general process in which these distinctions arise. 'Thus production, distribution, exchange and consumption form a regular syllogism; production is the generality, distribution and exchange the particularity, and consumption the singularity in which the whole is joined together' (1973, 89). But this is, at best, a 'shallow coherence'. Neither the distinctiveness of each sphere nor their reciprocal interrelations should be analysed into an interaction of equivalent elements: 'The person objectifies himself in production, the thing subjectifies itself in the person; in distribution, society mediates between production and consumption in the form of general, dominant determinants' (1973, 89). All production is also and simultaneously consumption (of nature and labour power), and all consumption is also production (of the person); 'each is immediately its opposite'. A product only becomes a product, he points out, in the act of consumption: 'a garment becomes a real garment only in the act of being worn' (1973, 91). And the product 'is production not as objectified activity, but rather only as object for the active subject'. 'Consumption creates the (economic) motive for production' and, at the same time, production 'produces not only the object but also the manner of production' and, crucially, also creates 'the need felt by the consumer' (1973, 92). Consumption 'produces the producer's *inclination* by beckoning to him as an aim-determining need' (1973, 92). Exchange mediates between the spheres of production and consumption. However, as the possibility and necessity of exchange, as well as its specific character, are aspects of the division of labour, this process is also a moment of production.

The social character of production is, of course, the central theme of *Capital* where it is given a more precise conceptual and historical location and, more significantly from the present perspective, the modern character of production as the *phenomenon* of society is expressed more clearly. Volume One of *Capital* opens where the unpublished *Grundrisse* had been interrupted a decade earlier in 1857–8, with an account of the commodity. This, in fact, is a fine piece of phenomenological analysis and highlights the affinity between Marx and the Romantic movement. For Marx the commodity is a *fragment* of society; a seemingly simple, detachable object, but one in which, like the literary fragment so loved by Novalis and Schlegel, an entire world, society, is hidden (Schlegel 1971; Novalis 1997; Lacoue-Labarthe and Nancy 1988). Marx shows that what is given *in* the commodity is by no means identical with what is given *as* the commodity. For the natural attitude of everyday life, as for the science of political economy, the commodity appears as an external object and as a bearer of value. The value of a commodity appears to be linked directly to its sensuous qualities and its relative availability. Commodities that are desirable and/or scarce are of higher value than those that are less wanted and/or common. However, if we 'bracket' this attitude, the genuinely phenomenal character of the commodity as the constituted reality of human labour becomes evident. The dual character of the commodity, as thing and as value, cannot fully be understood within the natural attitude; within that perspective value appears only in a process of exchange in which 'All its sensuous characteristics are extinguished' (Marx 1976a, 128). This apparent duality is dissolved, however, when we grasp the essential character of the commodity as a product of labour. Both the sensuous qualities of the object and its value in the process of exchange are expressions of productive labour. But the social and creative character of that labour is concealed. In capitalist society the intimate bond of possession, the corporeal expressiveness of labour, and its immanent freedom, have been corrupted and turned into a new form of oppression. Labour itself has become a commodity and, therefore, acquired the characteristics of a 'thing', transferable, exchangeable, and saleable. The human being lives now in a sphere of circulating commodities, that is to say in an unreality devoid of both humanity and society:

> Objects of utility become commodities only because they are the products of the labour of private individuals who work independently of each other ... It is only by being exchanged that the products of labour acquire a socially uniform objectivity as values, which is distinct from their sensuously varied objectivity as articles of utility. Value does not have its description branded on its forehead; it rather transforms every product of labour into a social hieroglyphic ... It is the finished form of the world of commodities – the money form – which conceals the social character of private labour and the social relations between the individual workers, by making those relations appear as relations between material objects, instead of revealing them plainly ... The categories of bourgeois economics consist precisely of forms of this kind. They are forms of thought which are socially valid, and therefore objective, for the relations of production belonging to this historically determined mode of social production, i.e. commodity production. The whole mystery of commodities, all the magic and necromancy that surrounds the products of labour on the basis of commodity production, vanishes therefore as soon as we come to other forms of production. (1976a, 163)

For Marx the fateful disjunction of freedom and authenticity is the rupture in which *society* takes root in the modern world. And because society is now made *present* in the *commodity* mode of production, the social world is *represented* as an impersonal system of exchange governed by universal laws of equivalence. Marx refers to this relation as the 'fetishism of commodities':

> It is nothing but the definite social relation between men themselves which assumes here, for them, the fantastic form of a relation between things. In order, therefore, to find an analogy we must take flight into the misty realm of religion. There the products of the human brain appear as autonomous figures endowed with a life of their own, which enter into relations both with each other and with the human race. So it is in the world of commodities with the products of men's hands. I call this the fetishism which attaches itself to the products of labour as soon as they are produced as commodities, and is therefore inseparable from the production of commodities. (1976a, 164)

The reduction to production is both a methodological procedure, the essential viewing in which production appears as the phenomenon of society, and a historical process, the emergence and development of modernity in which society conceals itself in the capitalist mode of production. *Capital*, thus, presents a substantial historical account of the transition to capitalism not only as the development of new productive means but as their withdrawal into the *private* world of the capitalist. The progressive appropriation of productive means and their sequestration as private property, and

175

the subsequent development of new means within the 'ontological region' of ownership, gives rise to a fatal, but almost invisible, duality in modern society. On the one hand society constitutes itself as a secret process of inhuman and exploitative production and, on the other hand, it generates a public realm of liberated market relations.

The social process emerges from and dissolves into the hidden inwardness of human being. Modern society is a product, and the process of production is nothing other than an expression of the private interests and private world of the capitalist; modern society is, as it were, the *hysteria* of capitalism; a mass of symptoms that at once conceals and reveals its forgotten body and hidden, secret longings. And its public life, validly conceived in political economy as the general exchange of equivalent values, finally collides with the unexaminable inner world of individual private wants.

Production is not the manufacture of things, or even of commodities, so much as the generation and regeneration of *society*. But, in capitalist society, this gives rise to an inverted world, an unreal objectivity, which conceals the real social character of the process itself. An abyss is opened between the appearance of society within the natural attitude of its members, and the phenomena of society revealed by the withdrawal of any positing conviction in the reality of what it seems.

Reduction to Consumption

Durkheim might plausibly be read as advancing a sociological reduction to consumption. Durkheim, among the classics in sociology, offers the most comprehensive and insightful treatment of sentiments, and it is in relation to the entire ontological region of feeling/presence that his view of consumption as the characteristic modern form of society can be understood. This perspective emerges in his critique of utilitarian political economy. For exchange to be possible, there must be an elementary *trust* binding the parties to any exchange, however limited and specific their contract. Society is viewed in terms of this 'background' assumption of trust; it is constituted as a 'moral community' defined by its shared 'beliefs and sentiment'. It is not the case, he insists, that modernity implies a withering away of sentiment and the development of calculative relations alone. Feeling – which is nothing other than collective subjectivity – becomes all the more evident in advanced societies, which are *also* characterized by individualism, rationalization, and impersonality. In the general process of the circulation of commodities, as in their production, the rational pursuit of private and group interests increasingly regulates social relations. But in the sphere of consumption 'society' is rediscovered in a spontaneous sharing of sentiment; in a newly energized *conscience collective*. Durkheim expresses this most clearly by contrast to the self-destructive feelings engendered in people suffering from social isolation and the anomic situation of unregulated and catastrophic social change. The linked forms of suicide have in common the absence in the immediate social context of those supportive relations which give rise to positive sentiments and the shared feeling in which selfhood is confirmed.

Much recent historical sociology has emphasized in a new way the role of consumption in the emergence and development of modern society. The 'consumer revolution' has been pushed back, from the recent past of post-war Europe and America, to Europe of the late nineteenth century, then to eighteenth-century England (Brewer and Porter 1993), and in an impressive way to early modern Europe of the late sixteenth and early seventeenth centuries (Braudel 1982). Certainly, the emergence of mass consumption forms an important background to Durkheim's sociology. For such a society value is sedimented in the material culture of things, and participation in the 'collective representations' of that culture, the sharing of sentiments, is most readily accomplished through the consumption of commodities. The sacred, in other words, has taken up residence in the new temples of consumption, and it is in this new urban setting that the direct force of collective life can be felt (Williams 1982; Zeldin 1980a; 1980b).

It is in relation to his own culture and its absorption in material consumption that Durkheim's most ambitious sociological work is best understood. When Durkheim outlines the character of 'mechanical solidarity' and its relation to the most elementary types of religious phenomena he is referring as much to late-nineteenth-century Paris as he is to aboriginal Australia. Durkheim's *Elementary Forms of the Religious Life* argues that religion is the essential phenomenon of society, and locates the religious in the distinction between the sacred and the profane, arguing that this is a universal and necessary distinction in which society is founded. The sacred is the symbol of society, and every society must make itself accessible to individual experience in some such abbreviated form. The difference between primitive archaic society and modern complex society turns out not to be so great. In simple society, also, 'society' has no permanent and continuous existence as a totality; rather, it comes fleetingly to life in those special occasions in which groups come together to celebrate specific festivals. Only then does the collective life manifest itself in its fullness.

Indeed, the unity of the social group, the interrelatedness of which is said to be founded on kinship, comes only from the assumption of a common name and emblem:

> for the members of a single clan are not united to each other by a common habitat or by common blood, as they are not necessarily consanguineous and are frequently scattered over different parts of the tribal territory. Their unity comes solely from their having the same name and the same emblem, their believing that they have the same relations with the same categories of things, their practising the same rites, or, in a word, from their participating in the same totemic cult. (Durkheim 1995, 167)

The 'figured representation of the totem' is treated in a special way; it is sacred. Similarly the totemic species and the clan are also considered sacred to varying and lesser degrees. Durkheim argues that totemism is not an animistic religion; rather 'an anonymous and impersonal force, found in each of these beings but not to be confounded with any of them' is the focus of sacred beliefs and practices (1995, 188). The totem is 'only the material form under which the imagination represents this immaterial substance, this energy diffused through all sorts of heterogeneous things, which alone is the real object of the cult' (1995, 189). This is no metaphorical force, but a real presence, experienced as an external pressure that 'is the source of the moral life of the clan' (1995, 190). In this totemism is not distinct, but shares with the more developed religions in a fundamentally common character. What is at the basis of all religious representations are not determined images, but 'indefinite powers, anonymous forces'.

The sacred, that is to say, is a specific representation of impersonal forces which, it is inescapably suggested to the primitive, shape the world in which they live. Thus 'the totem is before all a symbol, a material expression of something else'. Durkheim coyly and quite rhetorically asks 'Of what else?' But it is clear from the outset that the answer to this question will be 'society'. The totem is simply the 'outward and visible form' of the group.

As in Schleiermacher's view of religion, Durkheim argues that society 'gives us the sensation of a perpetual dependence' (Schleiermacher 1958; Durkheim 1995, 206). 'Since it has a nature which is peculiar to itself and different from our individual nature, it pursues ends which are likewise special to it', but ends realized imperiously through our action. It is society which exercises moral control over us, and which forces from us acknowledgement of its own supremacy and superiority (Nielsen 1999).

Furthermore, a god 'is not merely an authority upon whom we depend; it is a force upon which our strength relies' (Durkheim 1995, 209). Religious ritual vivifies sentiments through which society can maintain this superiority and provide this strength:

> in the midst of an assembly animated by a common passion, we become susceptible of acts and sentiments of which we are incapable when reduced to our own forces. (1995, 209–10)

A general effervescence, which is a strengthening influence of society, makes itself felt through the cult.

But if the totem represents the collective force of the group, its superiority and independence from the individual, what does the profane represent? The difficulty here is that Durkheim had already argued cogently that modern society is increasingly made up of individual representations; but that these are, as much as collective representations, social conventions in which must be incarnated the powers of social life. He had also argued that in primitive societies there are very few individual representations, that social life is more of a piece than modern society. So the profane, in primitive societies, must *also* represent society to its members; it could hardly be otherwise. Hence the difficulty: what is the meaning of the profane?; and how can the whole basis of Durkheim's argument be sustained if the distinction upon which everything is erected has an unfortunate tendency to break down? To put it otherwise; the profane is *also* a religious category.

The situation becomes a little clearer if the discussion is refocused on what is implicit in *The Elementary Forms*, but quite explicit in the rest of Durkheim's work; namely, that it is the character of *modern* society which is his central preoccupation and continuous subject matter. His study of primitive religion, indeed, is only an exercise in conceptual clarification; an exercise which has signally failed. But read as a meditation inspired by his experience of modernity, rather than by the confrontation with the primitive, it perhaps makes more sense.

Now in his other works Durkheim had argued for the view that individualism is both the subjective form of the advanced division of labour, and the foundation of organic solidarity. The individual, that is to say, is a formal creation of modern society, and neither the integrity of the individual nor the solidarity of society is threatened by its normal development. In modern society it is individual representations that are pre-eminently religious or sacred in nature; and the *conscience collective* of modern society is best seen as being crystallized within the individual. Efforts to rediscover the sacred in collective rituals of modern life have been singularly unconvincing, and Durkheim himself provides the best arguments against such a misapplication of his analysis of primitive religion.

Thus, although Durkheim began *The Elementary Forms* with what appeared to be the unambiguous difference between the sacred and the profane, as the work progressed, the boundary between these domains became more and more problematical. Not only, from the outside and in terms of his own theory, was there a tendency to slide into a monism of the sacred but, in terms of a more immediate, phenomenological understanding, his distinction became difficult to sustain.

The difference between the sacred and the profane is so radical that, in fact, it tends to disappear. This becomes evident in Durkheim's discussion of the origin of totemic beliefs. The effervescence of the group has a transforming power over experience: 'this exceptional increase of force is something very real'. It is clear that Durkheim is actually talking about a wholly modern situation as, for example, a speaker addressing a large crowd, in which 'he has succeeded in entering into communion with it' (1995, 210). Durkheim refers to 'the demon of oratorical inspiration':

> His language has a grandiloquence that would be ridiculous in ordinary circumstances; his gestures show a certain domination. It is because he feels within him an abnormal over-supply of force which overflows and tries to burst out from him; sometimes he even has the feeling that he is dominated by a moral force which is greater than he and of which he is only the interpreter. (1995, 210)

However, it is not only in exceptional circumstances that we feel this force, indeed, 'there is not, so to speak, a moment in our lives when some current of energy does not come to us from without'. The peculiarity of the sacred is in some way dispersed throughout the modern world such that, as efficacious as ever, it has been rendered invisible.

In the case of aboriginal society, on the other hand, he claims, the entire society alternates between profane and sacred states. The profane is dominated by economic activity and 'is generally of very mediocre intensity ... the dispersed condition in which the society finds itself results in making its life uniform, languishing and dull'. But during sacred rituals intensified interaction acts as a powerful stimulant; 'a sort of electricity is formed by their collecting which quickly transports them to an extraordinary degree of exaltation' (1995, 215). In this situation, heightened stimulation has dramatic consequences:

> This effervescence often reaches such a point that it causes unheard-of actions. The passions released are of such impetuosity that they can be restrained by nothing. They are so far removed from their ordinary conditions of life, and they are so thoroughly conscious of it, that they feel that they must set themselves outside of and above their ordinary morals. (1995, 216)

This transformation is complete:

> One can readily conceive how, when arrived at this state of exaltation, a man does not recognise himself any longer. Feeling himself dominated and carried away by some sort of external power which makes him think and act differently than in normal times, he naturally has the impression of being himself no longer. It seems that he has become a new being ... And at the same time all his companions feel themselves transformed in the same way ... everything is just as though he really were transported into a special world, entirely different from the one where he ordinarily lives, and into an environment filled with exceptionally intense forces that take hold of him and metamorphose him. (1995, 218)

But if these worlds are so radically distinct, entering the sacred effectively abolishes the profane and becomes itself an all-inclusive reality. Like a dream, for which the waking world does not exist, the sacred is a division within the profane which, paradoxically, includes everything within itself.

Modern society, thus, rather than being seen in terms of the gradual, but more or less complete secularization for which the sacred exists as a memory or as a theoretical, unrealizable possibility, is viewed as a condition in which the sacred becomes so pervasive that it is no longer visible. Our absorption in the sacred means that we imagine ourselves to be living within a secular world; but the frenzy of modern life, the continuous over-stimulation, the heightening of dynamic density, the sense of being carried along and carried away by mysterious external forces; all of this is Durkheim's way of characterizing modern society in general as an essentially sacred phenomenon: a collective reality characterized by mobile sentiments and unpredictable currents of feeling (Barrows 1981; Nielsen 1999; Van Ginneken 1992).

Synthesis and Interrelation

Phenomenological insight and historical-sociological analysis together articulate the constituting processes of modern society in terms of three irreducible ontological regions: sensing/representation/exchange; willing/presentation/production; feeling/presence/consumption. Each of these regions is also associated with a particular phenomenological method and a characteristic type of sociological perspective. The first links Husserl with Weber and Simmel; the second brings together Heidegger and Marx; the third finds a path from Levinas to Durkheim.

The limitations of this trinitarian structure are evident. Each construes society in different and incompatible ways. That these methodological positions correspond in some way to the actual history of modernity testifies to the scope and ubiquity of modern trinitarianism, but does not clarify the issue. Is the society that may appear to us in any of three different ways not in some ultimate sense always the same? If this is the case, and we persist in the sociological ambition to grasp society, how can we grasp its reality as a synthesis beyond experience? Must we, in fact, abandon phenomenology and return to speculation? Put another way; if society has become differentiated from itself and its past in a radical way and now comprises three distinct *worlds* of experience, how can this trinitarian structure reveal itself?; how can this become evident? Where does a phenomenological sociology of modernity *locate* itself if not in one of the delimited zones of modernity itself? And, if it is thus located, how can it see 'essentially' outside the constituting processes of that specific region? Finally, to put an end to an anxious surge of questioning, if phenomenological observation is located *outside* the regional ontologies of modernity, has it not emptied itself into sheer abstraction and ignored its own injunction to 'follow the phenomena themselves'?

These questions can only be posed, however, because the historical character of modernity has already shifted. The trinitarianism of modernity is apparent just because it already lies in the past. Contemporary society, in other words, is no longer modern or, at least, no longer modern in the same way. From being constituted in terms of what appears within the natural attitude as a given variety of difference, society appears as indifference. And it is just in this process of dissolution that the categorical structure of the recent past becomes visible; and what had been lived through as mutually exclusive realities (and not just different views of the same reality) become available as more or less interesting points of view, perspectives, and attitudes.

Contemporary understandings of the distinctions that were central to the development of each version of modernity now stress the instability of their immanent regulative principles, the incoherence of their forms of self-understanding, and the limitations of their sensibility. In retrospect the process of dedifferentiation manifests itself in an unambiguous way from the 1870s onwards. In relation to every aspect of culture and society, what now seems clear is the relatively short duration of modernity's confident maturity. The clarity and confidence of its central period have now evaporated and the world appears to as, in many respects, quite the opposite of what had been regarded as its most fundamental and well-established principles. This can be grasped, first of all, within each phenomenological region separately, then as a more general process that characterizes contemporary experience. The immanent regulative principle that had seemed to be on the point of a final and absolute clarification once again became obscure. Suspicion of reason, despair over selfhood, and fear of pleasure united in a general distrust of the present and its inherent possibilities.

The impasse reached within the development of each phenomenological domain was compounded and integrated into a culture of decadence and nihilism. In surprising ways, however, these obstacles proved to be points of departure for the emergence of unadumbrated novelties; original activity broke out in every field and, again with the advantage of hindsight, took form in ways that can be seen as embryonic in the earliest stages of modernity.

8

Indifference: Towards Contemporary Inexperience

> He inhabited a whole world of his own, totally self-contained, created in a haze of Pernod or brandy, in which he wandered around totally indifferent to the real world. It was a formless world, a teeming ant-hill of flitting shadows where nothing mattered, nothing had any purpose, where it was possible to wander aimlessly, effortlessly, feeling neither joy nor sadness, cocooned in a thick mist.
>
> Simenon, *The Bar on the Seine*

> They seemed uninvolved ... seemed rather to be watching themselves in the glass of the windshield where, superimposed on the varied confusion of park and sky, a few of their features were reflected at random: their eyes, their mouths, Carla's childish cheeks, Leo's felt hat – detached and suspended in the void like a mirage, impossible to comprehend.
>
> Moravia, *The Time of Indifference*

> The wakeful egoic life is distinguished from the egoic life that is not awake, from the ego that is 'in a stupor' in the broadest sense, and the two are distinguished by the fact that in the latter, no lived-experience in the specific sense of wakefulness is there at all and no present ego is there at all as its subject.
>
> Husserl, *Active and Passive Synthesis*

The trinitarian structure of modernity gives rise to three distinctive sociological reductions. The characterization of society through exchange, production, or consumption describes three distinctive historical processes rather than a single process from three different points of view. The common-sense view that sociology can arrive at a valid, comprehensive view of modern society by combining these different accounts must be rejected. Such an approach is almost certainly guided by a prior and unexamined commitment to a position justified as the implicit convergence of distinctive traditions. More significantly, any method of combination, interrelation, synthesis, and so on moves away from the 'phenomena themselves' towards an abstract and, therefore, non-experienced totality. Contrary to any such approach, the phenomenological import of the classical traditions in sociology is just that it is *society* that is experienced as exchange, or production, or consumption. Society as an exhaustive totality of social activities is no more open to experience as a unity than is the field of consciousness for the ego.

Yet convergence of another sort does emerge. Phenomenological sociology characterizes experience in and of contemporary society as *indifference*. In the indistinction of the present the difference in which consciousness takes root – the disparity between experiencing an object and the object of experience – is dissolved. All difference becomes inconsequential. That is to say, society itself dissolves into diffuse states and indeterminate forms of being. This process can be followed through each region in which society had previously constituted itself through difference and determination. Exchange and the sphere of sensing and reason come up against the contradiction between law and cause, which is solved by running them together as chance. Production and the practical articulation of the will and self come up against the paradox of selfhood, which is resolved by a growing disinterest. Consumption and the heightening of pleasure end in hysteria, which is dissolved in melancholy. The process of differentiation, which hitherto had described the trajectory of modernity, goes into reverse. Each distinctive sphere empties its forms, first into indeterminate phenomena that belong to their own region, then into a general indeterminateness, which characterizes contemporary experience as indifference, disembodiment, banality, and boredom. The astonishment in which, and with which, modernity first appeared – the manifestation of its strange and unfamiliar world – ultimately became utterly mundane, unremarkable, and dull.

Chance: Indifferent Reason

For the order of sensing, representation, and exchange the regulative principle of reason was both a systematic model of reality and an embodied force; it was an ideal law of conservation and the determining condition of every particular event. As law and cause together, empirical reality was explained in terms of the interaction of an indefinite number of 'point mass' interactions. Matter, as well as time and space, was drained of substantial qualities and conceptualized as the indifferent bearer of primary qualities. The substance of nature, empirical reality, was held to be everywhere the same; simple extension. Individual forms were a result, on the one hand, of the localization of matter in space and time and, on the other, of 'secondary qualities' arising from acts of perception themselves. The science of nature dealt with the idealized 'point mass' and its equally idealized interactions in a geometrized void. These interactions, like the accountant's formalization of market transactions, could be conceptualized independently of the phenomenal forms in which natural beings and objects actually appeared to us; they were abstract and, in terms of their mathematical description, reversible in time.

The first serious scientific investigations of industrial technology, however, which took place in post-revolutionary France where Napoleonic reforms in higher education had raised the academic and career status of engineers, found the classical 'mechanical philosophy' to be an analytically and practically inadequate basis for explaining the operation of actual machinery. Sadi Carnot's pioneering studies in the 1830s (around the same time as Andrew Ure's *Philosophy of Manufacture*, an equally pioneering sociological account of factory production) focused on the *inefficiency* of all machines and developed systematic concepts and methods for investigating its sources and measuring their effects. This was a mechanics of the 'real' world where operating mechanisms meant metal forced against metal, pistons grinding against cylinders, cogs meshing and sometimes slipping against cogs, levers and wheels turning on bearings, drive belts tightened against flywheels. In every moving part and point of contact friction impeded 'theoretically' effortless inertial motion; indeed, many mechanical operations were possible only because of the frictional forces generated within the machinery itself. The operation of every machine could be described precisely in terms of its 'loss' of energy or, more accurately, its 'conversion' of mechanical movement into heat; by the extent, in other words, from which it apparently departed from the theoretical model of 'conservation laws'. Of course, as Carnot and the subsequent development of the physics of heat elucidated, no energy was actually 'lost'; the heat energy generated exactly balanced the loss of mechanical energy. But the shift in focus was important and had long-term implications for the development of the physical sciences. Carnot attended to the inevitable and substantial 'experimental error' observed in the performance of every machine (the degree to which in practice its performance deviated from the theoretical model of the conservation laws) and made it the subject matter of his science. This might be described as another kind of 'reduction'; bringing forward into the foreground of active consideration aspects of the phenomenological field known as 'machinery' that had hitherto been overlooked and relinquishing to the background what previously had held the scientific gaze.

A particularly significant implication of the new mechanics of heat lay in the recognition that all empirical systems – even when 'reduced' to mechanical interactions – were inscribed with the arrow of time. Every mechanical action was essentially directional; mechanical energy was continuously lost, heat constantly generated. Machines, unlike Newtonian laws, could not be put into reverse; they operated and could be 'read' in one direction only. This was the case, as Clausius pointed out, even if we considered planetary systems or the entire cosmos. As a machine the cosmos was inherently inefficient and ceaselessly lost energy, which was 'wasted' in heating interstellar space. Frictional forces, the loss of mechanical energy in every particle collision, meant the universe as a whole was 'running down' and, as its original energetic creation was not renewable, would ultimately decay. *Entropy* could only be reversed locally; the machine of the universe would slowly and irrevocably come to a standstill. The Galilean and Newtonian image of the cosmos as a perpetual motion mechanism, its sum of motions conserved in the effortless continuity of inertia, gave way to a new (rather, renewed) vision of unremitting effort, ceaselessly mounting fatigue, and death as its fateful character (Clark and Henderson 2002).

Carnot was not alone in attending in a new way to 'experimental error'. At the same time the great French astronomer Pierre Simon Laplace recognized that the determination of the exact location of planetary bodies was subject to 'observational error' that could be analysed in a systematic fashion. Of course it had long been understood that all astronomical observations were subject to a number of sources of error of which the limitations of instruments, moment-to-moment changes in temperature and humidity, and 'human error' were the most significant. In spite of improvements in equipment and technique such sources of variation could never wholly be eliminated. However, Laplace noticed that if a large number of observations of the same object were made, the variations were distributed in a distinctive and regular pattern. The 'error curve' could be described with mathematical precision and used to establish an estimate of the 'true' position; a result that, even if it did not match any particular event, could be treated with greater confidence than even the most carefully conducted single observation.

The development of probability theory in the natural sciences shares an important context in the rise of statistical thinking in the practical 'management' of modern 'mass' social phenomena. Laplace was influenced by Adolphe Quételet's studies in 'social statistics' as, later, was Maxwell. The mathematical techniques of 'political arithmetic' and modern engineering emerged in observations of demographic data, notably in John Graunt's *Observations upon Bills of Mortality* in the 1660s and in the development of the insurance business (Porter 1986).

The 'error curve' in observational data was soon found to be characteristic of the distribution of many naturally occurring phenomena, such as the height and weight of individuals, and became known as the 'normal distribution'. The mathematical techniques that Laplace and others developed for the precise analysis of such data placed at the disposal of investigators in every field of empirical research powerful new research tools. At the same time the rapid development of statistical analysis made general an assumption that subverted the classically modern image of nature. The 'error curve' yielded to mathematical description only on the assumption of the independence of each observation. Each recorded event was regarded as *unconnected* with any other, and the resulting distribution was regarded as the outcome of *random* variation. This was a principle already well established in the mathematical study of gambling and games of chance that had begun in the Renaissance and developed in sophistication throughout the eighteenth century (Daston 1988; Kavanagh 1993; Reith 1999). But if the mathematically identical distribution also describes *natural* phenomena, does this not mean that nature, rather than being constituted as a mechanical system in which every part is physically connected to every other part in an unbroken continuity of efficient causes, is made up, in fact, of randomly occurring events?

The idea of randomness in nature, that is to say, was introduced into the physical sciences, natural history, and the social sciences as an apparently innocuous, and extremely useful, method of 'controlling error'. But a fuller examination of the assumptions and applications of statistical method led inescapably to radical change in the understanding of both nature and the architectonics of reason that had encompassed nature.

Darwin's theory of evolution by natural selection led the way with an impressive accumulation of examples in which differences within and among species could be grasped (in a nice irony) as the 'mechanical' (that is, blind) consequences of randomly occurring variations in particular populations of living beings. Adaptation to different and changing environments was possible only because the individuals of every species were not identical, and their variations in any particular feature were distributed randomly throughout the population. This aspect of Darwin's theory, which in other respects excited enormous interest and strong reactions, was not immediately grasped for the radical development in scientific thought that it subsequently proved to be.

It was the convergence of the physics of heat and new statistical thinking that finally provoked a more thorough examination of the implications of randomness for the classical scientific world view. Rudolf Clausius, and later Ludwig Boltzmann, developed a statistical approach to the understanding of radiant heat and conductivity. The way in which heat 'spread' through a medium from 'hot' regions to 'cool' regions until the temperature throughout the body was uniform had long been understood in terms of the purely mechanical transfer of energy from vibrating particles as they collided; in each collision some of the 'heat' (vibration) was transferred from the more active to the less active particle. What emerged in the latter part of the nineteenth century, however, was that the precise mathematical description of this process required that all transfers of energy were conceptualized as random and that no purely mechanical explanation in terms of the laws of physical contact was adequate (Brush 1976; 1978; Von Plato 1994; Krüger et al. 1996; Gigerenzer 1989).

In a related way the phenomenon of Brownian motion – the movement of pollen grains suspended in fluid – seemed to give direct observational evidence of the underlying randomness of particulate motion. Many scientists clung to the conviction that this was nothing more than a methodological device to deal in a formal way with extremely complex interactions that always operated in strict conformity with classical laws of mechanism. Others took the radical step of supposing randomness was embedded in nature in a way that ultimately was at odds with both the systematic idealization of mechanism and the notion of efficient cause. In either case randomness, rather than the unbroken chain of physical causality, became the generalized model of natural phenomena. Rather than 'explain' deviations from an expected outcome as random error, therefore, randomness became the 'natural' state of affairs, any departure from which called for specific explanation. For the modern sciences 'the indeterminism of probability is so reliable and highly structured that randomness seems to disappear from the end result' (Porter 1986, 150). But the apparent success of statistical thinking implied nothing less than the overthrow of the classical modern conception of nature.

This view made *chance* the new operative principle of nature, and this was quite simply the antithesis of reason. The notions of causality and mechanism had to be drastically amended if not overthrown. In the process science did not stop to draw breath and reflect on its philosophical rupture with the past. Rather, liberated from what suddenly seemed intolerable and narrow-minded constraints, it developed in the most dramatic fashion. In the early twentieth century the revolution in science was more thoroughgoing and radical than had been any of its previous incarnations. The randomness of cause and the systematic 'dematerialization' of nature, now transformed into a complex flux of unevenly distributed *energy*, made the universe a quite different and strange phenomenon (Clarke and Henderson 2002; Asendorf 1993). The success of science depended on the ever more rigorous application of fewer guiding principles; and its formal success meant ultimately the exclusion of nature from the phenomenological domain of sensing. This, in fact, had been immanent in the scientific mode of thought from the inception of its modern form, but was now presented with unavoidable starkness. Science had stepped beyond the rational, driven there by reason itself. And nature, no longer revealing itself in phenomenal forms, became at once transparent and thoroughly incomprehensible. Reason, or at least the classically modern notion of reason as systematic unity, was the obstacle rather than the means to a more adequate grasp of reality.

These considerations, of course, are central to a critical historical understanding of science rather than to phenomenological issues directly, but they illustrate important aspects of the cultural transformation of modernity that phenomenology describes. Again it must be stressed that this transformation cannot be understood as a willed change of attitude; rather, it has to be seen as a development 'forced' by the immanent development of the sciences themselves. We can reasonably ask, however, what was it around the turn of the nineteenth to the twentieth century that made randomness, chance, and the chaos of causes a *plausible* and satisfying view of nature; sufficiently so, indeed, to justify overturning the classical synthesis? And in this regard scientific innovation has an exemplary value no less than that provided by the frequently described novelties in music, dance, painting, and literature (Conrad 1998; Burrow 2000). In particular it provides a highly suggestive illustration of the sudden reversal of foreground and background; a change that amounts to an articulation within a particular cultural field of a general transformation in the 'natural attitude'.

Dissociation: Indifferent Selves

The modern construction of willing as the substantial quality of the soul was always unstable and ambiguous. Quite apart from the paradox of freedom and self-determination, and of interiority and communication, a residual sense of the term hinted at quite a different sphere of meaningfulness. The sense of 'to be willing' to do something, meaning to 'go along with' other people's plans or to be a 'willing helper' in some joint project, suggested the idea of willing also referred to compliance rather than self-assertion and constituted, in fact, an obscure background in relation to which self-determining agency stood out.

The transition from the classical *experience of* modernity as selfhood, to contemporary *self-experiencing*, can be characterized as a double movement; a receding of the phenomenon into the haziness of its background and, at the same time, an engulfing advance of the background, absorbing into a misty indetermination what had appeared to be the natural obstinacy of the ego.

In recent years impressive scholarship has excavated the rich sediments of pre-Freudian psychology and, in particular, has suggested fresh ways of grasping both the phenomenon of hysteria and the variety of theories its suddenly widespread incidence provoked. In the context of the present discussion this work is particularly suggestive as a phenomenological sociology of the important transition from authentic willing to insincere wishing (Ellenberger 1970; Showalter 1987; 1997; Bronfen 1998; Micale 1995). Related to the study of hysteria new investigative and therapeutic techniques emerged. Among these hypnosis took on particular significance for its demonstrative and forensic possibilities, and also offers itself as a particularly apt example of new forms and experiences (as well as new theories) of willing.

Hypnosis, like the technological innovations and natural discoveries of an earlier period of modernity, was fascinatingly strange. Initial astonishment at the phenomenon of hypnotism, which made it a staple of popular entertainment as well as a focus of scientific investigation, was tinged with uneasiness. Hypnotism strikingly illustrated a disturbing mobility and lack of independence of the individuated will; its possibility seemed to rest on assumptions that ran contrary to the fundamental developmental tendencies of modernity (Gauld 1992).

Charlatans and publicists from the beginning exploited the strangeness of hypnosis. Its popularity as entertainment, indeed, for many years delayed its serious investigation. An unconventional medical practitioner, Mesmer, sought a new therapeutics founded upon astrological and animistic superstitions. He held that an insensible 'magnetic fluid' (a subtle and pervasive version of the Homeric life-giving *psyche*) flowed through the entire natural world, its direction and intensity depending upon astral influences. Mesmer claimed to be able to 'attract' such astral forces, and thus, like the hermetic magician, act as a kind of focus of magnetic forces. Typically he would 'magnetize' a tree, or a large barrel of water, and a group of 'clients' would simultaneously touch the tree, or put their hands in the water, allowing the magnetic forces to flow into their bodies. The results were frequently dramatic. Individuals might lose consciousness, and on awaking be unable to recall anything of the 'séance'. Not infrequently people suffering from a wide variety of illnesses claimed to feel much better afterwards, and not a few to be completely cured.

From somewhat obscure beginnings in the Swiss countryside Mesmer rapidly acquired a profitable celebrity. He moved to Paris and for a season or two enjoyed an extravagantly fashionable success. He ministered, mostly, to aristocratic ladies over many of whom he exercised a fascinating allure. It was this fascination, in fact, which led to a somewhat abrupt change in his fortunes. In a magnetized state many of his women clients apparently abandoned themselves to shameless sexual displays. The suspicion that his medical practice was little more than an excuse to indulge in orgies quickly provoked the outraged, and ill-informed, criticism of respectable bourgeois citizens. His fall from grace was swift and complete but, surviving in the more sober researches of his immediate followers, as well as in the nagging doubt raised by the spectacle of the popular stage shows that spread his fame more quickly, a new view of the functioning body emerged (Gauld 1992; Winter 1998).

Mesmerism inaugurated a tradition, in both scientific and popular thought, which effectively ended the divorce between 'mind' and 'body'; and, in focusing on the 'body image' as the primary reality of experience, at the same time cast doubt on the natural unity and wholeness of this reality.

Enthusiasts of mesmerism, indeed, declared vivid demonstrations of its effects to be evidence for transmigration of souls, life after death, and spiritual communication without sensory intermediary. The Rev. Chauncy Townshend, for example, writing in 1839, after a generation of mesmerists had refined their skills to regularly produce 'induced mesmeric sleepwalking', believed this state of 'delirium' to be 'capable of eliciting the highest state of moral and intellectual advancement to which man, in this existence, can probably attain' (1844, ix). The ecstatic states, convulsions and alarming fits into which the early subjects of mesmeric trance had fallen were no longer so evident. Mesmeric sleep was now advertised as tranquil, soothing and therapeutic, even for the healthy. A Dr Ennemoser, for example, had treated a painful lumbar abscess by mesmeric sleep, with great success. Townshend claimed all this was due to the effect of the human imagination, rather than any presumed 'magnetic fluid'. In sensitizing the imagination, and, as it were, bringing it into a greater prominence in the maintenance of the body image, Townshend claims mesmerism has provided conditions for the observation of telepathy, clairvoyance, fantastic feats of memory and refined and heightened perceptions of all kinds.

Braid suggested that mesmerism amounted to an 'artificial' means of inducing a state of consciousness between waking and sleeping. In his treatise on 'Neurypnology' (1843), he argued additionally that these states were, in effect, self-induced. The 'hypnotic' state, as he for the first time termed it, 'depended on the physical and psychical condition of the patient ... and not at all on the volition, or passes of the operator, throwing out a magnetic fluid, or exciting into activity some mystical universal fluid or medium' (Braid 1899, 102).

Natural 'somnambulistic states' had been observed in the past and Braid viewed them, along with deliberately provoked mesmeric sleep, as a voluntary withdrawal of attention; 'it is a law in the animal economy, that by continual fixation of the mental and visual eye, on any object which is not of itself of an exciting nature, with absolute repose of body, and general quietude, they become wearied … a state of somnolency is induced' (1899, 112).

Braid's view, in principle, allowed a 'scientific' approach to hypnotism. A new understanding of both the sensory and the motor functions of the body, through the physiology of the central nervous system, begun by Bell and Solly, and extended by Helmholtz and others, offered a plausible account of spontaneous nervous reactions and unconscious automatism. Nervous tissue, capable of sensitivity and irritability, they suggested, displayed an inbuilt hierarchical form of organization, and consciousness was associated exclusively with 'higher' levels of integrated nervous activity.

In Britain the scientific study of mesmerism and related phenomena, which had begun with the work of Braid and Elliotson, was dominated by the more extravagant speculations of the forerunners of the Psychical Society which, towards the end of the century, championed what in retrospect seems to be an absurd mixture of scientific psychology, charlatanism, and spiritualism. It is worth seeing this, rather than the more sober approach of Braid and his scientific followers, as the significant legacy of Mesmer's career. For most people there was no clear distinction between science and spiritualism, and Mesmer's techniques, somewhat adapted and toned down, were embraced just because they seemed to offer a controlled experimental technique for investigating spiritual phenomena (Winter 1998). What fascinated so many people were the little tested claims of clairvoyance and telepathy in the somnambulistic state, and the 'mesmerizing' power exercised over the powerless subject by the apparently omnipotent hypnotizer. A good deal of discussion, both literary and academic, centred on the question of whether the hypnotizer could 'make' the hypnotized subject obey his every command. One imagines that the whole situation provided a respectable milieu for the exercise (if not satisfaction) of male fantasies of total control over a passive woman (Dijkstra 1986).

Most dramatically of all, the demonstration of post-hypnotic suggestion, the favourite of music-hall and scientific laboratory alike, presented the puzzling spectacle of an alien body image, or portion of the body image, imposing itself as if by some demonic force. The subject could be made to act, apparently in a normal and lucid state, in perfect conformity with a prearranged signal of which they claimed no conscious knowledge. It was as if they acted automatically, or suffered some spontaneous local motion in an arm or a leg, or found themselves momentarily unable to move in a particular fashion. Their bodies were no longer responsive to their will; the unthought interlocking of organism and body image was ruptured.

It was not until the latter part of the nineteenth century that the serious scientific study of hypnotic phenomena caught up with more popular speculation. It was in France, through the rival researches of Charcot and Bernheim, that this occurred. In different ways they attempted to understand hypnotic phenomena by linking them to other fields of psychological research with which they believed them to be systematically related. Jean-Martin Charcot, the greatest of nineteenth-century clinical psychopathologists, spent his internship at La Salpêtrière, in Paris, from 1848 to 1852, returning ten years later as attending physician and professor. This huge hospital, which his assistant Gilles de la Tourette called a 'pandemonium of human infirmities' (Charcot 1987, xxiv) was for Charcot 'a sort of museum of living pathology' (1987, xxiii), which contained some five thousand patients upon which he could exercise his diagnostic and taxonomic skills.

In what were themselves somewhat theatrical performances, Charcot would remove hysterical symptoms from hypnotized patients (prepared prior to the lecture by an assistant). Under hypnosis he could suggest the symptom had disappeared; an apparently paralysed limb would suddenly move, or feeling would return to an anaesthetized area of skin. This 'recovery' would continue for some time at least after the patient had been awakened. Conversely, Charcot demonstrated that apparently hysterical symptoms could be induced in a normal, hypnotized subject, and would persist on waking. The connection between hysteria and hypnosis, Charcot suggested, lay in a constitutional weakness of the individual. Only potential hysterics could be hypnotized, and in this abnormal state, the latent disorder would manifest itself.

The hysteric was characteristically, though not universally, female because women, especially young women, were suggestible, excitable, and subject to 'nervous attacks'. In comparison the majority of adult men were more in control of their affections, less impressionable and affected less intensely and less immediately by their surroundings. Charcot's therapy, thus, consisted in efforts to calm the patient, primarily by removing her, or him, from the source of excitation. He frequently advised separation from the family which, in most cases, 'serves only to perpetuate the excitable nervous condition' (1889, vol. 3, 94). The controlled use of static electricity and hydrotherapy was also recommended. Charcot argued that hysteria was often consequential on a traumatic accident of some sort. The new phenomena of railway-spine and railway-brain were in fact hysterical symptoms precipitated by the 'psycho-motor commotion' of the accident, rather than the drama of hypnosis (Micale and Lerner 2001).

On this view, hysteria, though an ancient disease, was increasing dramatically due to the intense pace of modern life. Many potential hysterics, who in premodern society might well have gone through life without developing any symptoms whatever, fell ill as a result of the 'nervous shock' of modern living.

Charcot's conception became the point of departure for an important tradition in French psychology, neurology, and psychiatry. In the present context his significance lies primarily in drawing attention to the dissociative effects of modern life on the body image. The primary features of hysteria were a loss of control, or sensitivity (alternatively hypersensitivity) and responsiveness, of some part of the body. It was as if part of the body 'had a mind of its own' and refused to respond spontaneously and effortlessly to the unitary will of the patient. Hysteria was the fragmentation and splintering of the body image; its classical wholeness effectively shattered by the experience of contemporary urban chaos (Beard 1881; Prince 1906).

If Charcot's elaborate botanizing in La Salpêtrière had its alarming aspect, hinting at a deeply disintegrative tendency in modern life, he at least confined its effects to a minority of unfortunate constitutional sufferers. Some bodies were naturally formed to respond in this way to the overburdening stimulation of life. But Bernheim placed no such optimistic limit on the spread of hysteria. Or, rather, there were no constitutional limitations on suggestibility, which, Bernheim argued, was the real foundation of Charcot's observations.

Bernheim insisted that 'suggestibility' was the fundamental phenomenon of hypnosis, and that 'Nothing could be further from the truth than the assertion that only hysterics are hypnotizable' (1980, 122). And that the classic diagnostic portraits from La Salpêtrière were 'cultivated hysteria'. Charcot's patients may have been unusually suggestible and, unwittingly prompted by Charcot's own discourse and his assistants' diligent preparation of the subject, produced the symptoms as an artificial construct of the situation. 'We do not realize how easy it is to make unconscious suggestions,' he argues, and 'by projecting onto the patient our own conceptions, we fabricate an observation with the preconceived ideas that we have in mind' (1980, 127). It was hardly surprising, therefore, to find that, in La Salpêtrière at least, 'it is rare for hypnotic suggestion not to rid the patient of the principal manifestations of hysteria' (1980, 160).

If, for Charcot, hypnosis is assimilated to a general notion of 'nervous shock', for Bernheim it is simply a form of suggestion. Charcot regarded the physical deformation of hysteria as the reality actualized through hypnosis. Bernheim, however, viewed suggestibility as the underlying reality masked by hysteria. Bernheim had been directly influenced by Liebault in Nancy and, unlike Charcot, was not an academic engaged in studying a captive group of patients. Bernheim describes the distinctive approach of the Nancy school as 'the systematic and reasoned application of suggestion in the treatment of the ill' (1980, 18). For them suggestion was not a passive act, 'not a simple imprint deposited within the brain' (1980, 22), but always a form of 'autosuggestion'. 'Suggestion is in everything' (1980, 46) was, for them, the fundamental principle of 'ideodynamism'. 'Sensation' is always formed into ideas, and ideas can frequently give rise to direct sensation, and their therapeutic effort was directed at exploiting the 'considerable action of the morale on the physique, of the mind on the body, of the psychic functions of the brain on all organic functions' (1980, 36). Hypnosis, which is a type of sleep, 'in suppressing control, creates suggestibility' (1980, 37). In a state of physical torpor our imagination is more active, and we are more receptive to suggestions arising from outside ourselves. This, Bernheim insists, is an old insight which has been revived by the enthusiastic and often misguided followers of Mesmer. In fact, he claims, the valid method of hypnosis was clearly outlined by the Abbot Faria (*Traité du Somnambulisme* 1823), which Liebault followed. The method of hypnosis is very simple. As outlined by Liebault, it is primarily a matter of speech. 'The simplest and best method for impressing the subject is by words' (1980, 65).

In fact there is no special hypnotic state, only various levels and forms of suggestibility. And as external impressions can only become suggestions through the inward transformation into images by the subject himself or herself – that is to say 'somnambulists can only accomplish what they can imagine' (1980, 89) – then it follows that 'the sole characteristic of natural somnambulism is active hallucinating or dreams in action' (1980, 73).

Charcot's patients, thus, like the subjects of popular entertainments, imagine the 'symptoms' described to them, and transform these images into corresponding sensations (or anaesthesias). Suggestion is the inversion of the process of perception as it had been conceptualized by the empirical psychologists from Locke and Hartley onwards. Bernheim's notion of 'ideo-dynamics' suggested there was some means by which parts of the external world became internal to the body image.

In the popular tradition of interest in hypnosis the phenomena were construed on the basis of classical bourgeois assumptions. There was, as a result, something fundamentally strange about it. Two intact egos within enclosed bodies ought not to be related by mesmeric trance. Charcot and Bernheim presented two alternative pictures, involving significant alterations in the classical body image. For Charcot hysteria became a typically modern disease; it was a bodily protest against the unnatural excitement of modern life. For Bernheim hypnotism was a phenomenon of suggestion, and suggestion was increasingly a feature of public life. More and more people were being urged to walk about in a 'waking dream'. The somnambulist was, in many respects, an ideal citizen of the modern world. The 'dream world' of modern consumption depended upon suggestibility, and encouraged it in every possible way. The visitor to the new department store was entranced by the variety and luxury of the displays, lulled into a physical torpor in which the slightest external stimulus was sufficient to create a potent mental image of a desirable object, and the sensation of an urgent longing for its possession (Williams 1982; Stewart 1984; Cormack 2002).

Dissociated states of consciousness, the surrender to wishfulness, as distinct from determined self-realization, are the psychological context for the development of consumerism, fashion, and the transformation of utopian longing. It is the *indifference* of commodities that stimulates their consumption. The equivalence of all commodities makes every consumer choice an arbitrary and ultimately random event. Wishes are mobile, insincere, and inconsequential; they alight on and reflect objects in fleeting, promiscuous unions. The commodity is not a focus of desire, either directly or through the intermediary of the desire of another (Girard 1976); it is rather a contemporary dream image in which the flux of collective wishfulness momentarily takes form. The romantic dialectic of desire and self-realization gives way to selfless, continually varying wishes. The demand for solidity, persistence, individuality, and style – qualities, that is, which adequately reflect the character of selfhood validated by ownership – dissolve into a general sensitivity to fashion.

Melancholy: Indifferent Pleasure

Wishing unites willing and feeling in a new way. The process of production no longer calls for the active support of a 'willing' and self-possessed worker, nor does the process of circulation depend upon the continuous application of awakened reason; these processes are automatic, and have slipped into the background of routinized social practices. It seems that the development of advanced capitalist society might be written as a series of transformations in sensing, then in willing, and finally in feeling. Certainly, each phenomenological domain, in turn, rose to prominence and temporarily lent the social process a specious aura of unity. But the realm of feeling for the twentieth century no more offers itself as an adequate 'model' of society than does the domain of sensing for the eighteenth century, or of willing for the nineteenth century. The waves of feeling that accompanied the seemingly inexhaustible range of cultural and social novelties that spelled the end of classical modernity in the early twentieth century are aspects of the general reconstruction of the phenomenological field. This reconstruction brought the realm of feeling, however briefly, out of its lengthy modern hibernation, but only the more effectively to assign it a new kind of insignificance.

The impasse of modernity found its expression in feeling as *mystery* and, just as the contradictions of reason and the paradox of selfhood faded (without being resolved) into the background forgetfulness of contemporary excitement, so the mystery of pleasure was overtaken by new kinds of experience. The indifference of feeling is related to the general reduction of experience to pure experience. The character of contemporary feelings is just that we 'see through' them; that they can appear to us as so many, equivalent, and interchangeable forms of possible experiences; provided, along with every other soul-quenching object, in a ready-made commodity form. Towards the end of the nineteenth century the search for novel experiences, that is to say, included as one of its primary elements an experimental orientation to feeling. Feelings, like tourist sites, or novels, or musical entertainments, could be provided more or less on demand and in a wide range of types. They could be tried out, less in the spirit of the rational consumer testing the market before deciding on a purchase than simply because they *could* be. Feelings were detached from ongoing social practices and reconstructed in situations deliberately created in order to stimulate experiences otherwise suppressed by the increasingly mechanized, routinized and 'cold' character of everyday life. The theatricality of the early modern period was briefly reborn, not only in popular cultural entertainments that indulged tastes for melodrama and mawkish sentiment, but also in the staging of sporting events, cultural festivals and expositions, in the rapidly developing newspaper and magazine media and, not least, in military parades and exhibitions. 'Sentiments' from envy and greed, to patriotism and loyalty were manufactured with the same intensity and deliberation that characterized the production of commodities and the business of government (Zeldin 1980a; 1980b).

Of course, throughout the development of modern society, authorities had ever been mindful of the 'sentimental education' as well as the practical instruction of citizens. But this had been dealt with primarily as an educational imperative, inculcating through appropriate regimes of schooling – including Sunday schooling for which the churches provided – the supportive feelings as well as the requisite knowledge and skill demanded by the modern organization of life. The public face of feeling was moralized as duty, loyalty, and respect for the law; the private face of feeling, however, was regulated by an economy of pleasure alone. But even at its most sanctimonious only those who had not recognized the self-controlling character of modern pleasure, which tended of itself towards moderation and prudence, ardently pursued this concern for 'gentling the masses' and cultivating bourgeois sensibilities. The liberated economy of pleasure, like the mechanism of reason and the self-directed *telos* of selfhood, could be relied upon to regulate the passions. The state, the churches, the industrial enterprises, therefore, did not need to 'interfere' in the realm of feeling any more than they had legally to compel people to work. Most people, most of the time, could be trusted to feel, as well as act and think, 'normally' (Gay 1999).

The re-emergence of feeling as a proper and problematic academic issue went along with its rapid commercial and political exploitation. Durkheim's sociology, in particular, should be read in the context of widespread concern over, on the one hand, the manifestation of 'extreme' and 'perverse' feelings and, on the other, the withering of sentimental attachment to the state and its symbols of power. Durkheim, unusually, as well as recognizing the essentially restraining role of society in the experience (and not just in the expression) of feelings, also stressed its positive role in the stimulation of sentiments essential to the conduct of daily life.

Both academic psychology and cultural criticism in sociology viewed feeling as a disorienting intrusion, a source of instability and of potential disruption in social and psychic life. Freud, in particular, took the notion of an internal equilibrium, developed by Claude Bernard and well established in the Vienna school of medicine, as the 'normal' condition (Lessky 1976). Rooted in scientific naturalism the idea translated moderation into an organic law; the living being, consciously and unconsciously, shields itself from dangerous overstimulation. The problem with modern life was just that this stimulation continually broke through the protective screen of attention and inattention, forgetting and remembering. Feelings provided an immediate model of advanced forms of urban life; the continuous welling up of currents of life that threatened to overwhelm and dissolve the ego.

For the equilibrium model pleasure was the internal monitor and the natural orientation of the subject; a view integral with efforts to link and define feelings as specific organic processes. In the pragmatism of James, as well as the psychology of Freud, feeling is a 'psychic representative' of bodily processes. But these theories already attest to a phenomenological interest. The physicality of feeling is not lodged in the body as a centre or self-directing agency, rather, unannounced feelings sweep through the nervous system, throwing the person into a state of agitation, or heightened awareness, or readiness for decisive action and so on; then they ebb away, replaced by other feeling tones.

But now feeling is detached from any organic process; its physicality becomes a token of mysterious otherness rather than evidence of comforting selfhood. The subject is driven and devoured by feelings, however alien they appear. As if in the grip of a powerful instinct, feelings transport the subject and shake him or her free of residual selfhood. The novels of Zola were still couched in the eighteenth-century language of nature – the libertine sought to release nature within the self – but had in fact moved on to describe the successive waves of passion flowing aimlessly through contemporary life. The naturalism of reductionist accounts of criminality, perversion, addiction, and extreme feelings of all sorts had a similar and paradoxical intent. These feelings were encountered, in fact, as 'unnatural' and the academic commentator sought to contain and rationalize their threatening appearance by conversion into an organic process that, in a deeper sense, could be related to a wholly natural source. But the break with scientific naturalism had already occurred; science itself had broken free of restraining reason.

Just as monetary exchange made commodities the equivalent expressions of an abstract, universal value, and the mechanized process of production rendered arbitrary every creative striving after selfhood, so advanced mass consumption reduced the abundance of distinctive feelings to an array of commercially or culturally sponsored experiences. And at the same time individuals, where they disdained such manufactured sentiments, sought unofficial experiences that, in the end, were hardly different. In this transformation pleasure ceased to be a regulative principle and was thoroughly relativized (that is to say, made indistinguishable from any other feeling). Feelings bore, at best, temporary and provisional distinguishing features; marks of difference that were surrendered in the consumption of pure experience they promised.

The longing for 'pure' experience became part of popular, mass culture from the late nineteenth century; but it had been present in modernity from the beginning. It is evident, above all, in the melancholic self-reflection that characterized its first and finest psychologists, Montaigne, Shakespeare, and Burton. As early as Albrecht Dürer's *Melancholia* (1517) the feeling was stripped of its premodern religious significance as acedia and given a new secular meaning as a depressed and disinterested mood. In Montaigne's *Essays*, Timothy Bright's *A Treatise on Melancholia* of 1585 which probably influenced Shakespeare, and, above all, in Burton's *Anatomy of Melancholy* (1607) it emerged as a new, general, and profound sickness of the modern spirit (Jackson 1986). To suffer melancholy was 'to be overwhelmed with heaviness' (Bright, quoted in Jackson 1986, 84). It was associated with torpid and obscure vapours 'rising from the spleen' and engulfing the soul in a dull and lethargic mist.

The dull and characterless mood of the present becomes a major theme in German tragic drama (*Trauerspiel*), a baroque cultural element specific to the early seventeenth century. Modernity was born both of a powerful assertion of human autonomy and self-worth and, because this very assertion separated the human world from the rest of creation, of a mournful loss of the world. The transformation of reality into a duality of object and subject meant the loss of intimate contact and participation through which the world had previously been lived. Melancholy arose as a feeling of loss of contact with the inner spirit of things including, most significantly, loss of contact with the inner spirit of human selfhood (Benjamin 1977, 155–7; Pensky 2001).

By the nineteenth century these themes had become commonplace. For Kierkegaard and contemporaneously Alexis de Tocqueville melancholy encompasses the entire mood of the present age. The mediocrity and relentless sameness of modern culture indicate a movement into the post-Romantic age; the dissolving of selfhood as the individual life-project. What Kierkegaard refers to as 'the present age' is characterized, rather, by a lack or loss of selfhood. This is the despair of the present, which Kierkegaard examined with unsurpassed precision and subtlety. The possibilities for modern life included an aesthetic existence, in which the individual 'hovered' above reality, engaged arbitrarily and at a whim in projects that soon lost their power to excite or fascinate. The possibility of a settled ethical life determined by choice and a clear goal of self-realization no longer raised the individual into a meaningful region of life interest. Guilt wrecked the ethical life and left the individuated self falling back into the aesthetic or losing itself in philosophical speculation. Religion, equally, is powerless to magnetize the self, it cannot be an *aim* and defining goal of life. Yet to live naively in the stream of everyday life seems absurd, is absurd. Every version of existence seems, equally, to carry within it the profound muffling of a melancholic spirit (Ferguson 1994; Westphal 1996; Matuštik and Westphal 1995). And a contemporary commentator describes 'the melancholy of the age' as the historical process which 'has lost its emotional force and consists for us only of mechanical acceleration, stasis, or repetition' (Bohrer 1994, 7).

The effortless interconnection of feeling and object has been broken, rent asunder, so that feeling lapses into so many self-experimenting states. The 'objectless' character of mood settles into dull background greyness. Melancholy encompasses the mood of nihilism and the loss of meaning endemic since the late nineteenth century. Where in Pascal there is still an acute sense of sadness over the modern, irrevocable loss of happiness that belongs to the past, in Baudelaire melancholy is a vague emptiness of the future and an emptying out of time's sacred promise (Kristeva 1989). The subject falls back upon itself; a self-experiencing self. But the self, deprived of a *world*, itself becomes vacant.

Feeling or mood is now detached from emotion as much as from objects; feelings 'break forth from the deepest interior of men and stream into the natural and social environment – in a completely planless and unintentional manner' (Strasser 1977, 82). 'The act which began as a dull, formless, unregulated disquietude' remains in this melancholic suspension (1977, 123).

Thus, for example, where in the eighteenth century the story of love was of forging a link between apparently isolated individuals, separated worlds of class, gender, age, and so on, love – irrationally – could bridge any gulf and form a new unity from the most heterogeneous elements. The contemporary story of love, however, is of playful narcissism; the creation of the other from the indifferent world. In Proust's great work, for example, love has the power to differentiate and distinguish, to isolate one of the fluid group of young girls the narrator comes across at Balbec and to impose upon her emerging silhouette the name and character of Albertine. Equally, the striking portrait of Robert Saint-Loup and the narrative of friendship – the richest since Montaigne's – is a process of 'othering', a progressive delineation of his absolute difference from the narrator. Now love and friendship introduce and sustain the absolute distinction to which consciousness clings.

Disembodiment: Indifferent Space

These cultural developments, and the reorientation of the phenomenological field outlined above that they adumbrate, involve and are implicated also in the emergence of new body images. It could hardly be otherwise; fundamental change does not stop at the artificial boundary of the skin. The individuated, closed, and self-disciplined corporeal form, the focus of sensing and bearer of reason, opened and stretched, sail-like, into the billowing currents of contemporary life. A sensitive membrane, rather than a protective shell, contemporary embodiment has undergone a process of dedifferentiation, desublimation, and deindividuation. Deleuze and Guattari refer to the 'body without organs', which is also to say 'organs in search of a body' – a body for which everything takes place on the surface. Contemporary life is embodied as skin. Anzieu (1989), thus, describes in psychoanalytic language the 'skin-ego', and the whole development of ego psychology from the wreckage of 'depth psychology' is part of the process of opening the body and bringing to its surface everything that had been separated from it as external and internal realities.

This process begins with the renewal of bodily awareness as a *flow* of sensibility. The 'stream of consciousness' is also, and principally, a 'stream of physicality'. In the latter part of the nineteenth century 'sensitivity' and 'nervousness' became commonplace (Beard 1881). At the same time a new freedom of movement and sensuousness was encouraged as both healthy and enjoyable. Sport, recreational exercise (cycling, walking, climbing, swimming), dancing, and gymnastic training all appeared and became popular aspects of the 'physical culture' of the most advanced societies. Typically these forms displayed the body in a vigorously active mode, in a public or semi-public place. And though it was usually a collective experience, many of the participants would be and would remain otherwise unknown to one another.

Marx, in a different context, had anticipated the emergence of the 'pure physicality' of the contemporary age; anonymous 'labour power', which was no more than the bare possibility of energetic movement, characterized the worker 'reduced' to the commodity form. The worker becomes indifferent, one from another; equivalent, interchangeable, and indistinguishable. Equally, the commodities the worker produces become indifferent; interchangeable, and equivalent; indistinguishably the same and, therefore, uninhibited in their circulation, defined by a single essential property of value expressed as money. This renewed physicality is quite distinct from the concentrated mass with its closed hard shell that characterized the classical modern period. This is physicality liberated from ponderous dead matter; *energetic* rather than statuesque. Energy, in fact, became the central *motif* of cultural innovation, the natural sciences, and popular culture. The body image of advanced society, like the transformed conception of space and matter in physics, was a local concentration of flowing energy rather than an isolated mass drifting in space. The body as an architectonic structure dissolved into various channels of conductivity and sensitivity. Fatigue and exhaustion became the characteristic disease of disembodiment. The human body, like any motor, suffered the exhaustion of entropy: 'Exhaustion was not merely the consequence of physical overexertion, but the cause of a variety of physical and mental pathologies born of the languid and torpid state of men, women, and especially school-age children. Fatigue was also a metaphor for the modern form of ontological suffering, for inertia, loss of will, and depletion of energy' (Rabinbach 1990, 20). Fatigue is disembodied weightiness. It is both the residue of physicality and the trace of spirit; the contemporary condition of the *flesh* (Chrétien 1996).

Body image and commodity have undergone a further reduction, in which their symmetry is sustained; both are local concentrations of circulating energy.

The senses, for such a body image, cease to explore the world on behalf of an imprisoned and remote self. Rather, they sensitize the subject to the presence of actual or potential energy flows (Deleuze and Guattari 1977). And, in registering the fluid oscillations of contemporary life, the senses become the new *locus* of experience. That is to say, where for classical modernity the sensing provided experience with its actual content – the image of objects – for contemporary culture sensing *is* experience. As in premodern society, the distance between sensing and the object sensed has been abolished, but unlike the premodern world, sensing now opens itself to the fluid energies of an ongoing collective life rather than the symbolic structure of creation. Now the 'object', if it is isolated at all, exists 'for us', as it were to provide us with an *experience*.

The structural differentiation and hierarchical ordering of the senses – already a disputed matter in relation to classical modernity – are now much less distinct. Sensing is a continuous 'multimedia' event; a chaos of impressions in which the once solid structures of both the world and the architectonics of the senses are dissolved (Berman 1982).

The theoretical sciences, in other words, take the actual, transforming character of contemporary experience as the dedifferentiated chaos of sensing as their 'model' of reality. They could hardly do otherwise; and it is from this experience – in which the *phenomenon* is also swallowed up by the uninterrupted flow of pure experience – that the strange and astonishing vision of contemporary science is born.

Here again we become aware of a switch in the relation of figure and ground. This is not simply the effect of a changing perspective; the latest frame revealed by the restless blinking of attention. Rather, it brings into the foreground what had been constituted as *essentially* background. It is not a matter of focusing on yet one more possible 'object' of attention and bringing it forward for momentary examination before passing to the next; now sensing – reduced to its pure form as experience – itself refuses artificially to be broken down and recombined into the apparently stable forms of an 'objective' world. The natural attitude is here taking on the character of its own reduction to the pure form of experience. We begin to sense the world in just the way that opened intuitively to Husserl only after a monumental effort of reflection. At the very moment Husserl was struggling to articulate the phenomenological reduction that very process was going on around him, or rather taking place through him, as the actual experience of contemporary life. This is quite unlike the disembodiment of modern *thought*; it is not a conceptualization of the body but a passing into inexperience of corporeal being.

In common with Freud, Simmel, Durkheim, and William James, Husserl experienced this transition as a fearful abyss. The 'natural attitude' of classical modernity was fragile and in an ultimate sense arbitrary and unfounded. But life was, for them, inconceivable without its continuous objectifications. *They* took for granted the necessity of a natural attitude that, in practice, was already dissolving. It was, indeed, just because it was dissolving that it had come into focus as a theoretical problem. But the natural attitude had become equivocal in more direct and immediate ways. In terms of sensing, the flux of impressions that the phenomenologist, as well as the pragmatist, psychologist and artist, had thrust into the background of experience and considered only as the unconstructed medium from which actual experience drew its materials and fashioned its content, thrust itself ever forward to claim the privilege of existing 'for itself'.

The transition to contemporary society is a process of merging, of breaking down barriers of all sorts. This, of course, is extremely limited in many respects and an 'ideal' condition and tendency rather than a description applying generally. But this is no more than to say that most people most of the time are both wholly immersed in contemporary society and live also in the several worlds of modernity and the many worlds of premodernity. It is just the peculiarity of contemporary society to make *all* these worlds, including its own, available on an apparently equal basis. But it is from the 'advanced' position of modernity that it becomes possible to reconstruct the multiplicity of dualities that absorbed the consciousness of modernity in itself, and thrust into the oblivion of the past those worlds that yet lingered in bodily practices and feelings of certain kinds.

Merging is an important reconstitution of the phenomenological field and, once again, a general social process. There are several mechanisms involved here. The use of money is highlighted by Simmel; the 'reduction' of all forms of rationality to the calculation of means, the general character of the commodity, are impressive accounts of aspects of this process. To this must be added the experience of illness – not only of hysteria among young affluent women in the late nineteenth century, but all those 'newer' forms of illness related to stress, fatigue, neurasthenia and nervousness. And, most significantly of all, the experience of warfare can be grasped as a brutal and irresistible 'reduction' of all experiential forms to their phenomenological purity. Warfare broke down the bodily resistance of young men to the advanced modern age, it *forced* upon them the reduction with which philosophers struggled. In an evident way the social context of Husserl's work is the experience of everyday urban life: walking along the street is an unfolding of new appearances, a receding and advancing horizon, fulfilled and unfulfilled expectations, shot through with possibility, modalization and so on; but in another context, the reduction imposed upon the consciousness of so many during the First World War is the more radical exposure to the 'pure' phenomena. And their merging becomes radical and complete; nothing exists other than pure phenomena. The senses become a kinaesthesia, feelings at once numbed and helplessly seized by waves of fear, willing indistinguishable from sensing that you are still alive. Here is the most complete shift from foreground to background, and the utter annihilation (literal and conceptual) of the object. Consciousness becomes consciousness of seeing, of hearing, of feeling, and so on, rather than consciousness of the object. The phenomenological golden rule – that all consciousness is consciousness of something – loses its force. Now all consciousness is consciousness of *being conscious* of something; anything.

Twentieth-century metaphysics orients itself towards indifference; towards death. It is the *inexperience* of death that fixes the gaze – the given that cannot appear. Death is a phenomenological limit. The removal of death, its sequestration more complete than was the great confinement at the beginning of modernity, rids the world of its unassimilated and indigestible substance. Death is denied because it cannot be experienced and, for the same reason, it becomes the only subject matter for any philosophy that still seeks its world outside experience.

Yet death also can be packaged, sold, and presented as a consumer good. The living person is removed from ordinary life, and later returned in a coffin. The moment of death becomes invisible and indeterminate; the funeral completes a rite of passage from living being to living memory of a deceased being. This involuntary modalization – the experience of inexperience – becomes emblematic.

In a related way the experience of pain is accorded a peculiar privilege in contemporary society – the immediate experience of indifference. We are not indifferent to pain, but pain is nothing other than 'pure' indifference. This is a phenomenological limit of a different sort, the farthest point it can reach. Pain is pure immediacy; it destroys time and forces the experience of eternity on the subject. Pain is a self-certifying; it cannot be verified other than in immediate experience. The authority of experience is here unchallenged. It also has the advantage of *demonstrating* existence. Kant declares existence does not require proof, and it is foolish to ask for or provide it; but in contemporary society proof of existence is precisely what is required. Pain is irrefutable. It brings into existence (proves in an older sense) the substance of the body, makes the pure physicality of experience something conspicuously real; brings into the foreground a body otherwise submerged in the indifference of contemporary life.

Boredom: Indifference of Time

The shift to essential viewing, evident in art as well as warfare, and the search for the pure experience of experience, is a last flaring of astonishment; something to shake everyone free of the melancholy and boredom that had descended like a damp fog over a culture that has lost its trust in reason, in selfhood, and in pleasure.

Heidegger characterizes the historically given orientation of *Dasein* as 'attunement', which is 'something we can least of all invent, something into which we slip unawares' (1990b, 59). We see that 'attunement is not at all inside, in some sort of the Other, and that it is not at all somewhere alongside in our soul … attunement imposes itself on everything … It is *not* at all "*inside*" in some interiority, only to appear in the flash of an eye, but for this reason it is *not at all outside either*' (1990b, 66). 'It seems as though an attunement is in each case already there, so to speak, like an atmosphere in which we first immerse ourselves' (1990b, 67).

Philosophy can be grasped in this perspective less as an active conceptualization of experience than as an 'awakening' to attunements. But the attunement of the present might then more properly be called 'falling' asleep, and modernity grasped essentially through the experience, or rather inexperience, of boredom (Goodstein 2005). Images of sleep and falling asleep are common in the modern western tradition of painting. Goya's *Sleep of Reason* with its powerfully ambiguous title is a nightmare vision on the far side of enlightenment. The 'awakening' to reason, the gradual disentangling of experience from the residues of sleep that begins in Descartes and Cervantes, runs its course and the subject slips back into inconclusive drowsiness. The exploration of reality becomes the investigation of dreams and shadows (Amiel 1906). Freud's masterwork, like Proust's, and the haunting images of de Chirico link philosophy and sleep in a new way. The modern history of painting, as of philosophical 'reflection', can be in terms of its clouds and shadows rather than its luminescence; a growing, engulfing, obscurity to which the ego finally surrenders (Damisch 2002; Stoichita 1997; Baxandall 1995; Gombrich 1995; Belting 2001).

Husserl, notwithstanding his predominant focus on the experience of wide-awakeness, acknowledges the specific character of drowsy indifference that now might well be taken as prescient of contemporary life in general:

> In the course of our psychic life, waking life is only one type; there is another one besides this one, deep dreamless sleep, unconsciousness. We arrive at both these types in their contrast by presentifying actual lived-experience of awakening, by a retrospective intuitive grasping of preceding phases of consciousness in comparison with wakefulness itself. Even if we cannot say anything in more detail at all about the content of what is past and about what is experienced in a torpid manner, we can describe with evidence the typical essence of the contrast. There is an experience taking place when in a stupor, as well. But there is not perception in the genuine sense of or an experience of another sort; there is nothing of a cognitive theme; there is nothing of a judgment; there is nothing of an object of an emotional interest; there is nothing properly speaking of an object being loved or hated at present, there is nothing of a desiring or a willing. (2003, 16)

Here there is no ego, no 'I' living in and through its acts in a characteristic manner, as a 'center of life'. Insight into contemporary life as sleepiness, what might be thought of as the normalization of late-nineteenth-century somnambulism, provides a meaningful characterization of the contemporary *inexperience* of indifference.

The self-surrender to indifference, which is the slumbering consciousness of contemporary life, is a general process of dedifferentiation, drifting and the dissolution into inexperience; the self abandoned equally to currents of fashion and periodic calm 'like a feather down a stairwell' (Moravia 2000, 33; Lipovetsky 1983; 1994). The sharp boundary between inner and outer, self and other, perception and memory fades into a sheer transition. The indifference of time is the inexperience of boredom. Lost time is not regained; it passes into oblivion. The astonishing newness of the present appears to be nothing other than dull repetition. Time loses the arresting charge of anxiety. The emptiness of the future no longer stimulates a nameless dread; the fear of the next moment and what it might bring; it will bring nothing; nothing different.

The 'disquiet' of the present comes to rest in the *tedium* of everyday life (Harootunian 2000a; 2000b). Fernando Pessoa's unclassifiable *The Book of Disquiet* (2002) provides through its unfinished accumulation of fragments, written throughout the period from 1912 to 1935, the most precise phenomenology of the colourless persistence of mundane existence. Unlike the boredom described by Kierkegaard, which oscillates between lethargy and bursts of enthusiastic activity, Pessoa grasps contemporary life as 'a tedium that includes the expectation of nothing but more tedium' (2002, 22). Tedium is the identity of time with itself, the absence of difference and the otherness which life requires: 'The tedium of the forever new, the tedium of discovering – behind the specious differences of things and ideas – the unrelenting sameness of everything ... the eternal concordance of life with itself ... all of it equally condemned to change' (2002, 110).

Pessoa's baroque masterpiece snatches fragments of consciousness from the gathering oblivion of sleep, a consciousness of lethargic merging and the running together of every possible difference: 'my true being, of this being that has always sleepily wandered between what it feels and what it sees' (2002, 40). Contemporary life is a lethargic relaxation into the twilight state from which modernity had shaken itself free. 'There's a sleepiness of our conscious attention that I can't explain but that often attacks me, if anything so hazy can be said to attack ... my attention, although alert to everything, will have the inertia of a body completely at rest ... And this spiritless state, which would be natural and therefore comfortable in some-one lying down or reclining, is singularly uncomfortable, even painful, in a man walking down the street' (2002, 45).

Now, 'intoxicated with inertia', we live in a twilight consciousness in which everything becomes identical: 'Whether clever or stupid, they're all equally stupid. Whether old or young, they're all the same age. Whether men or women, all are the same sex that doesn't exist' (2002, 70).

The constituting and objectifying processes of consciousness are, as it were, put into reverse and phenomena fade into foggy indistinction: 'We look but don't see. The long street bustling with clothed animals is like a flat-lying signboard whose letters move around and make no sense. The buildings are just buildings. We're no longer able to give meaning to what we see, though we see perfectly well what's there' (2002, 76).

This is a strangely comforting and tensionless world: 'To suffer without suffering, to want without desire, to think without reason ... It's like being possessed by a negative demon, like being bewitched by nothing at all' (2002, 208). And it is a world, thus, of easy sociability: 'Knowing neither ourselves nor each other, and therefore cheerfully getting along, we keep twirling round in the dance and chatting during the intervals' (2002, 222). Tedium is the quiet accommodation to despair; life untroubled by longing and the melancholic restlessness that seeks selfhood. In this attunement to contemporary society Pessoa recognizes, as had Kierkegaard in the edifying power of patience (Ferguson 2003), an attenuated but still real humanism as 'the tenderness one feels for common human banality' (Pessoa 2002, 69).

Tedium is life suspended, waiting, as if for something to turn up. Pessoa, like Heidegger, describes waiting as an experience that was common during World War I: 'a night of rain and mud where, lost in the solitude of an out-of-the-way station, I wait interminably for the next third-class train' (2002, 38).

Fundamental attunement of the present is boredom. This has nothing to do with the extension of time; with a sense of interminable continuity. Nor should it be mistaken for an apparent slackening in its pace, as if it were running down. Boredom infects memory and imagination as much as it does the experience of the present: 'I recall having suffered always from boredom,' remarks Moravia's hero (1999, 5). For him, boredom, more than being a 'vague and indefinite state of mind', is a 'lack of contact with external things' (1999, 7, 16). This is still felt as a melancholic loss, but in his hero's lover a new consciousness emerges, one for which boredom has become a perfectly normal state; her indifference, which 'was simply a complete lack of contact very similar to the thing which caused me to suffer so much and which I called boredom', was for her 'a sane and normal fact' (1999, 102).

Time, detached and purified of human intentionality, becomes overwhelming boredom. Being bored with something means we are present to the object, 'given over to it, but not taken by it' (Heidegger 1990b, 86), and boredom might, thus, be regarded as the antithesis of play (Fink 1966): 'Profound boredom is the concealed fundamental attunement of the interpretation of our situation provided by the philosophy of culture' (Heidegger 1990b, 74). 'Man as soul and spirit, coming to expression in forms that bear an intrinsic meaning and which, on the basis of this meaning, give a sense of existence [Dasein] as it expresses itself: This roughly speaking, is the schema of contemporary philosophy of culture' and in this interpretation the human existence is utterly banal (1990b, 75). These interpretations fail to *take hold* of us; and remain insignificant because we have become insignificant to ourselves. 'Is it because *indifference* yawns at us out of all things, an indifference whose grounds we do not know? ... a profound boredom draws back and forth like a silent fog in the abysses of Dasein' (1990b, 77).

This is the foggy indifference described also by Albert Cohen in his masterwork, and before that by Chekhov. This is a seeing through of the stream of life and consciousness to its emptiness, an experience of nihilism in the mundane actualities of life: 'the pallid lack of mood – indifference – which is addicted to nothing, and has no urge for anything, and which abandons itself to whatever the day may bring ... Just living along ... is a way which "lets" everything "be" as it is, is based on forgetting and abandoning oneself to one's throwness' (Heidegger 1962, 396).

We act primarily to escape, rather to try to escape, boredom; we 'at all times make an effort, whether consciously or unconsciously, to pass the time, by welcoming highly important and essential preoccupations for the sole reason that they take up our time' (Heidegger 1990b, 78–9). Yet there is something truthful in boredom; this detachment and lack of interest, the lack of spirit and contact with the world, betray a reality into which we have receded with a comforting sigh. This is not an inner feeling. The fading, as it were, of phenomena before our eyes, is at the same time a strange reconnection with and participation in the world; but a world now bereft of interest, emptied of content and meaning. Boredom 'is not simply an inner spiritual experience' but something that comes to us and at us *'from out of things themselves'*.

Boredom makes *'everything of equally great and equally little worth'* (1990b, 137). Gripped by a general indifference, 'The *emptiness* increasingly here consists in the *indifference* enveloping being *as a whole*' (1990b, 138). Here the subject is outside the self and, thus, no longer bound to immediate temporal determinants. In relation to Kierkegaard we can now see that boredom is the twin of – patience. Patience is the absolute freedom of the subject within the temporalizing illusion of being. Patience also must have this objectifying time relation, this powerful illusion of being 'interminable', but here it is not averse, because being does not resist itself, but rather welcomes itself in its plenitude. Patience is full, free, finitude as compared to the bound, empty, infinitude of boredom.

Conclusion: Phenomenological Sociology

We have entered an age of historical consciousness. We feel surrounded by
our entire past.

Dilthey, *Poetry and Experience*

Just as I have not chosen my body, I have not chosen my historical situation, but both the one and the other are the locus of my responsibility.

Ricoeur, *Nature and Freedom*

The development of modern experience or, rather, *experiences* currently
designated as modern, has to be viewed as a continuous process of contention
and negotiation among a whole series of possible, partial, and overlapping
syntheses; as in many other cultures, a messy juxtaposition of forms that are
lived through and grasped reflectively in ways that remain incoherent to
each other (Turner and Bruner 1986; Geertz 1977). The varied forms and
possible syntheses that may be grasped as distinctively modern were each
present from the outset. It is not that the world of sensing and reason first
of all appeared, developed, and eventually lost its impetus as it came up
against its own inconsistencies and was *replaced* by the world brought into
focus through willing, which in due course itself foundered on unresolved
paradoxes, and was succeeded by the reality of resurgent feelings. These
syntheses became culturally dominant and gained authority, certainly, in
turn; and in retrospect they provide a convenient way of characterizing distinctive periods in the history of modernity. But they coexist, in mutual
incomprehension or, more usually, in mutual disregard and ignorance, and
have done so throughout the period that still seems to bear the marks of a
peculiar self-birth.

The early modern period, in fact, with its extravagant development of
metaphysical systems as well as its scientific and artistic innovations, provides in embryonic form images of every possible future for its own world.
Thus, in addition to Descartes who is often recognized as the philosopher
of both sensing and reason, Leibniz may be read as the modern philosopher
of willing, and Spinoza as the modern philosopher of feeling. And rather
than view the latter as logical responses to epistemological problems raised
by Descartes, their work can be read more sympathetically as comprehensive ethnographies of modern experience written from distinctive and *given*
phenomenological standpoints (Deleuze 1993, 199).

These worlds coexist, furthermore, with an accumulated series of 'premodern' experiences that modernity, for all its self-assertive boldness, failed

to abolish. Modern experiences become 'modern' by a process of excluding, and thrusting into the background, everything that is coloured by the past. But premodern forms are not annihilated in this process, they remain present but slip from attention. The worlds of modernity *include* the past within itself in a variety of ways that depend not on the past alone but, to a large extent, on the variety of present forms and the different roles they each allot to what is grasped as *their* prehistory. And, also coexisting with this dizzying multiplicity is a world of modernity that defines itself as the banal present; a present that makes available, in a wholly relativized way, every *other* world as so many possible 'experiences', and which is nothing in itself. The present is a plenitude of different kinds of experience, but in its careless tolerance of anything it is capable of imagining, neglects to acknowledge *itself* as something worthy of its own attention.

But does not this conclusion fly in the face of an abundance of both sociological evidence and philosophical criticism? Is not an arrogant disregard of or, worse, a domineering superiority over, every culture, period, and people other than what we have (fictionally) created as our *own*, overwhelmingly the orientation of the 'modern west'? Surely contemporary western society thinks much too highly of itself? Does not modern western humanity display the careless hubris of a culture wholly certain of its inherent superiority over any other, past or present? This view, indeed, is now so well attested as hardly to require justification. Nonetheless, a phenomenological sociology of the present yields quite an opposite and surprising insight; this is *its* justification.

Bombastic self-glorification, realized in economic power and enforced with overwhelming military force, characterized the entire development of modern western society and remains inseparable from its founding assumption of human autonomy from nature and God. Modernity in the west was thematically developed as the process of continuous accumulation of capital and unrestrained military and economic expansion that, like Descartes's *cogito*, constituted a given, self-justifying reality; but at the same time the free development of human autonomy *also* meant the radical questioning of every possible explanation, understanding, or interpretation of the world. Relentless self-criticism and the restless instability of all epistemological and ethical frameworks characterized modernity from the outset (Arnason 1995). This is clearly grasped, for example, by Hobbes and is the ultimate source of the unresolved 'problem of order'. In an equally radical way Montaigne's *Essays* inaugurates a 'postcolonial' literature and, like Burton's *Anatomy of Melancholy*, already proffers diagnostic insight and therapeutic advice in relation to the maladies attendant on life in a society that has become transparently conventional. It should be noted that a historicizing and deconstructive account of the colonial encounter is *also* ethnocentric. Undoing our own (never very effective) ideology carries with it an appeal to the hidden universalism of history. But for many 'other' cultures history has quite a different constitution and remains incompatible with the western self-critical, as well as the western triumphalist, view.

In the context of increasing globalization or, at least, of regionalization in production processes, exchange, and consumption, the revival of 'localism', the cultural politics of unfounded 'national' and 'ethnic' groups, and a nostalgic evocation of 'community' are akin to the progressive liberation of reason, the self, and feeling in the individual within metropolitan culture. Local culture is revived because it is now *too late* for it to have any impact beyond that of adding to consumer choice.

Can contemporary society any longer be called modern? If modernity is identified with the project of the Enlightenment and the construction of a *rational* society in which an ever enlarging domain of nature and human conduct is brought under the conscious control of scientifically validated, instrumental agencies, then the answer must be, and always was, in the negative. The most serious Enlightenment thinkers recognized the systematic limitations of reason, the impenetrability of nature and the irreducible irrationality or non-rationality of human conduct. In that respect, the *critique* of reason must be regarded as an aspect of the Enlightenment itself. The proximity of Hamann, Herder, and Kant in Königsberg is emblematic of the richness and variety of modernity, which gave birth both to the Enlightenment and Romanticism and to major figures who, taken singly, cannot be squeezed into the later conventions of rationality and, taken together, constitute a daring, many-sided exploration of the character of its humanity (Zammito 2002). In this respect the classical sociological critique of the Enlightenment, impressively articulated in different ways by Weber and Durkheim in particular, is less original than it appears, and its widespread contemporary dismissal is little more than an instance of the ignorance and error the Enlightenment's major figures sought (unsuccessfully) to dispel. The dismal history of the twentieth century – war, destruction, famine, disease, exploitation – proposes itself as conclusive evidence against, not just the hope inspired by the Enlightenment, but the notion of reason itself. But that it appears to be an indictment against reason (rather than God, or the past, or nature) and that such attacks continue to be made in the name of human *rights* is a measure of the implicit trust in the continuing task of the Enlightenment.

Conceived somewhat more broadly to include the emergence of the individuated subject whose inner life has been liberated from premodern constraints of authority and whose conduct increasingly comes under the control of internalized agencies of command, then the answer must also be in the negative. The recalcitrance of the self, its reluctance fully to step forward and become transparent to itself, its inability fully to express itself or communicate its inner truth, were rocks upon which all of the many versions of 'ego psychology' foundered. But here again it would be misleading simply to reject out of hand what might now seem to be the naïve aspirations of an earlier age. The obscurity of the self becomes evident only in relation to a continuing ideal of self-clarification that has its origins also in an enlightening conception of modernity. And here also the practical history of illness, political and religious suppression, censorship and artificial constraints on freedom of expression in all its forms imposed, pointlessly and from their own point of view self-destructively, by almost all modern regimes, has done little to dampen enthusiasm for liberation.

Equally, if modernity is considered in terms of the stabilization of pleasure and physical comfort as the normative feeling to be sought and enjoyed, then again, it must be admitted that we no longer live in that kind of world. And here it must be admitted that the strange, unsettling persistence of happiness, much more than the sadness that is all too easily, and mistakenly, grasped as an appropriate *response* to the ceaseless troubles of the world, effectively confounds the Enlightenment's sentimental vision of the future.

In a broader perspective modernity is characterized less by the process of rationalization than by the continuous unfolding of humanism, within which rationalization plays a decisive role during only one of its phases. It must also be recognized that in Europe, as in the rest of the world, modernity has taken on rather different forms and developed in different ways. In addition to important differences in the trajectory of modernity within Europe, one thinks especially of Japan here (Eisenstadt 1995; Arnason 1997; Jansen 2002). Only in some places and in some periods does rationalization play a leading role.

In this broader context it is the early modern period in southern and eastern Europe, with its baroque culture of sensuous excess, fluidity of forms, extravagant display, exploration, curiosity and collecting, that appears to break most decisively with the long tradition of Christianized thought and practice. And it is this culture that bears a more immediate resemblance to contemporary life than does the classical period of European modernity that is associated with the Enlightenment, Protestant culture, the development of market economies, capitalist enterprise, the bureaucratic centralized state, and so on.

A view of modernity as the continuous unfolding of the implications of humanism – what might be termed the multiple consequences of Copernicanism – rather than the progressive articulation of self-conscious reason, casts the debate over the Enlightenment in a different light. Humanity, stepping forward into the foreground of its own experience and its own consciousness, assumed the dignity of a self-moving and self-centred creature. But, in grasping its proper nature as autonomous being, humanity *both* cut itself off from the world *and* absorbed into itself the shadowy sources of that world's power. God and nature now stood outside the human and, hidden from view, were known only through representations and traces. Humanity, however, freeing itself through a process of self-exploration and self-creation, came up against these enigmatic powers within itself. Humanity encountered within itself something radically non-human. Humanity was both itself and not itself; it was other than itself. The human was at once human, inhuman and non-human. Humanity, creating itself in its own image as modern, encountered the intractable inner shadow cast by its own pre-history. Humanity could not know itself, or become itself, or *imagine* itself, in the midst of a world it had disowned.

211

The City of God was replaced by the City of Man; the familiar other gave way to the unfamiliar self (Manent 1998; Lambropoulos 1993). Phenomenology is the most radical development of humanism; an attempt to assimilate the unfamiliar to the self-transparency of *experience*. In defining humanity in terms of its own experience, rather than enigmatically in terms of putative 'nature' or a self-generated 'divine' that cannot be thought without presuming its reality outside humanity itself, it seemed that the project of modernity would indeed come to an end; by reaching its goal. But experience, in becoming the focus of attention, also became opaque; rendered impenetrable by the act of looking. It is just the reflection of this look, the glassy stare of experience objectified, which instigated and resisted phenomenological analysis. It is in surprise at this reflection that philosophy briefly rediscovers itself. Phenomenology is the momentary efflorescence of astonishment in which experience reveals itself to be something utterly incomprehensible.

But the moment of drama passed; both the world and experience fade into an indifferent gloom. The strange and fascinating newness of the modern grows stale and every new thing appears as a copy of an already existing thing, every other thing as a replica of a historic past.

The astonishing, which had already become merely surprising, is swallowed up into the dull immensity of contemporary existence. Can the absolute naïvety of the present escape the annihilating momentum of society's rush towards oblivion and offer itself as the point of departure for a new, mundane humanism? Perhaps; the 'perhaps' is nothing, but the 'perhaps' may be all we have to outwit modernity's self-destructive hubris.

References

Aboulafia, Mitchell (1991) *Philosophy, Social Theory, and the Thought of George Herbert Mead* (Albany NY: State University of New York Press).

Adorno, Theodor W. (1999) *Sound Figures* trans. Rodney Livingstone (Stanford CA: Stanford University Press).

Agnew, Jean-Christophe (1986) *Worlds Apart: The Market and the Theater in Anglo-American Thought, 1550–1750* (Cambridge: Cambridge University Press).

Alpers, Svetlana (1983) *The Art of Describing: Dutch Art in the Seventeenth Century* (Chicago: University of Chicago Press).

Ameriks, Karl (2000) *Kant and the Fate of Autonomy* (Cambridge: Cambridge University Press).

Amiel, Henri-Frédéric (1906) *Amiel's Journal* trans. Mrs Humphry Ward (London: Macmillan).

Amrine, Frederick, Francis Zucker, and Harvey Wheeler eds (1987) *Goethe and the Sciences: A Reappraisal* (Dordrecht: Reider).

Anderson, Amanda and Joseph Valente eds (2002) *Disciplinarity at the Fin de Siècle* (Princeton NJ: Princeton University Press).

Anzieu, Didier (1989) *The Skin Ego* trans. Chris Turner (New Haven CT: Yale University Press).

Appadurai, Arjun (1986) *The Social Life of Things* (Cambridge: Cambridge University Press).

Ariès, Phillippe and George Duby eds (1991) *A History of Private Life* vol. V (Cambridge MA: Harvard University Press).

Aristotle (1996) *Poetics* trans. Malcolm Heath (Harmondsworth: Penguin).

Aristotle (1998) *The Metaphysics* ed. Hugh Lawson-Tancred (Harmondsworth: Penguin).

Arnason, Johann P. (1995) 'Modernity, Postmodernity and the Japanese Experience', in Johann Arnason and Yoshio Sugimoto *Japan Faces Postmodernity* (London: Kegan Paul).

Arnason, Johann P. (1997) *Social Theory and Japanese Experience* (London: Kegan Paul).

Arnason, Johann P., S. N. Eisenstadt and B. Wittrock eds (2004) *Axial Age Civilizations and World History* (Leiden: Brill).

Arnason, Johann P. and Peter Murphy eds (2001) *Agon, Logos, Polis: The Greek Achievement and its Aftermath* (Stuttgart: Steiner).

Arnason, Johann P. and Yoshio Sugimoto (1995) *Japan Faces Postmodernity* (London: Kegan Paul).

Asendorf, Christoph (1993) *Batteries of Life* (Berkeley CA: University of California Press).

Attali, Jacques (1985) *Noise: Political Economy of Music* (Minneapolis: University of Minnesota Press).

Auerbach, Jeffrey A. (1999) *The Great Exhibition 1851: A Nation on Display* (New Haven CT: Yale University Press).

Auslander, Leora (1996) *Taste and Power: Furnishing Modern France* (Berkeley CA: University of California Press).

Bachelard, Gaston (1969) *The Poetics of Space* (New York: Beacon).

Balzac, Honoré (1968) *Cousin Pons* trans. Herbert J. Hunt (Harmondsworth: Penguin).

Barasch, Moshe (2000) *Theories of Art. 2: From Winckelmann to Baudelaire* (New York: Routledge).

Barasch, Moshe (2001) *Blindness: The History of a Mental Image in Western Thought* (New York: Routledge).

Barrows, Susanna (1981) *Distorting Mirrors: Vision of the Crowd in Late Nineteenth-Century France* (New Haven CT: Yale University Press).

Barthes, Roland (1982) *Barthes: Selected Writings* ed. Susan Sontag (London: Fontana).

Bataille, Georges (1991) *The Accursed Share*: Volume 1 trans. Robert Hurley (New York: Zone).

Bauman, Zygmunt (2003) *Liquid Love: On the Frailty of Human Bonds* (Cambridge: Polity).

Bauman, Zygmunt (2005) *Liquid Life* (Cambridge: Polity).

Baxandall, Michael (1995) *Shadows and Enlightenment* (New Haven CT: Yale University Press).

Beard, George Miller (1881) *American Nervousness: Its Causes and Consequences* (New York: Putnam's).

Becker, Marvin B. (1988) *Civility and Society in Western Europe, 1300–1600* (Bloomington IN: Indiana University Press).

Beiser, Frederick C. (1987) *The Fate of Reason: German Philosophy from Kant to Fichte* (Cambridge MA: Harvard University Press).

Bell, Matthew (1994) *Goethe's Naturalistic Anthropology* (Oxford: Clarendon).

Belting, Hans (1994) *Likeness and Presence* trans. Edmund Jephcott (Chicago: University of Chicago Press).

Belting, Hans (2001) *The Invisible Masterpiece* (London: Reaktion).

Benedict, Burton (1983) *The Anthropology of World's Fairs* (London: Lewis Museum of Anthropology and Scholar).

Benjamin, Walter (1977) *The Origin of German Tragic Drama* trans. John Osborne (London: Verso).

Ben-Ze'ev, Aaron (2000) *The Subtlety of Emotions* (Cambridge MA: MIT Press).

Berger, Peter L. and Thomas Luckmann (1966) *The Social Construction of Reality* (London: Allen Lane).

Berman, Marshall (1982) *All that is Solid Melts into Air: The Experience of Modernity* (London: Verso).

Bernheim, H. (1980) *Bernheim's New Studies in Hypnotism* trans. Richard S. Sander (New York: International Universities Press).

Bianconi, Lorenzo (1987) *Music in the Seventeenth Century* trans. David Bryant (Cambridge: Cambridge University Press).

Blanchot, Maurice (1997) *Friendship* trans. Elizabeth Rottenberg (Stanford CA: Stanford University Press).

Bloch, Ernst (1995) *The Principle of Hope* trans. Neville Plaice, Stephen Plaice, and Paul Knight (Cambridge MA: MIT Press).

Bloch, Ernst (1999) *Literary Essays* trans. Andrew Joron (Stanford CA: Stanford University Press).

Bloch, Ernst (2000) *The Spirit of Utopia* trans. Anthony A. Nassar (Stanford CA: Stanford University Press).

Bloch, Marc (1962) *Feudal Society* trans. L. A. Manyon (London: Routledge and Kegan Paul).

Blumenberg, Hans (1985) *The Legitimacy of the Modern Age* (Cambridge MA: MIT Press).

Bohrer, Karl Heinz (1994) *Suddenness: On the Moment of Aesthetic Appearing* (New York: Columbia University Press).

Bourdieu, Pierre (1978) *Distinction* trans. Richard Nice (London: Routledge and Kegan Paul).

Bourke, Joanna (1996) *Dismembering the Male: Men's Bodies, Britain and the Great War* (London: Reaktion).

Bouwsma, William J. (2000) *The Waning of the Renaissance 1550–1640* (New Haven CT: Yale University Press).

Bowie, Andrew (1997) *From Romanticism to Critical Theory* (London: Routledge).

Bowie, Andrew (2003) *Aesthetics and Subjectivity: From Kant to Nietzsche* (Manchester: Manchester University Press).

Božouě, Miran (2000) *An Utterly Dark Spot: Gaze and Body in Early Modern Philosophy* (Ann Arbor MI: University of Michigan Press).

Braid, James (1899) *Braid on Hypnotism: Neurypnology* (London: Redway).

Brainard, Marcus (2002) *Belief and its Neutralization* (Albany NY: State University of New York Press).

Braudel, Fernand (1982) *The Wheels of Commerce* trans. Siân Reynolds (London: Collins).
Braudel, Fernand (1984) *The Perspective of the World* trans. Siân Reynolds (London: Collins).
Braudel, Fernand (1985) *The Structures of Everyday Life* trans. Siân Reynolds (London: Collins).
Brentano, Franz (1973) *Psychology from an Empirical Standpoint* trans. A. C. Rancurello, D. B. Terrell, and L. L. McAllister (London: Routledge).
Brewer, John and Roy Porter eds (1993) *Consumption and the World of Goods* (London: Routledge).
Briggs, Asa (1990) *Victorian Things* (Harmondsworth: Penguin).
Bronfen, Elizabeth (1998) *The Knotted Subject: Hysteria and its Discontents* (Princeton NJ: Princeton University Press).
Brush, Stephen G. (1976) *The Kind of Motion We Call Heat* 2 vols (New York: North-Holland).
Brush, Stephen G. (1978) *The Temperature of History* (New York: Franklin).
Bryson, Norman (1990) *Looking at the Overlooked: Four Essays on Still Life Painting* (London: Reaktion).
Buber, Martin (1937) *I and Thou* trans. Ronald Gregor Smith (Edinburgh: Clark).
Buber, Martin (1946) *Moses* (Oxford: Phaidon).
Buci-Glucksmann, Christine (1994) *Baroque Reason: The Aesthetics of Modernity* (London: Sage).
Bumke, Joachim (2000) *Courtly Culture* trans. Thomas Dunlap (New York: Overlook Duckworth).
Burke, Peter (1995) *The Fortune of the Courtier* (Cambridge: Polity).
Burrow, J. W. (2000) *The Crisis of Reason: European Thought, 1848–1914* (New Haven CT: Yale University Press).
Buxton, Richard ed. (1999) *From Mythos to Reason?* (Oxford: Oxford University Press).
Caillois, Roger (2001) *Man, Play and Games* trans. Meyer Barash (Urbana IL: University of Illinois Press).
Campbell, Mary Baine (1999) *Wonder and Science: Imaginary Worlds in Early Modern Europe* (Ithaca NY: Cornell University Press).
Camporesi, Piero (1988) *The Incorruptible Flesh* trans. Tania Croft-Murray and Helen Elson (Cambridge: Cambridge University Press).
Camporesi, Piero (1994) *The Anatomy of the Senses* trans. Allan Cameron (Cambridge: Polity).
Caputo, John D. and Michael J. Scanlon eds (2001) *God, the Gift, and Postmodernism* (Bloomington IN: Indiana University Press).
Carruthers, Mary (1990) *The Book of Memory* (Cambridge: Cambridge University Press).
Casey, Edward S. (1997) *The Fate of Place* (Berkeley CA: University of California Press).
Castiglione, Baldesar (1976) *The Book of the Courtier* trans. George Bull (Harmondsworth: Penguin).
Certeau, Michel de (1984) *The Practice of Everyday Life* trans. Steven Rendall (Berkeley and Los Angeles: University of California Press).
Certeau, Michel de (1986) *Heterologies: Discourse on the Other* trans. Brian Massumi (Manchester: Manchester University Press).
Certeau, Michel de (1998) *The Practice of Everyday Life* vol. 2 (Minneapolis: University of Minnesota Press).
Cézanne, Paul (1995) *Paul Cézanne's Letters* ed. John Rewald, trans. Marguerite Kay (New York: De Capo Press).
Charcot, Jean-Martin (1889) *Clinical Lectures on Diseases of the Nervous System* 3 vols, trans. Thomas Savill (London: New Sydenham Society).
Charcot, Jean-Martin (1987) *Charcot the Clinician: The Tuesday Lessons (1887/88)* trans. Christopher G. Gretz (New York: Raven).
Chartier, Roger (1994) *The Order of Books* trans. Lydia C. Cochrane (Cambridge: Polity).
Chaudhuri, K. N. (1985) *Trade and Civilization in the Indian Ocean* (New York: Cambridge University Press).
Cheney, Margaret (1981) *Tesla: Man Out of Time* (New York: Simon and Schuster).

215

Chong, Alan and Wouter Kloek with Celeste Brusati (1999) *Still-Life Paintings from the Netherlands 1550–1720* (Amsterdam: Rijksmuseum and Cleveland: The Cleveland Museum of Art).

Chrétien, Jean-Louis (1996) *De la Fatigue* (Paris: Minuit).

Chua, Daniel K. L. (1999) *Absolute Music: And the Construction of Meaning* (Cambridge: Cambridge University Press).

Cicourel, Aaron (1964) *Method and Measurement in Sociology* (New York: Free).

Cicourel, Aaron (1974) *Cognitive Sociology: Language and Meaning in Social Interaction* (Harmondsworth: Penguin).

Clarke, Bruce and Linda Dalrymple Henderson eds (2002) *From Energy to Information: Representation in Science and Technology, Art, and Literature* (Stanford CA: Stanford University Press).

Classen, Constance (1993) *Worlds of Sense* (London: Routledge).

Classen, Constance ed. (2005) *The Book of Touch* (Oxford: Berg).

Classen, Constance, David Howes, and Anthony Synnott (1994) *Aroma: The Cultural History of Smell* (London: Routledge).

Cohen, H. F. (1984) *Quantifying Music: The Science of Music at the First Stage of the Scientific Revolution, 1580–1650* (Dordrecht: Reidel).

Conrad, Peter (1998) *Modern Times, Modern Places* (London: Thames and Hudson).

Cooper, David E. (2002) *The Measure of Things* (Oxford: Clarendon).

Corbin, Alain (1996) *The Foul and the Fragrant: Odour and the Social Imagination* (London: Macmillan).

Corbin, Alain (1998) *Village Bells: Sound and Meaning in the 19th-Century French Countryside* trans. Martin Thom (New York: Columbia University Press).

Cormack, Patricia (2002) *Sociology and Mass Culture* (Toronto: Toronto University Press).

Cox, Ronald R. (1978) *Schutz's Theory of Relevance: A Phenomenological Critique* (The Hague: Nijhoff).

Crary, Jonathan (2001) *Suspensions of Attention: Attention, Spectacle, and Modern Culture* (Cambridge MA: MIT Press).

Crombie, A. C. (1990) *Science, Optics and Music in Medieval and Early Modern Thought* (London: The Hambledon Press).

Crosby, Alfred W. (1997) *The Measure of Reality: Quantification and Western Society, 1250–1600* (Cambridge: Cambridge University Press).

Crowell, Steven Galt (2001) *Husserl, Heidegger, and the Space of Meaning* (Evanston IL: Northwestern University Press).

Curtin, Philip D. (1984) *Cross-Cultural Trade in World History* (New York: Cambridge University Press).

Dahlhaus, Carl (1989) *The Idea of Absolute Music* trans. Roger Lustig (Chicago: University of Chicago Press).

Damisch, Hubert (1995) *Distance Points: The Origin of Perspective* (Cambridge MA: MIT Press).

Damisch, Hubert (2002) *A Theory of/Cloud/:Toward a History of Painting* trans. Janet Lloyd (Stanford CA: Stanford University Press).

Daston, Lorraine (1988) *Classical Probability in the Enlightenment* (Princeton NJ: Princeton University Press).

Daston, Lorraine and Katherine Park (1998) *Wonders and the Order of Nature, 1150–1750* (New York: Zone).

Davis, Natalie Zemon (2000) *The Gift in Sixteenth-Century France* (Madison WI: University of Wisconsin Press).

De Boer, Theodore (1978) *The Development of Husserl's Thought* trans. Theodore Plantinga (The Hague: Nijhoff).

Deleuze, Gilles (1993) *The Fold: Leibniz and the Baroque* trans. Tom Conley (London: Athlone).

Deleuze, Gilles and Félix Guattari (1977) *Anti-Oedipus: Capitalism and Schizophrenia*. Minneapolis: University of Minnesota Press.

Depraz, Natalie and Dan Zahavi eds (1998) *Alterity and Facticity: New Perspectives on Husserl* (Dordrecht: Kluwer).

Derrida, Jacques (1973) *Speech and Phenomena* trans. David B. Allison (Evanston IL: Northwestern University Press).

Derrida, Jacques (1976) *Of Grammatology* trans. Gayatri Chakravorty Spivak (Baltimore MD: Johns Hopkins University Press).

Derrida, Jacques (1981) *Dissemination* trans. Barbara Johnson (London: Athlone).

Derrida, Jacques (1992) *Given Time. 1: Counterfeit Money* trans. Peggy Kamuf (Chicago: University of Chicago Press).

Derrida, Jacques (1996) *The Gift of Death* trans. David Willis (Chicago: University of Chicago Press).

Derrida, Jacques (1997) *The Politics of Friendship* trans. George Collins (London: Verso).

Derrida, Jacques (2005) *On Touching: Jean-Luc Nancy* (Stanford CA: Stanford University Press).

Descartes, René (1985) *The Philosophical Writings*: 2 vols trans. John Cottingham, Robert Stoothoff, Dugald Murdoch (Cambridge: Cambridge University Press).

De Ste Croix, G. E. M. (1981) *The Class Struggle in the Ancient Greek World* (London: Duckworth).

Dijksterhuis, E. J. (1961) *The Mechanization of the World Picture* trans. C. Dikshoorn (Oxford: Oxford University Press).

Dijkstra, Bram (1986) *Idols of Perversity* (Oxford: Oxford University Press).

Dilthey, Wilhelm (1977) *Descriptive Psychology and Historical Understanding* trans. Richard M. Zaner and Kenneth L. Heiges (The Hague: Nijhoff).

Dilthey, Wilhelm (1985) *Poetry and Experience* trans. and ed. Rudolf A. Makkreel and Frithjof Rodi (Princeton NJ: Princeton University Press).

Dilthey, Wilhelm (1988) *Introduction to the Human Sciences* trans. Raman J. Batanzos (Brighton: Harvester).

Dilthey, Wilhelm (2002) *The Formation of the Historical World in the Human Sciences* trans. and ed. Rudolf A. Makkreel and Frithjof Rodi (Princeton NJ: Princeton University Press).

Donzelot, Jacques (1979) *The Policing of Families* trans. Robert Hurley (London: Hutcheson).

Douglas, Mary (1970) *Natural Symbols* (London: Cresset).

Durkheim, Émile (1995) *The Elementary Forms of the Religious Life* trans. Karen E. Fields (New York: Free Press).

Eamon, William (1994) *Science and the Secrets of Nature* (Princeton NJ: Princeton University Press).

Ebert-Schifferer, Sybille (1998) *Still Life: A History* trans. Russell Stockman (New York: Abrams).

Eisenstadt, S. N. ed. (1986) *Origin and Diversity of Axial Age Civilizations* (Albany: State University of New York Press).

Eisenstadt, S. N. (1995) *Japanese Civilization: A Comparative View* (Chicago: University of Chicago Press).

Eisenstein, Elizabeth (1983) *The Printing Revolution in Early Modern Europe* (Cambridge: Cambridge University Press).

Elias, Norbert (1983) *The Court Society* trans. Edmund Jephcott (Oxford: Blackwell).

Elias, Norbert (1994) *The Civilizing Process* trans. Edmund Jephcott (Oxford: Blackwell).

Ellenberger, Henri (1970) *The Discovery of the Unconscious* (London: Allen Lane).

Elster, Jon (1999) *Alchemies of the Mind: Rationality and the Emotions* (Cambridge: Cambridge University Press).

Elveton, R. O. (2000) *The Phenomenology of Husserl* (Seattle: Noesis).

Erasmus, Desiderius (1997) *Erasmus: The Education of a Christian Prince and the Panagyric for Archduke Philip of Austria* ed. Lisa Jardine, trans. Neil M. Cheshire and Michael J. Heath (Cambridge: Cambridge University Press).

Erlmann, Veit (2004) *Hearing Cultures: Essays on Sound, Listening and Modernity* (Oxford: Berg).

Ey, Henri (1978) *Consciousness* (Bloomington IN: Indiana University Press).

Febvre, Lucien and Henri-Jean Martin (1976) *The Coming of the Book* trans. David Gerard (London: NLB).

Ferguson, Harvie (1994) *Melancholy and Modernity: Søren Kierkegaard's Religious Psychology* (London: Routledge).

Ferguson, Harvie (1996) *The Lure of Dreams: Sigmund Freud and the Construction of Modernity* (London: Routledge).

Ferguson, Harvie (2000) *Modernity and Subjectivity: Body, Soul, Spirit* (Charlottesville VA: University Press of Virginia).

Ferguson, Harvie (2003) 'Patience: The Critique of Pure Naïveté' in Robert L. Perkins ed. *International Kierkegaard Commentary: Eighteen Upbuilding Discourses* (Macon, GA; Mercer University Press).

Findlen, Paula (1999) *Possessing Nature* (Berkeley CA: University of California Press).

Fink, Eugen (1966) *Le Jeu comme symbole du monde* trans Hans Hildenbrand and Alen Lindberg (Paris: Minuit).

Flandrin, Jean-Louis and Massimo Montanari eds (1999) *Food: A Culinary History* (New York: Columbia University Press).

Florike, Egmond and Peter Mason (1997) *The Mammoth and the Mouse: Microhistory and Morphology* (Baltimore and London: The Johns Hopkins University Press).

Foster Hal ed. (1988) *Vision and Visuality* (Seattle: Bay Press).

Foucault, Michel (1970) *The Order of Things* (London: Tavistock).

Foucault, Michel (1972) *The Archaeology of Knowledge* trans. A. M. Sheridan Smith (London: Tavistock).

Foucault, Michel (1977) *Discipline and Punish: The Birth of the Prison* trans. Alan Sheridan (London: Allen Lane).

Franks, David D. and E. Doyce McCarthy eds (1989) *The Sociology of Emotions* (Greenwich CT: JAI).

Frege, Gotlob (1953) *The Foundations of Arithmetic* trans. J. L. Austin (Oxford: Blackwell).

Frijda, Nico H. (1986) *The Emotions* (Cambridge: Cambridge University Press and Paris: Maison des Sciences de l'Homme).

Frisby, David (2001) *Cityscapes of Modernity* (Cambridge: Polity).

Funke, Gerhard (1987) *Phenomenology: Metaphysics or Method* trans. David J. Parent (Athens OH: Ohio University Press).

Gadamer, Hans-Georg (1975) *Truth and Method* (London: Sheed and Ward).

Gadamer, Hans-Georg (1976) *Philosophical Hermeneutics* trans. David E. Linge (Berkeley CA: University of California Press).

Galileo, Galilei (1967) *Dialogue Concerning the Two Chief World Systems* trans. Stillman Drake (Berkeley CA: University of California Press).

Garber, Frederick (1982) *The Autonomy of the Self from Richardson to Huysmans* (Princeton NJ: Princeton University Press).

Garber, Frederick (1992) *Descartes's Metaphysical Physics* (Chicago: University of Chicago Press).

Garfinkel, Harold (1967) *Studies in Ethnomethodology* (Englewood Cliffs NJ: Prentice-Hall).

Gauld, Alan (1992) *A History of Hypnotism* (Cambridge: Cambridge University Press).

Gay, Peter (1999) *The Bourgeois Experience: Victoria to Freud* 2 vols (New York: W. W. Norton).

Geertz, Clifford (1977) *The Interpretation of Cultures* (New York: Basic Books).

Giddens, Anthony (1992) *The Transformation of Intimacy* (Cambridge: Polity).

Giedion, Siegfried (1948) *Mechanization Takes Command* (New York: Oxford University Press).

Gigerenzer, Gerd ed. (1989) *The Empire of Chance* (Cambridge: Cambridge University Press).

Girard, René (1976) *Deceit, Desire and the Novel: Self and Other in Literary Structures* trans. Yvonne Freccero (Baltimore MD: The Johns Hopkins University Press).

Goehr, Lydia (1992) *The Imaginary Museum of Musical Works* (Oxford: Clarendon).

Goethe, Johann Wolfgang von (1971) *The Autobiography of Johann von Goethe: Dichtung und Wahrheit* trans. John Oxenford (London: Sidgwick and Jackson).

Goethe, Johann Wolfgang von (1982) *Wilhelm Meister* vol. 1 trans. H. M. Waidson (London: John Calder).

Goethe, Johann Wolfgang von (1989) *Goethe's Botanical Writings* trans. Bertha Mueller (Woodbridge CT: Ox Bow).

Gombrich, Ernst (1995) *Shadows: The Depiction of Cast Shadows in Western Art* (London: National Gallery).

Gooding-Williams, Robert (2001) *Nietzsche's Dionysian Modernism* (Stanford CA: Stanford University Press).

Goodstein, Elizabeth S. (2005) *Experience Without Qualities: Boredom and Modernity* (Stanford CA: Stanford University Press).

Gouldner, Alvin (1968) *Enter Plato: The Origins of Western Social Theory in Ancient Greece* (London: Routledge and Kegan Paul).

Gowing, Lawrence (1977) *Cézanne: The Late Years* (New York: The Museum of Modern Art).

Grathoff, Richard (1978) *The Theory of Social Action: The Correspondence of Alfred Schutz and Talcott Parsons* (Bloomington IN: Indiana University Press).

Greenblatt, Stephen (1980) *Renaissance Self-Fashioning* (Chicago: University of Chicago Press).

Greenblatt, Stephen (1991) *Marvellous Possessions: The Wonder of the New World* (Oxford: Clarendon Press).

Greenblatt, Stephen ed. (1993) *New World Encounters* (Berkeley CA: University of California Press).

Gregory, C. A. (1982) *Gifts and Commodities* (London: Academic).

Gurevich, A. J. (1985) *Categories of Medieval Culture* (London: Routledge).

Gurwitsch, Aron (1964) *The Field of Consciousness* (Pittsburgh PA: Duquesne University Press).

Gusdorf, Georges (1948) *La Découverte de Soi* (Paris: Presses Universitaires de France).

Gusdorf, Georges (1985) *Le Savoir Romantique de la Nature* (Paris: Payot).

Gusdorf, Georges (2002) *Le Romantisme* 2 vols (Paris: Broché).

Hadot, Pierre (1995) *Philosophy as a Way of Life* (Oxford: Blackwell).

Haley, Bruce (1978) *The Healthy Body and Victorian Culture* (Cambridge MA: Harvard University Press).

Harbison, Robert (2000) *Reflections on Baroque* (London: Reaktion).

Harman, Graham (2002) *Tool-Being: Heidegger and the Metaphysics of Objects* (Chicago: Open Court).

Harootunian, Harry (2000a) *Overcome by Modernity* (Princeton NJ: Princeton University Press).

Harootunian, Harry (2000b) *History's Disquiet* (New York: Columbia University Press).

Harrison, Charles and Paul Wood with Jason Geiger (1998) *Art in Theory 1815–1900: An Anthology of Changing Ideas* (Oxford: Blackwell).

Harvey, Elizabeth D. (2003) *Sensible Flesh: On Touch in Early Modern Culture* (Pittsburgh PA: University of Pennsylvania Press).

Hegel, G. W. F. (1977) *Phenomenology of Spirit* trans. A. V. Miller (Oxford: Clarendon).

Heidegger, Martin (1962) *Being and Time* trans. John Macquarrie and Edward Robinson (Oxford: Blackwell).

Heidegger, Martin (1967) *What is a Thing?* trans. W. B. Barton Jr and Vera Deutsche (Lanham MD: University Press of America).

Heidegger, Martin (1971) *Poetry, Language, Thought* trans. Albert Hofstadter (New York: Harper and Row).

Heidegger, Martin (1977) *The Question Concerning Technology and Other Essays* trans. William Levitt (New York: Harper and Row).

Heidegger, Martin (1982) *The Basic Problems of Phenomenology* trans. Albert Hofstadter (Bloomington IN: Indiana University Press).

Heidegger, Martin (1990a) *Kant and the Problem of Metaphysics* trans. Richard Taft (Bloomington IN: Indiana University Press).

Heidegger, Martin (1990b) *The Fundamental Concepts of Metaphysics* trans. William McNeill and Nicholas Webber (Bloomington IN: Indiana University Press).

Heidegger, Martin (2001) *Phenomenological Interpretation of Aristotle: Initiation into Phenomenological Research* trans. Richard Rojcewicz (Bloomington IN: Indiana University Press).

Heller, Thomas C., Morton Sosna, and David E. Wellbery eds (1986) *Reconstructing Individualism: Autonomy, Individuality, and the Self in Western Thought* (Stanford CA: Stanford University Press).

Hendrickson, Robert (1979) *The Grand Emporiums* (New York: Stein and Day).

Henry, Michel (1975) *Philosophy and Phenomenology of the Body* trans. Girard Etzkorn (The Hague: Nijhoff).

Henry, Michel (1983) *Marx: A Philosophy of Human Reality* trans. Kathleen McLaughlin (Bloomington IN: Indiana University Press).

Henry, Michel (2002) *Incarnation: Une Philosophie de la chair* (Paris: Seuil).

Herlihy, David ed. (1971) *The History of Feudalism* (London: Macmillan).

Hirschman, Albert O. (1977) *The Passions and the Interests* (Princeton NJ: Princeton University Press).

Hobbes, Thomas (1839, 1840) *The English Works of Thomas Hobbes* vols I and IV (London: Bohn).

Hoffenberg, Peter (2001) *An Empire on Display* (Berkeley and Los Angeles: University of California Press).

Honig, Elizabeth Alice (1998) *Painting and the Market in Early Modern Antwerp* (New Haven CT: Yale University Press).

Horner, Robyn (2001) *Rethinking God as Gift: Marion, Derrida, and the Limits of Phenomenology* (New York: Fordham University Press).

Howes, David ed. (2004) *Empire of the Senses: The Sensual Culture Reader* (Oxford: Berg).

Huizinga, J. (1955) *The Waning of the Middle Ages* trans. F. Hopman (Harmondsworth: Penguin).

Hundert, Edward M. (1989) *Philosophy, Psychiatry and Neuroscience: Three Approaches to the Mind* (Oxford: Clarendon Press).

Husserl, Edmund (1964) *The Idea of Phenomenology* trans. W. P. Alston and G. Nakhnikian (The Hague: Nijhoff).

Husserl, Edmund (1967) *Cartesian Meditations* trans. Dorion Cairns (The Hague: Nijhoff).

Husserl, Edmund (1969) *Formal and Transcendental Logic* trans. Dorion Cairns (The Hague: Nijhoff).

Husserl, Edmund (1970a) *The Crisis of European Sciences and Transcendental Phenomenology* trans. David Carr (Evanston IL: Northwestern University Press).

Husserl, Edmund (1970b) *Logical Investigations* 2 vols, trans. J. N. Findlay (London: Routledge).

Husserl, Edmund (1970c) *The Paris Lectures* trans. P. Koestenaum (The Hague: Nijhoff).

Husserl, Edmund (1973) *Experience and Judgment* trans. James S. Churchill and Karl Ameriks (Evanston IL: Northwestern University Press).

Husserl, Edmund (1977) *Phenomenological Psychology* trans. John Scanlon (The Hague: Nijhoff).

Husserl, Edmund (1980) *Ideas Pertaining to a Pure Phenomenology and to a Phenomenological Philosophy: Third Book* trans. Ted E. Klein and W. E. Pohl (The Hague: Nijhoff).

Husserl, Edmund (1981) *Husserl: Shorter Works* ed. and trans. Peter McCormick and Frederick A. Elliston (Notre Dame IN: University of Notre Dame Press).

Husserl, Edmund (1982) *Ideas Pertaining to a Pure Phenomenology and to a Phenomenological Philosophy: First Book* trans. F. Kersten (Dordrecht: Kluwer).

Husserl, Edmund (1989) *Ideas Pertaining to a Pure Phenomenology and to a Phenomenological Philosophy: Second Book* trans. R. Rojcewicz and A. Schuwer (Dordrecht: Kluwer).

Husserl, Edmund (1990) *On the Phenomenology of the Consciousness of Internal Time* trans. J. B. Brough (Dordrecht: Kluwer).

Husserl, Edmund (1997a) *Psychological and Transcendental Phenomenology and the Confrontation with Heidegger (1927–1931)* trans. T. Sheehan and R. E. Palmer (Dordrecht: Kluwer).

Husserl, Edmund (1997b) *Thing and Space: Lectures of 1907* trans. R. Rojcewicz (Dordrecht: Kluwer).

Husserl, Edmund (2001) *Analyses Concerning Passive and Active Synthesis* trans. Anthony J. Steinbock (Dordrecht: Kluwer).

Husserl, Edmund (2003) *Philosophy of Arithmetic: Psychological and Logical Investigations with Supplementary Texts from 1887–1901* trans. Dallas Willard (Dordrecht: Kluwer).

Hyde, Lewis (1979) *The Gift: Imagination and the Erotic Life of Property* (New York: Vintage).

Hyppolite, Jean (1969) *Studies on Marx and Hegel* trans. John O'Neill (London: Heinemann).

Ihde, Don (1993) *Postphenomenology: Essays in the Postmodern Context* (Evanston IL: Northwestern University Press).

Izenberg, Gerald N. (1992) *Impossible Individuality* (Princeton NJ: Princeton University Press).

Jackson, Stanley W. (1986) *Melancholia and Depression: From Hippocratic Times to Modern Times* (New Haven CT: Yale University Press).

Jacques-Dalcroze, Émile (1921) *Rhythm, Music, and Education* trans. Harold F. Rubinstein (London: Chatto and Windus).

James, William (1981) *The Principles of Psychology* (Cambridge MA: Harvard University Press).

Janicaud, Dominique, Jean-François Courtine, Jean-Louis Chrétien, Jean-Luc Marion, Michel Henry and Paul Ricoeur (2000) *Phenomenology and the 'Theological Turn': The French Debate* (New York: Fordham University Press).

Jankélévitch, Vladimir (2001) *La Mort* (Paris: Flammarion).

Jankélévitch, Vladimir (2003) *Music and the Ineffable* trans. Carolyn Abbate (Princeton NJ: Princeton University Press).

Jansen, Marius B. (2002) *The Making of Modern Japan* (Cambridge MA: Harvard University Press).

Jardine, N., J. A. Secord and E. C. Sparry eds (1996) *Cultures of Natural History* (Cambridge: Cambridge University Press).

Jeanrond, Werner (1991) *Theological Hermeneutics* (London: SCM).

Joas, Hans (1985) *G. H. Mead: A Contemporary Re-examination of his Work* (Oxford: Polity).

Johnson, Mark (1987) *The Body and the Mind* (Chicago: University of Chicago Press).

Jordan, John M. (1994) *Machine Age Ideology* (Chapel Hill NC: University of North Carolina Press).

Jordan, William B. (1985) *Spanish Still Life in the Golden Age 1600–1650* (Fort Worth TX: Kimbell Art Museum).

Judovitz, Dalia (1988) *Subjectivity and Representation in Descartes: The Origins of Modernity* (Cambridge: Cambridge University Press).

Judovitz, Dalia (2001) *The Culture of the Body: Genealogies of Modernity* (Ann Arbor MI: University of Michigan Press).

Jütte, Robert (2005) *A History of the Senses: From Antiquity to Cyberspace* (Cambridge: Polity).

Kahn, Douglas (2001) *Noise, Water, Meat: A History of Sound in the Arts* (Cambridge MA: MIT Press).

Kant, Immanuel (1997) *Critique of Pure Reason* trans. Paul Guyer and Allen W. Wood (Cambridge: Cambridge University Press).

Kant, Immanuel (2000) *Critique of the Power of Judgement* trans. Paul Guyer and Eric Matthews (Cambridge: Cambridge University Press).

Kantorowitz, Ernst H. (1957) *The King's Two Bodies* (Princeton NJ: Princeton University Press).

Kass, Leon R. (1999) *The Hungry Soul: Eating and the Perfecting of Our Nature* (Chicago: University of Chicago Press).

Katz, David (1935) *The World of Colour* (London: Kegan Paul, Trench and Trubner).

Katz, David (1989) *The World of Touch* ed. and trans. Lester E. Krueger (Hillsdale NJ: Erlbaum).

Kaufmann, Thomas DaCosta (1988) *The School of Prague* (Chicago: University of Chicago Press).

Kaufmann, Thomas DaCosta (1993) *The Mastery of Nature* (Princeton NJ: Princeton University Press).

Kaufmann, Thomas DaCosta (1995) *Court, Cloister and City: The Art and Culture of Central Europe, 1450–1800* (Chicago: University of Chicago Press).

Kavanagh, Thomas M. (1993) *Enlightenment and the Shadows of Chance* (Baltimore MD: The Johns Hopkins University Press).

Keller, Pierre (1999) *Husserl and Heidegger on Human Experience* (Cambridge: Cambridge University Press).

Kemp, Martin (1992) *The Science of Art* (New Haven CT: Yale University Press).

Kern, Stephen (1983) *The Culture of Time and Space, 1880–1918* (Cambridge MA: Harvard University Press).

Kleinschmidt, Harald (2000) *Understanding the Middle Ages* (Woodbridge: Boydell).

Kockelmans, Joseph J. (1987) *Phenomenological Psychology: The Dutch School* (Dordrecht: Nijhoff).

Kockelmans, Joseph J. (1994) *Edmund Husserl's Phenomenology* (West Lafayette IN: Purdue University Press).

Köhnke, Klaus Christian (1991) *The Rise of New Kantianism* trans. R. J. Hollingdale (Cambridge: Cambridge University Press).

Kojève, Alexandre (1969) *Introduction to the Reading of Hegel* trans. James H. Nichols Jr (New York: Basic Books).

Kolnai, Aurel (2004) *On Disgust* ed. Barry Smith and Carolyn Korsmeyer (Chicago: Open Court).

Konstan, David (1997) *Friendship in the Classical World* (Cambridge: Cambridge University Press).

Koselleck, Reinhart (2000) *Critique and Crisis: Enlightenment and the Pathogenesis of Modern Society* (Cambridge MA: MIT Press).

Koselleck, Reinhart (2004) *Futures Past* (New York: Columbia University Press).

Koyré, Alexandre (1957) *From the Closed World to the Infinite Universe* (Baltimore MD: Johns Hopkins University Press).

Kristeller, Paul Oskar (1972) *Renaissance Concepts of Man* (New York: Harper and Row).

Kristeller, Paul Oskar (1979) *Renaissance Thought and Its Sources* (New York: Harper and Row).

Kristeva, Julia (1989) *Black Sun: Depression and Melancholia* trans. Leon S. Roudiez (New York: Columbia University Press).

Krüger, Lorenz, Lorraine J. Daston, and Michael Heidelberger (1996) *The Probabilistic Revolution* 2 vols (Cambridge MA: MIT Press).

Kuriyama, Shigehisa ed. (2001) *The Expressive Body* (New York: Zone).

Kwinter, Sanford (2002) *Architectures of Time: Towards a Theory of the Event in Modernist Culture* (Cambridge MA: MIT Press).

Laban, Rudolf (1963) *Modern Educational Dance* (London: Macdonald).

Lacoue-Labarthe, Philippe and Jean-Luc Nancy (1988) *The Literary Absolute* trans. Philip Bernard and Cheryl Lester (Albany NY: State University of New York Press).

Lakoff, George and Johnson, Mark (1980) *Metaphors We Live By* (Chicago: University of Chicago Press).

Lambropoulos, Vassilis (1993) *The Rise of Eurocentrism* (Princeton NJ: Princeton University Press).

Landes, David S. (1983) *Revolution in Time* (Cambridge MA: Harvard University Press).

Larson, James L. (1994) *Interpreting Nature* (Baltimore MD: Johns Hopkins University Press).

Lawrence, C. H. (1998) *Medieval Monasticism* (London: Longman).

Lawrence, Nathaniel and Daniel O'Connor (1967) *Readings in Existential Phenomenology* (Englewood Cliffs NJ: Prentice Hall).

Leclerq, J. (1978) *The Love of Learning and the Desire for God* (New York: Fordham University Press).

Lefebvre, Henri (1971) *Everyday Life in the Modern World* trans. Sacha Rabinovitch (London: Allen Lane).

Lefebvre, Henri (1991) *The Production of Space* trans. Donald Nicholson-Smith (Oxford: Blackwell).

Lefebvre, Henri (1992, 2001) *Critique of Everyday Life* 2 vols (London: Verso).

Le Goff, Jacques (1982) *Time, Work, and Culture in the Middle Ages* (Chicago: University of Chicago Press).

Le Goff, Jacques (1988) *The Medieval Imagination* trans. Arthur Goldhammer (Chicago: University of Chicago Press).

Le Goff, Jacques (1990) *Medieval Civilization 400–1100* trans. Julia Barrow (Oxford: Basil Blackwell).

Leibniz, G. W. and Samuel Clark (1956) *The Leibniz–Clarke Correspondence* (Manchester: Manchester University Press).

Lenoir, Timothy (1982) *The Strategy of Life* (Dordrecht: Reidel).

Lepenies, Wolf (1988) *Between Literature and Science: The Rise of Sociology* (Cambridge: Cambridge University Press).

Lessky, Erna (1976) *The Vienna Medical School of the Nineteenth Century* trans. L. Williams and I. S. Levy MD (Baltimore MD: The Johns Hopkins University Press).

Levin, David Michael (1970) *Reason and Evidence in Husserl's Phenomenology* (Evanston IL: Northwestern University Press).

Levin, David Michael (1985) *The Body's Recollection of Being* (London: Routledge and Kegan Paul).

Levin, David Michael ed. (1993) *Modernity and the Hegemony of Vision* (Berkeley and Los Angeles: University of California Press).

Levin, David Michael ed. (1997) *Sites of Vision* (Cambridge, MA: MIT Press).

Levinas, Emmanuel (1969) *Totality and Infinity* trans. Alphonso Lingis (Pittsburgh PA: Dusquesne University Press).

Levinas, Emmanuel (1993) *Outside the Subject* trans. Michael B. Smith (London: Athlone).

Levinas, Emmanuel (1995) *The Theory of Intuition in Husserl's Phenomenology* trans. André Orianne (Evanston IL: Northwestern University Press).

Levinas, Emmanuel (1998a) *Discovering Existence with Husserl* trans. Richard A. Cohen and Michael B. Smith (Evanston IL: Northwestern University Press).

Levinas, Emmanuel (1998b) *Otherwise Than Being* trans. Alphonso Lingis (Pittsburgh PA: Duquesne University Press).

Lhermite, Jean (1960) *L'Image de notre corps* (Paris: Nouvelle Revue Critique).

Lindberg, David C. (1992) *The Beginnings of Western Science: European Scientific Tradition in Philosophical, Religious and Institutional Context, 600 B.C. to A.D. 1450* (Chicago: University of Chicago Press).

Lipovetsky, Gilles (1983) *L'Ère du vide* (Paris: Gallimard).

Lipovetsky, Gilles (1994) *The Empire of Fashion: Dressing Modern Democracy* trans. Catherine Porter (Princeton NJ: Princeton University Press).

Locke, John (1975) *An Essay Concerning Human Understanding* ed. Peter H. Niddich (Oxford: Clarendon).

Lonergan, Bernard J. F. (1957) *Insight* (London: Darton. Longman and Todd).

Löwith, Karl (1964) *From Hegel to Nietzsche: The Revolution in 19th Century Thought* trans. David E. Green (London: Constable).

Löwith, Karl (1998) *Martin Heidegger and European Nihilism* (New York: Columbia University Press).

Löwy, Michael and Robert Sayre (2002) *Romanticism Against the Tide of Modernity* trans. Catherine Porter (Durham NC: Duke University Press).

Lüdtke, Alf (1995) *The History of Everyday Life* trans. William Templer (Princeton NJ: Princeton University Press).

Luhmann, Niklas (1986) *Love as Passion: The Codification of Intimacy* trans. Jeremy Gaines and Doris L. Jones (Stanford CA: Stanford University Press).

Lukes, Steven (1973) *Émile Durkheim: His Life and Work* (London: Allen Lane).

Makkreel, Rudolf and John Scanlon eds (1987) *Dilthey and Phenomenology* (Washington DC: Center for Advanced Research in Phenomenology and University Press of America).

Mâle, Emle (1958) *The Gothic Image: Religious Art in France of the Thirteenth Century* (New York: Harper).

Maletic, Vera (1987) *Body–Space–Expression: The Development of Rudolf Laban's Movement and Dance Concepts* (Berlin: Mouton de Gruyter).

Malinowski, Bronislaw (1978) *Argonauts of the Western Pacific* (London: Routledge).

Mallarmé, Stéphane (2001) *Mallarmé in Prose* ed. Mary Ann Caws (New York: New Directions).

Mandelstam, Osip (1991) *The Collected Critical Prose and Letters* trans. Jane Gary Harris and Constance Link (London: Collins Harvill).

Manent, Pierre (1998) *The City of Man* trans. Marc A. LePain (Princeton NJ: Princeton University Press).

Maravall, José Antonio (1986) *Culture of the Baroque* trans. Terry Cochran (Manchester: Manchester University Press).

Marcel, Gabriel (1949a) *Being and Having* trans. Katharine Farrer (Glasgow: MacLehouse and Glasgow University Press).

Marcel, Gabriel (1949b, 1950) *The Mystery of Being* 2 vols (London: Harvill).

Marin, Louis (1988) *Portrait of the King* trans. Martha M. Houle (London: Macmillan).

Marion, Jean-Luc (1998) *Reduction and Givenness* (Evanston IL: Northwestern University Press).

Marion, Jean-Luc (2002) *Being Given: Toward a Phenomenology of Givenness* (Stanford CA: Stanford University Press).

Martin, Henri-Jean (1994) *The History and Power of Writing* trans. Lydia C. Cochrane (Chicago: University of Chicago Press).

Marx, Karl (1970) *The German Ideology* ed. C. J. Arthur (London: Lawrence and Wishart).

Marx, Karl (1973) *Grundrisse: Foundations of a Critique of Political Economy* trans. Martin Nicolaus (London: Allen Lane; New Left Review).

Marx, Karl (1976a) *Capital:* Volume 1 trans. Ben Fowkes (Harmondsworth: Penguin).

Marx, Karl (1976b) *Early Works* ed. Lucio Colletti (Harmondsworth: Penguin).

Marx, Karl and Friedrich Engels (1969) *Basic Writings in Politics and Philosophy* ed. Lewis S. Feuer (London: Fontana).

Matuštík, Martin J. and Merold Westphal eds (1995) *Kierkegaard in Post/Modernity* (Bloomington IN: Indiana University Press).

Mauriès, Patrick (2002) *Cabinets of Curiosities* (London: Thames and Hudson).

Mauss, Marcel (1970) *The Gift: Forms and Functions of Exchange in Archaic Society* trans. Ian Cunnison (London: Cohen and West).

May, Rollo, Ernest Angel and Henri F. Ellenberger eds (1958) *Existence: A New Dimension in Psychiatry and Psychology* (New York: Basic Books).

Mayr, Otto (1986) *Authority, Liberty, and Automatic Machinery in Early Modern Europe* (Baltimore MD: Johns Hopkins University Press).

McGinn, Bernard (1992) *The Foundations of Mysticism*. Volume I: *The Presence of God* (London: SCM).

Melucci, Alberto (1996) *The Playing Self* (Cambridge: Cambridge University Press).

Mensch, James Richard (2001) *Postfoundational Phenomenology* (University Park PA: Pennsylvania University Press).

Merleau-Ponty, Maurice (1962) *The Phenomenology of Perception* trans. Colin Smith (London: Routledge).

Merleau-Ponty, Maurice (1963) *The Structure of Behaviour* trans. Alden L. Fisher (Boston: Beacon).

Merleau-Ponty, Maurice (1974) *Phenomenology, Language, and Sociology* (London: Heinemann).

Meštrovič, Stjepan G. (1992) *Durkheim and Postmodern Culture* (New York: Aldine de Gruyter).

Meyerson, Emile (1989) *Identity and Reality* trans. Kate Loewenberg (New York: Gordon and Breach).

Micale, Mark S. (1995) *Approaching Hysteria: Disease and Its Interpretation* (Princeton NJ: Princeton University Press).

Micale, Mark S. and Paul Lerner eds. (2001) *Traumatic Pasts: History, Psychiatry and Trauma in the Modern Age, 1870–1930* (Cambridge: Cambridge University Press).

Mill, John Stuart (1973) *A System of Logic* 2 vols, ed. J. M. Robson (Toronto: Toronto University Press and Routledge and Kegan Paul).

Miller, William Ian (1997) *The Anatomy of Disgust* (Cambridge MA: Harvard University Press).

Minkowski, Eugene (1970) *Lived Time: Phenomenological and Psychopathological Studies* trans. Nancy Metzel (Evanston IL: Northwestern University Press).

Mintz, Sidney (1985) *Sweetness and Power: The Place of Sugar in Modern History* (New York: Penguin).

Mohanty, J. N. (1982) *Husserl and Frege* (Bloomington IN: Indiana University Press).

Mohanty, J. N. (1989) *Transcendental Phenomenology: An Analytic Account* (Oxford: Blackwell).

Montagu, Ashley (1986) *Touching: Human Significance of the Skin* (New York: Harper & Row).

Montaigne, Michel de (1991) *The Essays of Michel de Montaigne* trans. and ed. M. A. Screech (London: Allen Lane).

Moran, Dermot (2000) *Introduction to Phenomenology* (London: Routledge).

Moravia, Alberto (1999) *Boredom* trans. Angus Davidson (New York: New York Review of Books).

Moravia, Alberto (2000) *The Time of Indifference* trans. Tami Calliope (South Royalton, Vermont: Steerforth Press).

Moretti, Franco (1987) *The Way of the World* (London: Verso).

Muchembled, Robert (1988) *L'Invention de l'homme moderne: Sensibilités, mœurs et comportements collectives sous l'Ancien Régime* (Paris: Fayard).

Mueller-Vollmer, Kurt (1997) *The Hermeneutics Reader* (New York: Continuum).

Müller-Sievers, Helmut (1997) *Self-Generation: Biology, Philosophy, and Literature around 1800* (Stanford CA: Stanford University Press).

Mumford, Lewis (1963) *Technics and Civilization* (San Diego CA: Harcourt Brace and World).

Nancy, Jean-Luc (1993) *The Birth to Presence* trans. Brian Holmes (Stanford CA: Stanford University Press).

Nancy, Jean-Luc (1994) *The Experience of Freedom* trans. Bridget McDonald (Stanford CA: Stanford University Press).

Naphy, William G. and Penny Roberts eds (1997) *Fear in Early Modern Society* (Manchester: Manchester University Press).

Neubauer, John (1986) *The Emancipation of Music from Language* (New Haven CT: Yale University Press).

Newsome, David (1997) *The Victorian World Picture* (London: Murray).

Nielsen, Donald A. (1999) *Three Faces of God* (Albany NY: State University of New York Press).

Nietzsche, Friedrich (1999) *The Birth of Tragedy and Other Writings* ed. Raymond Geuss and Ronald Spiers, trans. Ronald Spiers (Cambridge: Cambridge University Press).

Nordau, Max Simon (1994) *Degeneration* (Lincoln NE: University of Nebraska Press).

Norton, Robert E. (1995) *The Beautiful Soul* (Ithaca NY: Cornell University Press).

Novalis (Friedrich von Hardenberg) (1989) *Pollen and fragments* trans. Arthur Versluis (Grand Rapids MI: Phanes Press).

Novalis (1997) *Novalis: Philosophical Writings* trans. and ed. Margaret Mahony Stoljar (Albany NY: SUNY Press).

Nussbaum, Martha C. (2001) *Upheavals of Thought: The Intelligence of Emotions* (Cambridge: Cambridge University Press).

Nye, David E. (1992) *Electrifying America: Social Meanings of a New Technology* (Cambridge MA: MIT Press).

Nye, David E. (1999) *American Technological Sublime* (Cambridge MA: MIT Press).

Oakes, Guy (1988) *Weber and Rickert: Concept Formation in the Cultural Sciences* (Cambridge MA: MIT Press).

Ollman, Bertell (1976) *Alienation: Marx's Conception of Man in Capitalist Society* (Cambridge: Cambridge University Press).

Oppenheim, Janet (1991) *'Shattered Nerves': Doctors, Patients, and Depression in Victorian England* (Oxford: Oxford University Press).

Pagden, Anthony (1994) *European Encounters with the New World: From Renaissance to Romanticism* (New Haven CT: Yale University Press).

Patočka, Jan (1998) *Body, Community, Language, World* trans. Erazim Kohák, ed. James Dodd (Chicago: Open Court).

Pensky, Max (2001) *Melancholy Dialectics: Water Benjamin and the Play of Mourning* (Amherst MA: University of Massachusetts Press).

Perec, Georges (1997) *Species of Spaces and Other Pieces* trans. John Sturrock (Harmondsworth: Penguin).

Perella, N. J. (1969) *The Kiss: Sacred and Profane* (Berkeley CA: University of California Press).

Pessoa, Fernando (2002) *The Book of Disquiet* trans. Richard Zenith (Harmondsworth: Penguin).

Petitot, Jean, Bernard Pachoud, Jean-Michel Rey and Francesco J. Varela eds (1999) *Naturalizing Phenomenology: Issues in Contemporary Phenomenology and Cognitive Science* (Stanford CA: Stanford University Press).

Plato (1987) *Thaetetus* trans. Robin A. H. Waterfield (Harmondsworth: Penguin).

Poggi, Stefan and Maurizio Bossi eds (1994) *Romanticism in Science* (Dordrecht: Kluwer).

Pomeranz, Kenneth (2001) *The Great Divergence: China, Europe, and the Making of the Modern World Economy* (Princeton NJ: Princeton University Press).

Pomeranz, Kenneth and Steven Topik (1999) *The World that Trade Created* (Armonk NY: M.E. Sharpe).

Pomian, Krzysztof (1984) *L'Ordre du temps* (Paris: Gallimard).

Pomian, Krzysztof (1987) *Collectors and Curiosities: Paris and Vienna, 1500–1800* trans. Elizabeth Wiles-Portier (Cambridge: Polity).

Poovey, Mary (1995) *Making a Social Body: British Cultural Formation, 1830–1864* (Chicago: Chicago University Press).

Poovey, Mary (1998) *A History of the Modern Fact: Problems of Knowledge in the Sciences of Wealth and Society* (Chicago: University of Chicago Press).

Porter, Theodore M. (1986) *The Rise of Statistical Thinking 1820–1900* (Princeton NJ: Princeton University Press).

Prince, Morton (1906) *The Dissociation of a Personality* (New York: Longman, Green & Co).

Psathas, George (1973) *Phenomenological Sociology: Issues and Applications* (New York: Wiley).

Rabinbach, Anson (1990) *The Human Motor: Energy, Fatigue, and the Origins of Modernity* (New York: Basic Books).

Randles, W. G. L. (1999) *The Unmaking of the Medieval Christian Cosmos, 1500–1760* (Aldershot: Ashgate).

Rawson, Claude (2001) *God, Gulliver, and Genocide: Barbarism and the European Imagination, 1492–1945* (Oxford: Oxford University Press).

Reddy, William M. (2001) *The Navigation of Feeling: A Framework for the History of Emotions* (Cambridge: Cambridge University Press).

Reiss, Timothy J. (1997) *Knowledge, Discovery, and Imagination in Early Modern Europe* (Cambridge: Cambridge University Press).

Reith, Gerda (1999) *The Age of Chance: Gambling in Western Culture* (London: Routledge).

Renaut, Alain (1997) *The Era of the Individual* trans. M. B. DeBeroise and Franklin Philip (Princeton NJ: Princeton University Press).

Reymert, Martin L. ed. (1967) *Feelings and Emotions* (New York: Hafner).

Richards, Graham (1992) *Mental Machinery: The Origins and Consequences of Psychological Ideas* (London: Athlone).

Richards, Robert J. (2002) *The Romantic Conception of Life* (Chicago: University of Chicago Press).

Ricoeur, Paul (1966) *Freedom and Nature: The Voluntary and the Involuntary* trans. Erazim V. Kohák (Evanston IL: Northwestern University Press).

Ricoeur, Paul (1967a) *The Symbolism of Evil* trans. Emerson Buchanan (Boston: Beacon).

Ricoeur, Paul (1967b) *Husserl: An Analysis of His Phenomenology* trans. Edward G. Ballard and Lester E. Embree (Evanston IL: Northwestern University Press).

Ricoeur, Paul (1969) *The Conflict of Interpretations* (Evanston IL: Northwestern University Press).

Ricoeur, Paul (1970) *Freud and Philosophy* (New Haven CT: Yale University Press).

Ricoeur, Paul (1986) *Fallible Man* trans. Charles A. Kelbley (New York: Fordham University Press).

Ricoeur, Paul (1990) *Time and Narrative* 3 vols trans. Kathleen McLaughlin and David Pellauer (Chicago: University of Chicago Press).

Ricoeur, Paul (1991) *From Text to Action* trans. Kathleen Blamey and John B. Thompson (London: Athlone).

Ricoeur, Paul (1992) *Oneself as Another* trans. Kathleen Blamey (Chicago: University of Chicago Press).

Ricoeur, Paul (2000) *La Mémoire, l'histoire, l'oubli* (Paris: Seuil).

Rivière, Jacques (1983) 'Le Sacre du Printemps' in Roger Copeland and Marshall Cohen *What is Dance? Readings in Theory and Criticism* (Oxford: Oxford University Press), pp. 115–23.

Rockmore, Tom (1995) *Heidegger and French Philosophy* (London: Routledge).

Rose, Nikolas (1990) *Governing the Soul: The Shaping of the Private Self* (London: Routledge).

Rosen, Charles (1999) *The Romantic Generation* (London: Fontana).

Rosenzweig, Franz (1985) *The Star of Redemption* trans. William W. Hall (Notre Dame IN: University of Notre Dame Press).

Rossum, Gerhard Dohrn-Van (1996) *History of the Hour* trans. Thomas Dunlap (Chicago: University of Chicago Press).

Rousseau, Jean-Jacques (1970) *The Confessions* trans. J. M. Cohen (Harmondsworth: Penguin).

Rousseau, Jean-Jacques (1973) *The Social Contract and Discourses* trans. G. D. H. Cole (London: Dent).

Sallis, John (1995) *Delimitations: Phenomenology and the End of Metaphysics* (Evanston IL: Northwestern University Press).

Sartre, Jean-Paul (1969) *Being and Nothingness* trans. Hazel E. Barnes (London: Methuen).

Sartre, Jean-Paul (1976) *Critique of Dialectical Reason* trans. Allan Sheridan-Smith (London: NLB).

Sartre, Jean-Paul (1999) *Essays in Existentialism* (Secaucus NJ: Carol Publishing Group).

Saussure, Ferdinand de (1986) *Course in General Linguistics* trans. Roy Harris (Chicago: Open Court).

Scheler, Max (1954) *The Nature of Sympathy* trans. Peter Heath (London: Routledge and Kegan Paul).

Scheler, Max (1973) *Formalism in Ethics and Non-Formal Ethics of Values* trans. Manfred S. Frings and Roger L. Funk (Evanston IL: Northwestern University Press).

Scheler, Max (1987) *Person and Self-Value* trans. Manfred S. Frings (Dordrecht: Nijhoff).

Schelling, Friedrich Wilhelm Joseph von (1988) *Ideas for a Philosophy of Nature* trans. Errol E. Harris and Peter Heath (Cambridge: Cambridge University Press).

Schilder, Paul (1964) *The Image and Appearance of the Human Body* (New York: Humanities Press).

Schiller, Friedrich (1967) *On the Aesthetic Education of Man* ed. and trans. Elizabeth M. Wilkinson and L. A. Willoughby (Oxford: Oxford University Press).

Schivelbusch, Wolfgang (1993) *Tastes of Paradise: A Social History of Spices, Stimulants, and Intoxicants* trans. D. Jacobson (New York: Vintage).

Schivelbusch, Wolfgang (1995) *Disenchanted Night: The Industrialization of Light in the Nineteenth Century* trans. Angela Davies (Berkeley CA: University of California Press).

Schlegel, Friedrich (1971) *Lucinde and Fragments* trans. Peter Firchow (Minneapolis: University of Minnesota Press).

Schleiermacher, Friedrich (1958) *On Religion: Speeches to its Cultured Despisers* trans. John Oman (New York: Harper).

Schluchter, Wolfgang (1996) *Paradoxes of Modernity: Culture and Conduct in the Theory of Max Weber* trans. Neil Solomon (Stanford CA: Stanford University Press).

Schmidt, James ed. (1996) *What is Enlightenment?: Eighteenth-Century Answers and Twentieth-Century Questions* (Berkeley and Los Angeles: University of California Press).

Schneewind, J. B. (1998) *The Invention of Autonomy* (Cambridge: Cambridge University Press).

Schneider, Norbert (1999) *Still Life* (Cologne: Taschen).

Schutz, Alfred (1962) *Collected Papers* 3 vols, ed. Maurice Natanson (The Hague: Nijhoff).

Schutz, Alfred (1967) *The Phenomenology of the Social World* trans. George Walsh and Frederick Lehnert (Evanston IL: Northwestern University Press).

Schutz, Alfred (1970a) *Reflections on the Problem of Relevance* ed. Richard M. Zaner (New Haven CT: Yale University Press).

Schutz, Alfred (1970b) *On Phenomenology and Social Relations* ed. Helmut R. Wagner (Chicago: University of Chicago Press).

Schutz, Alfred and Thomas Luckmann (1974) *Structure of the Life World* (London: Heineman).

Schwartz, Hillel (1998) *The Culture of the Copy* (New York: Zone).

Segal, Naomi (1981) *The Banal Object* (London: University of London, Institute of German Studies).

Segal, Sam (1988) *A Prosperous Past: The Sumptuous Still Life in the Netherlands, 1600–1700* (The Hague: SDU Publishers).

Shapin, Steven and Simon Schaffer (1985) *Leviathan and the Air-Pump: Hobbes, Boyle, and the Experimental Life* (Princeton NJ: Princeton University Press).

Shapiro, Gary (2003) *Archaeologies of Vision* (Chicago: University of Chicago Press).

Showalter, Elaine (1987) *The Female Malady: Women, Madness and English Culture, 1830–1980* (London: Virago).

Showalter, Elaine (1997) *Hystories: Hysterical Epidemics and Modern Culture* (London: Picador).

Sigwart, Christoph (1895) *Logic* trans. Helen Dandy (New York: Macmillan).

Simmel, Georg (1950) *The Sociology of Georg Simmel* trans. Kurt H. Wolf (New York: Free Press of Glencoe).

Simmel, Georg (1978) *The Philosophy of Money* trans. Tom Bottomore and David Frisby (London: Routledge and Kegan Paul).

Simmel, Georg (1997) *Simmel on Culture* ed David Frisby and Mike Featherstone (London: Sage).

Smith, Barry and David Woodruff Smith eds (1995) *The Cambridge Companion to Husserl* (Cambridge: Cambridge University Press).

Sokolowski, Robert (2000) *Introduction to Phenomenology* (Cambridge: Cambridge University Press).

Solomon, Robert C. (1983) *The Passions: The Myth and Nature of Human Emotion* (Notre Dame IN: University of Notre Dame Press).

Sorabji, Richard (2000) *Emotion and Peace of Mind* (Oxford: Oxford University Press).

Spariosu, Mihai I. (1989) *Dionysus Reborn: Play and the Aesthetic Dimension in Modern Philosophical and Scientific Discourse* (Ithaca NY: Cornell University Press).

Spariosu, Mihai I. (1997) *The Wreath of Wild Olive: Play, Liminality, and the Study of Literature* (Albany NY: State University of New York Press).

Spiegelberg, Herbert (1969) *The Phenomenological Movement* (The Hague: Nijhoff).

Stafford, Barbara Maria (1994) *Artful Science: Enlightenment Entertainment and the Eclipse of Visual Education* (Cambridge MA: MIT Press).

Starobinski, Jean (1988) *Jean-Jacques Rousseau: Transparency and Obstruction* trans. Arthur Goldhammer (Chicago: University of Chicago Press).

Starobinski, Jean (2003) *Action and Reaction* (New York: Zone).

Steinbock, Anthony J. (1995) *Home and Beyond* (Evanston IL: Northwestern University Press).

Sterling, Charles (1981) *Still Life Painting from Antiquity to the Twentieth Century* (New York: Harper and Row).

Stewart, Susan (1984) *On Longing* (Baltimore MD: Johns Hopkins University Press).

Stoichita, Victor I. (1997) *A Short History of the Shadow* (London: Reaktion).

Stoichita, Victor I. (1998) *The Self-Aware Image: Insight into Early Modern Meta-Painting* trans. Anne-Marie Glasheen (Cambridge: Cambridge University Press).

Strasser, Stephen (1957) *The Soul in Metaphysical and Empirical Psychology* (Louvain: Nauwelaerts).

Strasser, Stephen (1977) *Phenomenology of Feeling: An Essay on the Phenomena of the Heart* trans. Robert T. Wood (Pittsburgh PA: Duquesne University Press).

Strathern, Andrew (1971) *The Rope of Moka* (Cambridge: Cambridge University Press).

Strauss, Erwin (1963) *The Primary World of Senses* trans. Jacob Needleman (London: Free Press of Glencoe).

Strauss, Erwin (1966) *Phenomenological Psychology* trans. Erling Eng (London: Tavistock).

Szondi, Peter (1995) *Introduction to Literary Hermeneutics* trans. Martha Woodmansee (Cambridge: Cambridge University Press).

Thompson, George (1961) *The First Philosophers* (London: Lawrence and Wishart).

Thulstrup, Niels (1980) *Kierkegaard's Relation to Hegel* trans. George L. Stengren (Princeton NJ: Princeton University Press).

Tiffany, Daniel (2000) *Toy Medium* (Berkeley CA: University of California Press).

Todes, Samuel (2001) *Body and World* (Cambridge, MA: MIT Press).

Todorov, Tzvetan (1984) *The Conquest of America: The Question of the Other* trans. Richard Howard (New York: Harper & Row).

Todorov, Tzvetan (2002) *Imperfect Garden: The Legacy of Humanism* (Princeton NJ: Princeton University Press).

Toepfer, Karl (1997) *Empire of Ecstasy* (Berkeley CA: University of California Press).

Tomlinson, Gary (1999) *Metaphysical Song: An Essay on Opera* (Princeton NJ: Princeton University Press).

Tounshend, Chauncy (1844) *Facts in Mesmerism* (London: Bailliere).

Trân, Duc Thao (1986) *Phenomenology and Dialectical Materialism* trans. Daniel J. Herman and Donald V. Morano (Dordrecht: Reidel).

Turner, Victor (1982) *From Ritual to Theatre: The Human Seriousness of Play* (New York: PAS).

Turner, Victor and Edward M. Bruner (1986) *The Anthropology of Experience* (Urbana IL: University of Illinois Press).

Unger, Roberto Mangabeira (1975) *Knowledge and Politics* (New York: The Free Press).

Unger, Roberto Mangabeira (1984) *Passion: An Essay on Personality* (New York: Free Press).

Valéry, Paul (1989) *Dialogues* trans. William McCausland Stewart (Bollingen Series XLV, 4; Princeton NJ: Princeton University Press).

Van Ginneken, Jaap (1992) *Crowds, Psychology, and Politics 1871–1899* (Cambridge: Cambridge University Press).

Van Krieken, Robert (1998) *Norbert Elias* (London: Routledge).

Vernant, Jean-Pierre (1991) *Mortals and Immortals: Collected Essays* ed. Froma Zeitlin (Princeton NJ: Princeton University Press).

Voegelin, Eric (1956) *Order and History* Vols 1 & 2 (Baton Rouge LA: Louisiana State University Press).

Von Plato, Jan (1994) *Creating Modern Probability: Its Mathematics, Physics and Philosophy in Historical Perspective* (Cambridge: Cambridge University Press).

Weber, Max (1930) *The Protestant Ethic and the Spirit of Capitalism* trans. Talcott Parsons (London: Routledge).

Weber, Max (1975) *Roscher and Knies: The Logical Problems of Historical Economics* trans. Guy Oakes (New York: Free Press).

Welton, Don (2000) *The Other Husserl* (Bloomington IN: Indiana University Press).

Westphal, Merold (1996) *Becoming a Self* (West Lafayette IN: Purdue University Press).

White, John (1961) *The Birth and Rebirth of Pictorial Space* (London: Faber and Faber).

Whitebook, Joel (1996) *Perversion and Utopia* (Cambridge MA: MIT Press).

Williams, Rosaalind (1982) *Dream Worlds: Mass Consumption in Late Nineteenth-Century France* (Berkeley CA: University of California Press).

Williams, Simon (2001) *Emotion and Social Theory* (London: Sage).

Wimbush, Vincent L. ed. (1995) *Asceticism* (Oxford: Oxford University Press).

Winter, Alison (1998) *Mesmerized: Powers of Mind in Victorian Britain* (Chicago: University of Chicago Press).

Wyschogorod, Edith, Jean-Joseph Goux, and Eric Boynton eds (2002) *The Enigma of Gift and Sacrifice* (New York: Fordham University Press).

Yates, Frances (1964) *Giordano Bruno and the Hermetic Tradition* (London: Routledge and Kegan Paul).

Young, Robert M. (1994) *Mental Space* (London: Process Press).

Zaehner, R. C. (1957) *Mysticism: Sacred and Profane* (Oxford: Oxford University Press).

Zahavi, Dan (2003) *Husserl's Phenomenology* (Stanford CA: Stanford University Press).

Zammito, John H. (1992) *The Genesis of Kant's Critique of Judgment* (Chicago: University of Chicago Press).

Zammito, John H. (2002) *Kant, Herder, and the Birth of Anthropology* (Chicago: University of Chicago Press).

Zaner, Richard M. (1970) *The Way of Phenomenology* (New York: Pegasus).

Zaner, Richard M. (1971) *The Problem of Embodiment* (The Hague: Martinus Nijhoff).

Zeldin, Theodore (1980a) *France 1848–1945: Taste and Corruption* (Oxford: Oxford University Press).

Zeldin, Theodore (1980b) *France 1848–1945: Anxiety and Hypocrisy* (Oxford: Oxford University Press).

Žižek, Slavoj (1996) *The Indivisible Remainder: An Essay on Schelling and Related Matters* (London: Verso).

Žižek, Slavoj (2000) *The Abyss of Freedom/Ages of the World* (Ann Arbor MI: University of Michigan Press).

Name Index

Subject Index